HOW STUPID ARE WE?

Cliff Somers

HOW STUPID ARE WE?

Paperback: (979-8-950072-22-2)
Hardcover: (979-8-950072-23-9)

Table of Contents

Foreword......6

Introduction......8

Acknowledgment......15

Chapter 1 17
The Enemy

Chapter 2 61
From Their Own Mouths

Chapter 3 81
The Background Story

Chapter 4 93
The Legacy of the Past Thirty-Five Years

Chapter 5 122
Unhealthy and Poorly Educated

Chapter 6 134
The Rape of North Carolina

Chapter 7 145
Global Warming

Chapter 8 169
How Did It Get This Way?

Chapter 9 180
Motivations

Chapter 10 190
Invading Education

Chapter 11 204
The Money Machine

Chapter 12 213
The Effect on Politics

Chapter 13 246
What about the Climate?

Chapter 14 255
How About that Republican Platform?

Chapter 15 307
The Catastrophe of November 8, 2016

Chapter 16 317
Resolving this Mess

Bibliography 324

Total liberty for wolves is death to the lambs.

Isaiah Berlin

Foreword

Here you have a book that begins with a foreword, an introduction and then an acknowledgement. It was not my intent to write a foreword at the outset. But then, I started writing this book in May of 2016, before the November 8th election. It took me weeks to recover from that disaster and more weeks to decide how to deal with the result in this, which is undeniably a book about politics. I was torn between extensively rewriting the book and dealing with the election and resulting administration in brief. Finally, I decided that the election did not change my message in any way; it simply heightened the urgency of the problem. Further, although I would like to write a tome on what I perceive as the shortcomings of our new president and those he has surrounded himself with, any detailed treatment of those topics would be a book in itself. Finally, I guess I should admit that I really did not want to do the work of tearing an almost completed book apart and totally rewriting it – which is known as laziness, I guess.

As a result of my conclusion about how to handle the rise of Mr. Trump and his presidency, I have simply added chapter 15 dealing briefly with what they mean to the overall message of the book. Despite wanting to vent about the demeanor, xenophobia, misogyny, bombasticism and juvenility of the man, I have opted not to spend time on those factors because they are outside the core issues I set out to deal with. They are unique to this man, and this book is not about any one person, not even our president. Thus, you will seldom see Mr. Trump's name in any chapter before chapter 15. No matter whether the reader loves Trump or hates him, both will no doubt be relieved to know that.

Introduction

Let me start by quoting from the movie *Network:* "I'm mad as hell and I'm not going to take this anymore." That is a fair description of my state of mind over how stupid we who are not members of the top 1% richest people in America are about our government and our politics. We are being conned and lied to in order to get us to vote for and accept political leaders who then do nothing at all for us and everything for the elite rich and the powerful corporations who own the lion's share of the wealth and the power in this which we only think is our country. We allow this for a number of reasons. One of them, of course, is apathy on our part. We don't look hard at what is actually happening in our government and our economy outside our immediate affairs. We don't try to parse out the truth of what our politicians tell us, what our corporations tell us and what various vested interests tell us. That is, we tend to take what we hear from these sources at face value or, in the alternative, we say that we don't believe anything we hear from them, which excuses us in either case from needing to do the hard work of finding out what is true and what is not. Certainly I include myself in this category. I have lived a long time. During that time, this country has gone from being one with a growing middle class, the best health care in the world, the best educational system in the world, a robust infrastructure, a well-regulated and strong economy, a concern for the individual which was inclusive of the poorest among us, a growing concern for the well-being of our environment and a belief that each American was entitled to a fair opportunity to better him or herself to something far less than that. I didn't notice it because I was, like most of us, too busy living my life. Over the course of the last fifty years, I have slowly changed from a "conservative" and a Republican to a "liberal" and a Democrat. My parents, you see, were Republicans back when the Republican Party was much different from what it is today. As a result, I didn't notice the problems which I will describe in some detail in this book. I didn't take in the meaning of economic and political changes that took place that were slowly strangling the middle class, slowly degrading our health care, slowly, but increasingly more rapidly, poisoning our environment and slowly relegating the bottom 99% of American citizens to the category of "takers" in the eyes of the elite 1% who dream that they are the "makers". What they and the increasingly enormous and wealthy monopolistic corporations have done to us and are continuing to do to us is criminal in my eyes. It is my intent with this book to render it criminal in the eyes of the readers and to inspire you folks to realize that the only way out is to throw out the bastards in office who have conspired with the powerful to do this and want to do more and worse and then elect people who actually do care about all of America and not just the 1%.

For those who pay attention to the politics of the moment, you will have noticed that both the Republican and the Democratic Parties say they want to help the middle class and provide opportunities for all. They can be very disparaging of each other's plans for doing this and they can sound like they both want to help us. Depending on our party affiliation, we will tend to believe "our" party and disbelieve the other party. So, those of you reading this book may well wonder what is different about it and how it could help sort these things out. The answer is that, while both parties have their warts, one of them has been purchased by the rich and powerful and is lying through its teeth while the other is weak, and spiritless as well as being, at times, just as venal as the other, but the hope of the average American still lies with that party.. What I intend to do is to show which is which and what the rich and powerful really want to accomplish so that we, the 99%, can see clearly where our real interests lie.

For more than forty years, we have been subjected to a world view espoused by the rich and powerful that involves many working parts. It started in the administration of Jimmy Carter when we were mired in what was called "stagflation" in which the economy was experiencing stagnant growth but also experiencing high inflation, a rather bad situation resulting from a number of factors, not the least of which was the oil embargo by OPEC. This led to the onset of the troika of policies that have so beggared us since then. These are the idea that tax cuts can enrich us, that the government is our enemy and should be deprived of its power to regulate the market forces and that it should be "shrunk" to keep it from intruding into our day-to-day lives. These concepts don't really belong to the Republican Party so much as they belong to the Libertarian Party, which has never been very popular in itself, but which is the ideal of the rich and powerful who have been pushing its agenda in the more mainstream political world. Notice today that the Libertarian Party seems to be receiving much better press than it used to get. The mechanism used in the economic field to achieve the aims of the elite is the so-called "supply-side" economics. Putting that in terms I understand is the concept that we should allow the market to proceed without regulatory restraint so that it can produce the greatest amount of goods which will enrich us by employing more people, and providing more goods for the buying public which will purchase them and thus it will lift all boats. Of course, the boats that will first be lifted will be those of the rich, but then the wealth will "trickle down" to the rest of us. The market will adjust for the good of all automatically, they say, and does not need to be regulated by government. They also say that we are the most taxed people on earth and should have the government out of our pockets. Some go so far as to say that taxation is theft by the government. It certainly sounds nice doesn't it? The problem is that it is all one big lie.

Despite the reiteration of so many that we are the most taxed people on earth, it is not true. We are not even in the top ten most taxed among the most advanced nations in the world. But the real bug-a-boo in these propositions is the idea that an unfettered or "free" market is the solution to all our problems. In the first place, there is no such thing as a "free" market in which the means of production and finance are free of all regulation. In such a situation, the richest and most powerful commercial entities will "eat" their competition and will treat the consuming public just as they wish. No such system has existed in any civilized country since the dawn of time. Furthermore, it is not really what the rich and powerful want. What they want is a system that protects their "property" to the exclusion of anyone else. The only real government entities they want to exist are those which promulgate legal protections for their interests and the courts in which they can sue each other and us over their claims to "their" property. I will support these claims and expand on these points in this book. These ideas are not mine alone but are also the product of some very intelligent and knowledgeable people to whom I will cite as we go.

The concept that the government is our enemy is easy to sell. Almost all Americans harbor the suspicion that there is in government too much power over our lives. Further, it is easy to resent the power of the government to take from us in taxes and fees that which we labored to earn. But, the fact is that the government is all that makes our civilization possible. The absence of government is anarchy. In such a situation, the strong can and will prey on the weak and will suffer no ill from it unless by way of revenge. Civilization is defined by a group of people having a government to regulate and control the behavior of its citizens. It can only do that if it has the funds to do it. Thus, as the old saw has it, the only thing inevitable besides death is taxes. Adam Smith, whose books *"An Inquiry into the Nature and Causes of the Wealth of Nations"* constitute one of the iconic texts on economics, published in 1843 and much quoted by the elite, said therein "Every tax is to the person who pays it a badge, not of slavery but of liberty." (Bk. I Ch. 10; Bk. V Ch. 2) Without taxes, the government cannot protect its citizens from outside aggressors, from criminals within or from oppression by the powerful. Without taxes, the government (at every level) cannot build roads and bridges, provide water and sewer services, regulate growth, provide education to its citizens or otherwise do the many things needed by its citizens. And as nations become more populous and crowded and the world becomes vastly more complex, the extent of needed regulation grows. In a world with billions and billions of people, it is increasingly difficult to provide a milieu in which we are not stepping on one another's toes in a myriad of different ways. Only government can do this. In order to do it, government must also grow and have the power to see to it that we continue to live in a safe and workable environment. The government is not only not our enemy, it is the only entity capable of restraining the powerful and the rich from totally wiping out the benefits of civilization to the great mass of people.

Speaking, as I just was of "environment", the wish of the rich and powerful is to be free of any regulation of their commercial and industrial activities so that they can do as they will regardless of the effect on our environment. They despise the Environmental Protection Agency (the EPA) and want to abolish it. In the meantime, they want Congress to deprive it of its regulatory power and to reduce its budget in order to render it powerless to do its job. They have tried to prevent the EPA from regulating the production of sulfur dioxide by the fossil fuel burning industries, especially the electric companies that burn coal and oil so as to limit the resulting acid rain. They fought the regulation of chlorofluorocarbons (CFC's) that were producing holes in our ozone layer. And they are presently fighting all efforts to limit the emission of carbon dioxide by the same industries that is leading to global warming. In each case they have argued that the problems didn't exist and if they did, they weren't caused by human activity and if they were, then it was too expensive to fix the problem. In each case, every position taken by the coal industry, the oil industry, the natural gas industry, the power companies, etc. was a BIG LIE. I use caps here because I will be using this term a lot and I want to distinguish the BIG LIE from the usual prevarication. A BIG LIE is a lie propagated to mislead the public that is well known by the liars to be untrue and is known by most thinking people to be untrue, but which is promulgated in such massive ways so as to cause people to believe there must be truth here in the same way as "where there's smoke there must be fire". After all, the liars here can afford all the media coverage they need and, in fact, they own some of the media such as Fox News the Washington Times and talk radio bloviators such as Rush Limbaugh. The rich and powerful, which I will henceforth refer to as the "rich bitches", the "bums", the "enemy" and other fond epithets, do not care whether they damage our environment or poison us or cause world flooding, or any of the other environmental horrors they are causing.

What the rich bitches have done, are doing and wish to continue to do are the subject of this book. Further, the methods used to accomplish their ends are also the subject of the book. Finally, a very short section of the book is devoted to the solution to the majority of these problems. There is something very simple we can all do. We can understand what is going on and we can get out in huge numbers to vote the bastards out of office. The only lever we, the 99%, have is government. We outnumber these people massively. We live in a democracy (sort of) and we can use the ballot to do what needs to be done. Our future lies in our own hands if we will but take hold of it. After all, we are the ones who will suffer the consequences. The rich and powerful can all afford to live in a chalet in the Alps.

And just a note about why I have written this book. As you will note in the acknowledgment, I have cited in this book to the works of other, very well informed authors who have written more exhaustive books on these subjects. You could read those books and skip this one and be just fine. But most folks probably haven't read them just because they are so scholarly and so dense in content. Or perhaps they haven't been aware of them. My aim in this book is to make the subjects even easier for those, like me, who are not so well informed as these folks. The other difference between this book and the underlying works is that I am pissed and I intend to call it as I see it in this book. My language will be a good deal blunter than that of the others. I, after all, don't have an academic or journalistic reputation to uphold.

Acknowledgment

This book is crammed full of facts. I am not expert in the areas from which these facts come. I am but a retired trial lawyer. Many of the facts I provide come from the authors of several erudite books. If this book should cause you, the reader, to also read the underlying books, I will be content because there is so much to learn from them. I will not use footnotes because this is not an academic work. If I cite to something or quote something, I will put the citation in parentheses immediately following the quote or cite. With respect to many works, I will refer to them by an acronym with a following page number or page numbers. I wish to acknowledge my debt to these writers who come from academia, the media, politics and other areas. I stand on their shoulders. If I make errors, and that seems inevitable, those errors are my fault, not that of anyone else. I will list below some of the sources I relied upon and the acronyms I use to cite them. And, let me say to them once more, thank you for your wonderful efforts and may you truly educate those who need to know. More complete citations to these works may be found in the bibliography.

The authors, their books and the acronyms I will use are as follows:

1. Jacob S. Hacker and Paul Pierson, *American Amnesia* (AA).

2. David Brock, *Blinded by the Right* (BBR)

3. Jane Mayer, *Dark Money* (DM)

4. Michael E. Mann, *The Hockey Stick and the Climate Wars: Dispatches from the Front Lines* (THS)

5. Naomi Oreskes and Erik M. Conway, *Merchants of Doubt* (MD)

6. Kevin T. Leicht and Scott T. Fitzgerald, *Middle Class Meltdown in America* (MCM)

7. Robert B. Reich, *Saving Capitalism* (SC)

8. Theda Skocpol and Vanessa Williamson, *The Tea Party and the Remaking of Republican Conservatism* (TTP)

9. Naomi Klein, *This Changes Everything* (TCE)

Read these books! You will be glad you did.

Finally, I wish to acknowledge my wife, Jennie, and my friends Ralph Swank, M. D. and Louis Hernandez who read the first draft of this book and provided me the benefit of their kind observations and thoughts on ways to improve it. CS

Chapter 1

The Enemy

This book is a labor, not of love, but of passion. The matters in it excite my passion to a high level. From the time I started research for it, I have been dying to write it. But when I sat down to actually start pounding the keys, I found myself stumped. There is so much to cover and it needs to do the job readably. That is, not just understandably, but, if possible, engagingly. Yet, as I have already said, there are these books that I am depending on so heavily for the facts. They are great books and they cover parts of what I want to say even better than I can do it, if somewhat more densely than I wish to do it. If I was to write a useful book, I needed to approach the subjects differently from the others. How to do it? What could I say that was different? I read and re-read the underlying authors. I sat down several times to try to write the thing and came up blank as to how to start and how to say something that properly reflected my position on the subject matter. Then one day, while reading the 2016 Libertarian Party platform, I had an epiphany (and boy was I glad). The Libertarian Party platform sets forth the clear position of the enemy. It does so unsparingly but disguised in pretty language. I knew that I needed to start there, and so I will.

Before I tackle the Libertarian Party platform, though, let me say briefly what it is that makes me so passionate. The rich and the powerful own this country, not the American people. The disparity between what they own and control and what we (the 99%) own, and control is worse now than it has been for most of a century and it is getting even worse at a rapid pace. The middle class is diminishing and the number of the working poor is increasing. Laws that might benefit the common folk are routinely stymied in the Congress and the state legislatures. Although I acknowledge that many Democratic office holders are involved in this charade, it is the Republican Party that is mainly responsible because it has become wholly owned by the enemy. Thus, 1% of the population and many large corporations, think tanks and associations such as the Chamber of Commerce control what the Congress of the United States does or does not do and the rot is rapidly spreading to all the state legislatures. I recognize that many readers will say or at least think at this point that my language is inflammatory and my position is wrong. If you stick with me through the book I will do my best to prove I am right. If I can but get you to read the underlying books, I don't believe many of you who think about what you have read can reach a differing conclusion. What I say is happening is simple. We are stupid. How stupid we are is the subject I wish to address. We are letting these folks sell us a bill of goods. They use many dirty tricks and lies to accomplish their goals. Their aim is to protect and further their own great fortunes with no regard whatever for the 99% whom they generally think of as "takers". It's a democracy, people. If we don't vote or we don't recognize what is in our own best interests, we cannot expect a good outcome for us or our children, their children and the human race. The problem is just exactly that critical. This, too, is a position I think I can prove to you if you stick with me.

Okay, let's talk about the Libertarian Party for a moment. Why that party if I say the problem is the Republican Party? It is because the people behind the Libertarian Party are the people who are now proud owners of the Republican Party. The Libertarian Party is a far, far right organization. It has been around for decades. It had a presidential and vice-presidential candidate in the 1980 race. The vice-presidential candidate was David Koch of "the Koch brother" as the media refers to them and as they are thought of these days. The other brother is Charles Koch, who is, in my opinion, a towering genius. While there are plenty of other individual enemies whom I will talk about, the Kochs are at the top of the heap right now and they stand as the leaders of the efforts to screw the rest of us. They are the principal owners of Koch Industries that has an annual gross income well north of $100,000,000,000 per year. Yep, that's one hundred billion, folks. Their net worth is currently estimated at around $48, 000,000,000 each. Together they own the largest single fortune in the world. The Libertarian Party lost the 1980 election by such a margin as to be pitiful. It was deemed to be far outside acceptable limits to the American people. The Kochs have been working hard and spending billions since that time to move the Libertarian Party into the mainstream of thought, or at least to move its aims into the Republican Party. The Party (Libertarian for the moment unless I say otherwise) nominated Gary Johnson for president, former governor of New Mexico and Bill Weld, former governor of Massachusetts for vice president. They also formulated a party platform which is very similar to all their platforms since 1980. Because they were so efficient in getting this done, they have handed me the document I need to help prove my point.

Before I delve into the Libertarian Party platform, let me explain my epiphany, because it is what I judge all of the document and most everything else in this book by. It is this: *human beings are born inherently unequal.* That sounds like a no-brainer, I know, but it is a guideline to understanding what is wrong with the party platform and the approach of all of the enemies. In the early days of the human race (and Homo erectus, etc. before us for that matter), strength and speed were survival traits. In general, that meant that adult males had a better chance to survive than women and children (feminists don't hate me – you know at that level it is true). Not only that, but the males who were faster and/or stronger were better able to survive than those who weren't. Those who were smarter had yet another leg up and that did include women. In order to survive, and successfully pass on their genes, our early ancestors had to cooperate with each other to increase their chances. As people began to congregate in larger groups, which further enhanced the chances of survival, the group had to adopt "rules" to control how they would work with one another to the desired end. From that point forward in human history, there have been rules and rulers to facilitate the function of the group, to protect the "weaker" members and to organize who does what and when. The bigger the group, the more complicated the interactions and the more rules were necessary to deal with all the complications that were introduced. Thus to governments. And from that time the ruling entities have decided how the wealth of the group would be distributed for the common good. Obviously many groups gave better protection to the weak than others, but they all did it. And they all distributed the food, clothing and other goods to the weaker members from the common wealth of the group. Thus, taxes have been with us forever and are essential to the survival of the group. As societies got wealthier, they were better able and willing to distribute goods to the weaker members because the wealthier members were getting richer and richer. In today's world, the complexities of societies and the more crowded in they are next to each other, the more rules, or to use the word that the Libertarians hate, regulations, were needed. In the present, advanced civilizations have the riches to care for all and still allow for some of us to be very rich. However, there has always been a segment of the population who were unwilling to give up anything for the common good and that group has grown numerically large even if not proportionately large. They are the predators. And they are the Libertarians. So, to my point: the party has set forth a manifesto in its platform that is perfectly designed to screw the weak and reward the rich and powerful while professing its love for the principle of freedom for every individual. Thus they exploit the inherent inequality of people.

Before I delve into the platform, one last thing; English philosopher Isaiah Berlin said the following which is painfully pertinent:

Both liberty and equality are among the primary goals pursued by human beings throughout many centuries; but total liberty for wolves is death to the lambs, total liberty of the powerful, the gifted, is not compatible with the right to a decent existence of the weak and the less gifted. (Isaiah Berlin, *The Crooked Timber of Humanity: Chapters in the History of Ideas*)

The Libertarian Party is trying to set up a situation in which the enemies are in a position to devour the goods of society and despoil the lives of the poorer and the weaker. This is the philosophy that we, the 99%, had better recognize and stop before it is too late for us to avoid all being destitute and, even worse, living in a planet raped of its assets and rendered unlivable in large areas if not all of them. It is becoming a matter of survival of the human race! The rich think they can avoid the unfavorable results of their actions and indeed they can for a while, but in the end, they need us and they can't survive it either.

So, let's deal with the Libertarian Party platform for 2016 (adopted in 2014 in convention). It starts with a preamble that contains this statement, among others:

We believe that respect for individual rights is the essential precondition for a free and prosperous world, that force and fraud must be banished from human relationships, and that only through freedom can peace and prosperity be realized.

Isn't this inspiring? It can hardly sound any better can it? Yet, hidden in this language lie many problems that concern us all. First off, this sets up the tenet that every individual must be free to do what he or she wishes (except for fraud and force). They want to be free to do what their power would otherwise allow them to do. They also want fraud and force banished from human relationships. Sounds good, doesn't it? The facts that it is only possible to even try to do this if government does it, no government from the dawn of time could do it and it is impossible to imagine a government that could accomplish it is handily elided over. The best that can be done is to give government the task of enforcing rules to achieve that end. Every society tries to do this. Thus the party tells us individual freedom is paramount (especially for wolves I say) and then gives us some pretty sounding phrases setting forth the impossible to look benevolent. Watch as we go along.

In case you think I have overstated the extent of freedom for the individual the party intends, check out the next paragraph of the preamble:

Consequently, we defend each person's right to engage in any activity that is peaceful and honest, and welcome the diversity that freedom brings. The world we seek to build is one where individuals are free to follow their own dreams in their own ways, without interference from government or any authoritarian power.

Once again, doesn't it sound great? But look carefully. They want each individual to have the right to engage in "any activity" that is "peaceful" and "honest". Take a look at the track record of Koch Industries for honesty. It has been sued and prosecuted for many activities such as stealing oil from Native American lands and shorting customers with fraudulent measuring of oil. These are the people who would decide what is peaceful and honest under their system. And don't even get me started on their environmental record. And, this language doesn't address how anyone born to poverty will ever have the chance to make the kinds of decisions that those who are already rich can make. They are beginning to set up an ideal wherein only the rich can benefit from their "freedom". Finally, they ignore the fact that only a government can enforce the obligation to be honest and peaceful (short of a Wild West vigilante justice which sort of obviates the peaceful part and probably the honest part because that would permit those with the biggest guns and the most talent and training to use them to enforce "peace" and "honesty"). You see where this is going?

Perhaps the most ominous thing they say is the concluding sentence of the preamble: "Our goal is nothing more or less than a world set free in our lifetime, and it is to this end that we take these stands." They want their freedom set in force in their lifetime. Putting aside the sheer impossibility of that goal, it is an almost terrifying thought. Believe me, we are just starting on the journey through their nightmarish tract. By the way, it is important to know that the enemies define "individual" to mean corporations as well as people. Check out their ridiculous (but nevertheless bought by the Court) position in the case of *Citizens United v. Federal Elections Commission* in which "Citizens United", a front group for the enemy and no true representative of citizens, obtained a ruling from the U. S. Supreme Court that corporations were entitled to free speech like other citizens, to include the right to spend as much on election campaigns as they wanted, whereby the purchasing of our government has been truly set free. Try competing against Exxon Mobil or even Koch Industries.

Now let us examine the first two paragraphs of the next section, the "Statement of Principles":

We, the members of the Libertarian Party challenge the cult of the omnipotent state and defend the rights of the individual.

We hold that all individuals have the right to exercise sole dominion over their own lives and have the right to live in whatever manner they choose so long as they do not forcibly interfere with the equal right of others to live in whatever manner they choose.

Again, these are pretty words until you examine what they mean. Consider the "cult" of the state. Government is not a "cult". It is absolutely essential to the survival of large groups of people. It is called a cult, apparently, to disparage it in the minds of the readers. It is also how the wolves would like to see government because it is the only thing big enough to restrain them. As for the rights of the individual, they mean them. The rest of us who can't keep up with them can shut up and take it or die if that is what must happen. If this sounds like I am exaggerating, just look at the next paragraph. Individuals (once you know that they mean them, this begins to make sense) have the right to live in whatever manner they choose. They mean in whatever manner they choose free from any restraint by government, of course. They deal with the basic impossibility of that in our huge societies by modifying this with the words "so long as they do not forcibly interfere with the equal right of others to live in whatever manner they choose". Now, who do they propose will decide whether such interference has taken place? How will they define such interference? The only entity that could do this is government. If a member of a residential neighborhood wants to exercise his right to live however he wants by erecting a house that fills his lot to the very edges and towers over its neighbors by three stories, is that forcibly interfering with the rights of his neighbors? Does zoning make any sense? What about a neighbor in such a neighborhood who wants to enjoy his second amendment "right" to have and use firearms by erecting a shooting range in his back yard? Is that a forcible infringement on the rights of his neighbors? (This is not a fanciful fact pattern, it actually happened in a Tampa Bay community.) What about a neighbor who has an amateur rock band which she has practicing in her garage until 2am every evening? Is that a forcible interference with the rights of her neighbors? What about a celebrity who plays on his name to create a "university" which specializes in ripping off its students to the tune of thousands of dollars? Is that a forcible interference with the rights of other citizens? What's that you say? That's fraud and Libertarians are against fraud? Two things. One, who is supposed to define fraud and who is supposed to enforce the ban on it? The government, you say? My, my. Further, what if the celebrity in question is so rich that he can keep a toothless government (isn't that what they want) from enforcing its rules? The point I am making is that in a large and complex society the freedom to live in whatever way we like is and has to be constrained by many different factors and only government can protect the peaceable enjoyment of one's life and property. To deprive it of the ability to do that is to set loose the wolves. There are, of course, much more egregious examples of the point to be discussed as we go along. But, even at this point, we can see several examples of the need, even within the words of the Libertarians for government action.

In the fourth paragraph of their Statement of Principles, they set forth many things they don't want the government to do. I am not going to quote it because I could nitpick every bit of it and I would like to get this critique to an end someday. However, they end that paragraph saying that they"… support the prohibition of robbery, trespass, fraud and misrepresentation". Look at what they support prohibiting. Every one of these prohibitions refers in some way to crimes against property. That is the only thing they really care about. They want there to be courts to protect their property. Not listed by them are rape, murder, battery or any other crime against the person. Now, I am sure they would say, of course they are against these things and their platform does have language to that effect. But when it comes to listing their priorities, it is property, property, property.

The last paragraph of their Statement of Principles is a doozy:

Since governments, when instituted, must not violate individual rights, we oppose all interference by government in the areas of voluntary and contractual relation among individuals. People should not be forced to sacrifice their lives and property for the benefit of others. They should be left free by government to deal with one another as free traders; and the resultant economic system, the only one compatible with the protection of individual rights, is the free market.

Here is where the inequality of the "traders" is totally ignored. It is axiomatic that people and businesses are of all sizes and power. If an individual person in our society wants to have many services offered by gigantic corporations, for instance, that individual will accept all of the terms set forth by the corporation or get no service. If an individual wants to have a job and survive, that individual will accept the terms under which the job is offered, or will not have a job. If that sounds fair, consider that the party is against the minimum wage (as we will see later). Thus, under their scheme, many huge employers such as McDonald's and Walmart could offer jobs for $5.00 per hour. Their employees need jobs to survive. Millions of Americans are stuck with such jobs. But, they can't live on $200 per week. And, if they are married and have children, they can't make it even if their spouse also makes $200 per week. These are not lazy people, nor are they "takers". They want to work and they do work. But, their employers would rather cheat them on salary so that they can make greater profits. This is perilously close to the old company store concept in which the employer controlled the employee's whole life and embedded him or her in a lifelong debt servitude. This is what unfettered free markets mean in the world of unmitigated inequality. Depending on the largesse of the employer is a fool's errand. Contrary to the party's express assertion, a market with no governmental protection for workers is a prescription for what was once called wage slavery. Adam Smith, the free marketer's hero, as quoted in *American Amnesia* said, "When…regulation…is in favor of the workmen, it is always just and equitable."(AA 5) They should heed their hero. But, this section of the party's platform deals with a broader segment than just workers. It deals with allowing the wolves to have their way with consumers, their smaller competitors, the environment and any other commercial transaction or activity. This will become clearer as we go through this document.

Under the heading of "Self-Ownership" we find these words:

Individuals own their bodies and have rights over them that other individuals, groups and governments may not violate. Individuals have the freedom and responsibility to decide what they knowingly and voluntarily consume, and what risks they accept to their own health, finances, safety, or life.

You can read at least two different areas of concern here. One is to the effect that individuals should be free to purchase and use any type of drug or substance they wish to use or consume. That would include all the drugs that are now illegal in this country. That would be a legitimate reading and the party intends that meaning. Frankly, as a value judgment, this one doesn't bother me too much, but it would bother a lot of Americans. The other area of meaning, however, is a different kettle of fish. It is that of "buyer beware". If you buy it, you take the risk that it ain't safe. They want the Consumer Protection Agency abolished. Consumers would be expected to understand the risks they are taking and the government is to stay out of it. The fact that even simple products such as children's toys may have unappreciated hazards, much less products such as power tools and automobiles is of no concern to them. They should be free to sell such things and if, as Takata has done, they sell defective air bags which no consumer could have known about, or, such as Volkswagen, they deliberately sell automobiles with fraudulent emissions devices, or they cover up safety hazards such as accelerators that malfunction and drive automobile drivers and passengers into collisions, well, that would be too bad. After all, they were free not to buy the product and they "accept the risk to their own health, finance safety or life". The same would be true if, at the urging of a broker, they invest in an incredibly complicated Wall Street investment which goes belly-up and was known to be likely to do that by the broker. Too bad. And that is what led to the 2008 great recession. Did you know that only one minor player from the brokers and Wall Street executives involved in the frauds that led to the meltdown of the economy in 2008 has been even indicted, much less convicted? Once the Libertarians get their way, the issue would never even be considered.

Under "Expressions and Communication", we find this first sentence:

We support full freedom of expression and oppose government censorship, regulation or control of communications media and technology.

This is followed by a sentence about freedom of religion so that it looks like just a freedom of speech and religion section. It is, however, a great deal more (or less, depending on your point of view). They oppose government control of communications media and technology. They also want to abolish the FCC. They want freedom to broadcast on any frequency they like regardless of who else might be using that frequency, for instance. They want to advertise Joe Camel to children and any other product they please. If it turns into a mess, and I guarantee it would, well, we should trust them because, after all they represent the holy free market and it can regulate itself and they wouldn't try to hurt us would they? Wolves will be wolves if we let them. End of sentence.

In order to eventually get to the end of this someday, I will skip to the section entitled "Crime and Justice". In this section they advocate the repeal of all "victimless crimes" which would clearly include all drug consumption offenses and prostitution. Guess who would then get to sell drugs and set up houses of ill repute? Given how they fought the truth on tobacco for decades after they knew better, how do you think they would approach the honest truth in the use of drugs? But, one of the real zingers in this section is the final sentence: "We assert the common law right of juries to judge not only the facts but also the justice of the law." Lawyers call this idea "jury nullification". What it means is if a particular jury doesn't like what the law is that pertains to a given case, they may decide not to accept or follow it. If that is allowed, why bother to have laws? After all, if any jury can decide that laws passed by the legislatures or determined by the courts don't suit them, and they make up their own law, then no law can survive in a jury trial. That, folks, is anarchy. Just imagine a huge case against an oil company that had spilled oil all over the Gulf of Mexico, or some similar body of water, being tried in a state with many oil workers in which the corporation puts a million dollars or so into an ad campaign extolling the disadvantage to the workers of having their industry punished for the offense. The media blitz could easily convince some of the folks on the jury to decide they didn't like the law against spilling oil into the environment and let the corporation off. Do we think any of our corporations would do such a thing? Does anyone think they wouldn't??? This jury nullification is a recipe for anarchy.

Next let's look at the first two sentences of the section entitled "Self-Defense." They read as follows:

The only legitimate use of force is in defense of individual rights-life, liberty, and justly acquired property-against aggression. This right inheres in the individual who may agree to be aided by any other individual or group.

The defense of property with force is a very tricky area. If we see someone stealing our car may we shoot at them? How about if they are stealing our cell phone? May we impose an on-the-spot death penalty for this? Actually, they are thinking more about their own property however they see fit to define "property". What about militias in this country that decide that land or facilities owned by the government is "their property"?

May they, as we have seen such groups threaten to do, shoot at government agents who come to evict them? Next question I have is how they define "aggression". Will they define the enforcement of the tax laws as aggression? They want the IRS abolished and no one convicted for tax evasion (more on that later). So, may some individual or powerful group simply refuse to pay taxes and hunker down to shoot at government agents who come to arrest them? This sort of approach favors the powerful and the crazies. The Libertarians don't seem to mind being in the company of the crazies if they can get their way.

Let's next consider the last two sentences of the "Self-Defense" section:

Private property owners should be free to establish their own conditions regarding the presence of personal defense weapons on their own property. We oppose all laws at any level of government restricting, registering or monitoring the ownership, manufacture, or transfer of firearms or ammunition.

So, if your neighbor is paranoid and decides that on his property the appropriate "defense weapons" would be automatically triggered machine guns, rocket propelled grenades and land mines, well that would be alright with the party. But look closely. What is almost hidden in this language is the word "manufacture". Guess who wants to make a fortune manufacturing this stuff? From the late sixties up to today, more Americans have died from domestically owned guns than in all the wars in which the U.S. has ever been engaged. They not only want to lift all restrictions, but they want to manufacture the guns, folks. It's very profitable

The next section of the platform is titled "Economic Liberty". Paragraph 2.0 of that section states the general idea:

Libertarians want all members of society to have abundant opportunities to achieve economic success. A free and competitive market allocates resources in the most efficient manner. Each person has the right to offer goods and services to others on the free market. The only proper role of government in the economic realm is to protect property rights, adjudicate disputes, and provide a legal framework in which voluntary trade is protected. All efforts by government to redistribute wealth, or to manage trade, are improper in a free society.

So, as you see, "A free and competitive market allocates resources in the most efficient manner". I suppose, from their point of view the issue is efficiency so long as that means they get the riches. Let's talk for a minute about how well that has worked. Just within this so awfully terribly regulated economy, how has that been working out? There is a fascinating report entitled "Billionaire Bonanza Report: The Forbes 400 and the Rest of Us". It comes from the Institute for Policy Studies, is dated December 2015 and was written by Chuck Collins and Josh Hoxie. It contains some incredible statistics. For instance, America's 20 wealthiest people own more wealth than the bottom half of the American population combined, a total of 152,000,000 people in 57,000,000 households. With a combined wealth of 2.34 trillion dollars, the Forbes 400 own more wealth than 61% of the country combined, a staggering 194,000,000 people. That is, 400 people in America own more wealth than nearly 200 million other Americans! The wealthiest 100 households now own about as much wealth as the entire African American population. The wealthiest 186 members of the 400 now own about as much wealth as the entire Latino population. For other comparisons, from 1978 to 2013, the average corporate CEO' pay rose 978% while the pay of the typical worker rose 10.2% (SC 97) From 1948 to 2012, the net productivity for a production/ non-supervisory worker rose 240.9% but the real hourly compensation rose 7.8%. (SC 116) During the first six years of the recovery from the 2008 great recession the income of the bottom 90% declined. (SC 117) Between 2010 and 2013 the average income of the bottom fifth dropped 8% and their average wealth dropped by 21%. According to a study by Oxfam America, more than half of America's 46 million users of food pantries and other charitable food programs in 2013 had jobs or were members of working families. (SC134) In 2003 over 34 million Americans lived below the official poverty level; by 2013, this number had grown to over 46 million. (MCM 9) And this was well into the so-called recovery! Only the rich have really been recovering. As an example, although the Koch brothers despise Obama and warned that he would cause economic disaster in America, during his two terms in office, the brothers have gone from a net worth of approximately $14 billion to approximately $48 billion in the Forbes listings. What an "economic disaster" – but for whom? And one more statistic. The share of wealth in America held by the bottom 50% has fallen from 3% in 1989 to 1% today. All of these facts point to the inescapable conclusion that the Libertarians are getting what they want right now, Goodness knows what they would get if they were allowed free rein in power in the U. S. government. Their "free market" will screw everyone not rich or powerful enough to prevent it. It is no wonder the Libertarians call it "efficient", not "fair". Finally, note that they do want the government to provide rules and courts to protect property rights. The only regulation they will abide is that which they can use for their own purposes. Certainly, they don't want the courts to protect us from them!

Under "Property and Contract", I would select just this sentence:

Libertarians would free property owners from government restrictions on their rights to control and enjoy their property, as long as their choices do not harm or infringe on the rights of others.

Think for a minute who owns most of the property in this country. It ain't the 99%! Think of who has the assets to go head to head with a one percenter or a major corporation. It ain't us! The only entity that can do it is the government. Bet they don't want "restrictions" on property by the government. And they are taking full control of all the governments in the U. S. from the federal government to the state governments as I will explain later. They are doing it by buying them. That is how they can use their property and you can't because you aren't mega rich. But you and I are part of the vast majority of voters in the country. If we vote together, we can stop this "free market" Libertarianism from its takeover. Finally, once again notice that they do add a caveat that we should be free to enjoy our property "as long as their choices do not harm or infringe on the rights of others'. Who is to decide if that is so? Obviously, only the courts of the government. Thus, there needs to be a legislature and laws, right? Further, what constitutes "harm" or "infringement" on the rights of others? It would have to be the government, right? So, would they accept that the surgeon general of the U. S. should issue a report to the effect that tobacco use causes cancer? Whose "property rights" do you think they would want to protect? I suggest that history shows they would want to protect the rights of the tobacco companies to make and sell their product and the rest of us are free to decide to smoke and take the risks inherent in that choice, even if we don't know about them. And, remember, folks, big tobacco fought for decades to publicly deny the danger of cigarette smoking even though it knew from its own scientists in the 1950's that the surgeon general was right. They did the same thing about secondhand smoke. Only the government had the power to disseminate contrary evidence on a wide scale, to pay for the studies to prove the point, to regulate who could buy cigarettes and where they could be smoked. With this sort of track record (and there are many more example discussed later) who could believe that the "free market" of the Libertarians would treat the rest of us fairly? It wouldn't. They have told us so. We make our own "free" choices and we assume the risk of harm or even death, remember?

Next, we come to one of my favorite section. It is a favorite because it concerns the environment, which they wish to be free to despoil to the point of destruction for the livability of the planet. The section is entitled simply "Environment". The first two sentences read as follows:

Competitive free markets and property rights stimulate the technological innovations and behavioral changes required to protect the environment and the ecosystems. Private landowners and conservation groups have a vested interest in maintaining natural resources.

I will give them this: industry *could* develop the technology to protect the environment and the ecosystems. But, you see, it won't do it unless it is required to do so by government and it will do everything it can, as it has done and will continue to do, to stop the government from entering the fray. These free marketers fought tooth and nail to stop the government from regulating acid rain emissions, to stop it from regulating the use of CFC's that were eating the protective ozone layer and they have so far hamstrung all government efforts to regulate the emission of carbon dioxide which is emitted by the burning of fossil fuels, especially coal and oil. They have fought the efforts of the government to foster the development and spread of alternative energy production by solar, wind, geothermal and other methods. And they have spent literally billions to prevent the public from recognizing the problem. They propagated the big lies that global warming ain't happening, or, maybe if it is, it ain't caused by humans, or, if it is, it will be too expensive and damaging to the economy to fix it, or, there ain't anything we can do to fix it (note that this is opposite of what the party platform says) or, global warming is good for us because many cold areas will warm up, never mind that most of us live in warmer areas, or, and, finally, it's too late and we just need to adapt. We can all migrate to safer areas!!! (How the billions of people on earth could do this, I have no idea and neither do they. Or, maybe we will live underground and develop curved spines to accommodate cramped spaces. Later in the book I will expand on this and tell you who says this, but some of them are named David and Charles Koch, the proto-Libertarians. These folks don't care what consequences the burning of their fossil fuels cause and they cannot be trusted with the future of the earth because, contrary to the pretty words of their platform, they are wolves and they will destroy us all without a second thought. And believe me folks, we can't buy enough Tesla cars or put enough solar panels on our roofs to solve this problem ourselves. Trust the "competitive free markets" to do what they steadfastly refuse to do? Don't you believe it.

The next sentence from "Environment reads: "Governments are unaccountable for damage done to our environment and have a terrible track record when it comes to environmental protection." To start with, it is true that the U. S. government has caused environmental problems itself on military bases and other government property. However, this is something voters can hold it responsible for and, in any event, government caused environmental damage is miniscule to the point of nonexistence in comparison to the damage done by industry. With respect to its "terrible track record", that would be funny if it weren't so damned painful. The government's efforts to control all environmental hazards have been fought ferociously by the environmental enemies and their lackeys such as Mr. Inhofe and Mr. Mitchell in the Congress (and many others) The best weapon they have is to continuously slash the budget of the Environmental Protection Agency (EPA) and appoint environmental protection enemies to its leadership. We can't trust these people because they lie and they buy our governments and they have no intention of helping their fellow human beings to live in a protected environment. How they can fail to care about the wellbeing of their own children and grandchildren is more than I can decipher, but I suppose they believe they can buy their way out of an overheated world situation somehow.

The next sentence is rich. It says: "Protecting the environment requires a clear definition and enforcements of individual rights and responsibilities regarding resources like land, water, air and wildlife." Who are they suggesting should "define" and "enforce" individual rights? Even they must concede that it could only be the government. What do they mean by "individual rights"? Are they suggesting that only individuals have any rights here? Doesn't the whole population of the nation and, indeed, the planet have rights here? Would they propose that only an individual could sue over global warming? How well do we suppose that would work? Don't forget, they are buying judicial candidates as well as legislators. And that says nothing about the unequal pocket books of the litigators. This sentence is window dressing. They don't want us to have any environmental rights.

Finally, they say: "Where damages can be proven and quantified in a court of law, restitution to the injured parties must be required." Sounds like they actually said something here, doesn't it? Never fear, they didn't say a thing of any benefit to us. Let me think like a lawyer here for a minute. Just how would one "prove" and "quantify" one's damages for global warming? Right now, I don't believe that I could prove that I have personally suffered any damage from global warming. There are people, such as those who live in Miami Beach in Florida and have had to raise their road beds to escape rising tides, who might try it, but I wish them well for two reasons. One is that the enemies have suborned a whole host of "experts" who will come to testify against the case. Another is that where there is a whole group of people who are complaining, it is difficult to identify the "individual" right in question. If a citizen won this case, how could the damages be "quantified"? Other than some slight increase in local tax load for the improvements, what would the "damages" be that could be "quantified" It certainly doesn't sound like they intend such damages as the loss of enjoyment of one's surroundings, or the increased risk of higher water to be quantifiable" damages. By the time that serious "individual damages can be proven, it is very likely to be too late to prevent a catastrophe (even assuming it isn't getting too late now to reverse or stop the process). And how will industry ever afford to pay damages for damage to the whole planet and all its human citizens? They can't and they won't. We should just develop curved spines and adapt.

The next section is entitled "Energy and Resources". It says: "While energy is needed to fuel a modern society, government should not be subsidizing any particular form of energy. We oppose all government control of energy pricing, allocation and production." This is also rich. Note the word "fuel". That is their concern. They possess the fuels we use now and the future fuels still in the ground. But, I digress. The reason this is rich is that the fossil fuel industry has had a history of government subsidies and tax breaks since the beginning of the twentieth century. Those subsidies have not stopped to date. What they really mean is that they do not want to allow competing forms of energy such as the renewable energy sources to be subsidized. And, they want the government to have nothing to do with the production of energy. Right now it really is not involved, but if you go back to the mid-thirties of the twentieth century you will find such government projects as the electrification program of the new deal, Hoover dam, and the Tennessee Valley Authority were government production plans that brought electricity to much of the nation. It is beginning to appear that no one, *but* government will be able to put us onto nonpolluting and renewable energy sources in the time we have left to get it done. Further, only government can get a handle on stopping the burning of fossil fuels. I recognize that such government action would cost the enemies a fortune in lost assets in the form of unburned and unburnable fossil fuel reserves, but I really don't care. Yes, there will be an economic cost which all of us will bear to some extent, but it is better than a planet we can't live on - the only planet we've got. The rich can use their riches right now to get on the bandwagon for the new energy sources and make a fortune that way. Or, they can try out mining the asteroids or do something else with their present fortunes and still be filthy rich.

The next section is entitled "Government Finance and Spending". The first three sentences are as follows:

All persons are entitled to keep the fruits of their labor. We call for the repeal of the income tax, the abolishment of the Internal Revenue Service and all government programs and services not required under the U. S. Constitution. We oppose any legal requirements forcing employers to serve as tax collectors.

This one requires some thought to understand just what the consequences would be and what it really means. Start with this: the U. S. government and many state governments depend to a very large degree on the income tax. It is a "progressive" tax that burdens each of us with at least some concern to how much we can give up in taxes and still survive. Those who make more can afford to and are required to pay more. Those who cannot pay as much are asked to pay less and those at the bottom who are working but not making it even get money out of the system in the form of the earned income tax credit. Without these taxes, our governments cannot provide roads, education, social security the armed forces, etc. Do the rich bitches care? Of course not. They want to be free of taxes (wouldn't we all), but they want what they want regardless of the consequences to others. Remember, they are the top of the inequality pyramid. Next they want to abolish all government programs not *required* by the U. S. Constitution. There is not a lot *required* by the U.S. Constitution. Such entities as the National Institutes of Health and the Centers for Disease control (the NIH and the CDC) are not constitutionally required. So, forget public health services. Social Security, Medicare and Medicaid are certainly not required by the constitution. So, millions of us who depend on them for any reason can just forget it, right? (And we are supposed to *want* this and *vote* for it?)

Certainly such frivolous programs as the EPA and the Occupational and Safety and Health Administration (OSHA) would be gone. We wouldn't want to protect the environment or the safety and health of workers, would we? Other agencies such as the FBI, the CIA and the Department of Homeland Security are certainly not constitutionally required agencies. All government relief services for the welfare of the poor, the hungry and the needy would be gone. Screw 'em, right? Let 'em get a job, right? What job that would be is hard to tell and, besides that, many who use these services are employed but not making enough to survive without help. This provision of the Libertarian platform more than any other shows the callous unconcern of those who have "got theirs" have for the rest of America. The wolves don't care and they don't want to have to be involved in making our society work for everyone even though the rest of us are their employees or their customers or even just their fellow human beings. I will give specific examples out of their own mouths later.

But look: Article I, section 8 of the U. S. Constitution sets forth the powers of Congress. These are stated as powers, not requirements. In its first paragraph, it says, in part:

The Congress shall have The Power To lay and collect Taxes, Duties, Imposts and Excises, to pay the Debts and provide for the common Defense and General Welfare of the United States…

There is no question that our constitution gives Congress the power to tax us for the common defense *and the general welfare* of the country. The sixteenth amendment gives it the power to levy income taxes. Thus, regardless of what the constitution *requires,* it *empowers* the government to do everything it is doing, including all the agencies I just mentioned as well as providing for what it determines is proper for general *welfare*! For those strict constructionists among us, the word "welfare" must be a hard nut to digest. You see, the Libertarians will try to con us at every step of the way in order to get out of their obligations to the general welfare of the country so that they can be ever richer and more powerful.

Skipping onward, we come to the section entitled "Money and Financial Markets". It says:

We favor free market banking, with unrestricted competition among banks and depository institutions of all types. Markets are not actually free unless fraud is vigorously combated. Those who enjoy the possibility of profits must not impose risks of losses upon others, such as through government guarantees or bailouts. Individuals engaged in voluntary exchange should be free to use as money any mutually agreeable commodity or item. We support a halt to inflationary monetary policies and unconstitutional legal tender laws.

Well, goodness me. What a mouthful they say here. They favor "free market banking". You know, that is what we had in 1929 and it nearly ruined our country when the depression exploded the economy. They cannot be trusted to regulate themselves. Greed will control, not good sense. Controls were put on banking after the collapse of 1929 and we got along fine for more than 50 years. Unfortunately, beginning with Reagan, the government began to relax the regulation of banking, allowing interstate banking and investment banking. This allowed banks to turn into monstrously large institutions, some of which now have assets of more than a trillion dollars. These behemoths became "too large to fail" not because they deserved to be protected, but because it would trash our economy and set off world-wide economic destruction. Further, allowing investment banking led to the Lehman Brothers travesty in which they nearly collapsed the economy all by themselves investing in bundled mortgage-backed investments which became (as they were always destined to do) nearly worthless when the real estate market imploded. Then, of course, for a while Lehman lied about the health of the bank until it suddenly went bankrupt. If you have seen the movie "The Big Short", you may have some sense of what was going on. This resulted from relaxing controls on the banks and letting them be "free". They cannot be trusted. And you should know that the Dodd-Frank Act which was enacted after the great recession of 2008 set in, which was intended to tighten the controls, has been strangled by the finance industry by starving the regulatory agencies' budgets and fighting all their proposed regulations in the courts. You may have noticed that the real estate market seems to be on the upslope of doing the same thing all over again. Sure, give these crooks a freer hand. After all, what could possibly go wrong? The free market will look out for us won't it? Or.... maybe not???

Then they say "those who enjoy the possibility of profits must not impose risks of losses on others.... What hypocrites. They want the "possibility of profits" (certainty is more like it) but they steadfastly refuse to admit that they are causing damage and destruction to others. Check out the environmental record of Koch Industries or Exxon Mobile or BP or Georgia Pacific (a Koch industries subsidiary now) or the nuclear power industry or DuPont, etc., etc. etc. They not only won't admit it but they will fight to the last gasp denying the damage and then claim it is nothing or, at least, worth nothing. Worse yet, they are heating up our world. How will they ever pay for that? And they have the gall to say that "those who enjoy the possibility of profits must not impose risks of losses on others"??? They don't mean it when it comes to them and they want the government divested of the power to hold their feet to the fire. Of course they do. On the other hand, when it comes time for the damage to be ameliorated in order to save the economy from true catastrophe, well, then they say: "...such as through government guarantees or bailouts". How dare they? It's OK if they break it but don't let the government try to save the rest of us from the effects of their actions. Incidentally, the financiers and bankers who did this in the past are strong right wing "free market" advocates and many are part of the Koch network.

Next, they say:

"Individuals engaged in voluntary exchange should be free to use as money any mutually agreeable commodity or item. We support a halt to inflationary monetary policies and unconstitutional legal tender laws."

What the heck are they talking about? It's really very simple. They want to do away with the U. S. currency and become the issuers of money themselves. This would take us back to the disastrous policies of the mid-nineteenth century. Far worse, it would destroy the universal acceptability of money within the U. S. and around the world. Why would they want this? It is really very simple. They want to profit from creating their own money. They also want consumers to accept whatever they designate as money when they are to pay out to us for any reason. Just imagine the effect on the world economy if the U. S. dollar were discontinued. Insofar as their constitutional argument goes, that has long been decided by the Supreme Court. Article I section 8 again of the constitution gives Congress the power to "coin" money. The courts find this a satisfactory basis for the government to issue greenbacks and declare them the only 'legal tender" in the country. How would you like to be paid in the currency of Lehman Brothers? You begin to see how this Libertarian Party platform and those who push it are out to steal the country out from under us and I promise they are sneering at us as they talk us into doing it to ourselves.

Their next section is labeled "Marketplace Freedom". It reads:

Libertarians support free markets. We defend the right of individuals to form corporations and other types of entities based on voluntary association. We oppose all forms of government subsidies and bailouts to business, labor, or any other special interest. Government should not compete with private enterprises.

What they mean is free for them. Just start up a business that begins to successfully compete with one of them and they will either try to destroy it or buy it out. They can't stand and will not tolerate competition. They also can't stand and are trying to eliminate the moderating power of the government because it is so far the one entity that can, if the right wing will let it, control these egomaniacs. With respect to subsidies, they have received and will continue to receive subsidies, special tax breaks and other goodies from governments, both national, state and local. They shop their plants and offices around the country and go with the location where the governments that pertain will give them the biggest break, for instance, putting aside the massive breaks the fossil fuel industry, agribusiness, big pharma and others have received from Congress. Perhaps you can see why I hate this Party and its platform. If not yet, you will. They next say that "Government should not compete with private enterprise. Well, perhaps then the pharmaceutical industry will get busy and develop a slew of new antibacterial drugs to replace the ones that are slowly being outfought by mutating bacteria? No, they won't. Such drugs are rapidly curative and there is not much profit in them because patients don't need much to do the job. They would rather put out drugs that people must take for years or for life or, in the alternative, drugs they can charge $1,000 a pill for such as certain cancer drugs and others. Or maybe they will compete with one another to produce flu vaccines and other such drugs? No, not so much. Again, not enough profit. So, who does this? Much comes from grants given by the NIH. Many other drugs such as penicillin were developed in usable form by the government. Don't forget, the government produced computers, the internet, lasers, radar, jet planes, etc. Industry now profits from these inventions. Government work has not hurt industry, it has enriched us all. On a day-to-day basis, government does not compete with private enterprise, but private enterprise has benefited hugely from subsidies, inventions, funding, public contracts for infrastructure and military armament and so on. The success of the twentieth century in enriching all Americans was due to the combined efforts of the government and private enterprise in what the authors of *American Amnesia* call the "mixed economy". I strongly urge every American to read that book. The authors are awesomely erudite, and they make their case with meticulously researched and footnoted data. Please, people, read that book. The rest of us are not in their league in understanding what is really happening in America today and whose fault it is. And notice that we are now seeing people and especially political commentators calling Obama's policies or FDR's policies or any other Democrat's policies "socialism" or "collectivism". They do grave harm to the meaning of those terms. Both refer to the collective ownership of the means of production and distribution by "the people" collectively or, same thing, by the government. This country has never had such collective ownership of the means of production or distribution in any meaningful sense. Did not, does not and will not. Later I will talk in some detail about the technique of the Big Lie used by the enemy. You will no doubt be interested in what exactly they have been up to.

The next goody in the platform is entitled "Labor Markets". It reads as follows:

Employment and compensation agreements between private employers and employees are outside the scope of government, and these contracts should not be encumbered by government-mandated benefits or social engineering. We support the right of private employers and employees to choose whether or not to bargain with each other through a labor union. Bargaining should be free of government interference, such as compulsory arbitration or imposing the obligation to bargain.

No government-mandated benefits mean they don't want the government to tell them that they should provide health insurance or vacations or parental leave or a minimum wage or government overseen safety on the job or any other benefit that makes life for an employee better. Every other rich country in the world does better by its people than we do. These low-lifes want the U. S. employee deprived of these benefits. And you know what? Almost every other advanced nation in the world has single-payer government-backed universal health care. If we had that, we could stop fighting over these "benefits" in employment contracts that they are bitching about. But they would never want that because they want control of health care to remain in the hands of those who can rape us to the tune of twice the cost of health care compared to any other advanced nation, lack of availability to many millions of Americans and prescription drugs that are so expensive that a large percentage of Americans don't buy or take them when prescribed because they can't afford them. That is the health care that they want to protect. And if you hear some bloviating politician, say we have the best health care system in the world know that they are lying. The statistics are undeniable. Again, look to *American Amnesia* or also *Saving Capitalism.* Great books. I will have more details on health care later.

Now let's talk about unions. When I was young and Harry Truman tried to nationalize the railroads to break a strike and force the industry and the unions to heel, I thought the unions were the worst thing in the world. And some of their tactics were pretty thuggish. It wasn't until I was much older and better educated that I realized that many if not most of the benefits of the ordinary employee, whether in a unionized industry or not, came as a result of unions. The free marketers hate them because they became big enough to go head-to-head with the giant corporations. Through the latter half of the twentieth century and into the twenty-first, the unions have steadily lost ground and it shows. The middle class is slowly disappearing, and the working poor are replacing it. It is almost not worth their time to put this in their platform because it is a fight that they have already won. And the rest of us are paying for it. So, if there are not going to be unions to stand up for us, then I say the government should be doing it. It should, in the words of the constitution, see to the general welfare. If they don't like unions, let them deal with that! The government has the power if the paid assassins in the Congress can only have their greedy fingers pried off the levers of control.

Next, we come to "Education" and this one is pure poison. Look at it:

Education is best provided by the free market, achieving greater quality, accountability and efficiency with more diversity of choice. Recognizing that the education of children is a parental responsibility, we would restore authority to parents to determine the education of their children, without interference from government. Parents should have control of and responsibility for all funds expended for their children's education.

Now, I don't know about other places, but putting private firms into the public education system has been a disaster in Florida. But what these rich bitches want is the profit from providing schooling. It is a massive undertaking with the potential to make billions for them. Yet all of this is trivial beside the central tenet here. The central point is this: "Parents should have *control of and responsibility for* all funds expended for their children's education". (My italics) Think about what this means. First, giving parents control of their children's education means that many who do not understand or care for the requirement for their children to be educated will be free to skip it altogether. Go back to the nineteenth century before compulsory education for an idea what that might mean. Compulsory education is what drove the boom of the late nineteenth century and the twentieth. It produced the most educated population in the world until the late twentieth century when we started ignoring education's priority. But the real bug-a-boo is this: the responsibility – mind you the *responsibility* -- for paying for education is to be that of the parent. This means whether we can afford it or not, we will each be responsible to pay these new private schools for our children's elementary, middle school and high school education ourselves! Hey, folks, if we could all afford this, no doubt many of us would. It is certainly true that education in the upper tier of private schools is exemplary. But those schools are hideously expensive. What could be afforded by those without thousands to spend every year on each child's education would certainly not be top-tier education. In fact, most of us could not do it at all. The horrendous effect on the education of the next generations cannot be overstated. You would think that these idiots might be worried about getting sufficiently educated employees, but I guess not. And, by the way, they would like to basically wipe out the public institutions of higher learning. The colleges and universities that have provided the vast bulk of our educated citizens would disappear. According to Koch buddy Art Pope in North Carolina who masterminded the rape of that state with the purchase of the state legislature and its governor and then became director of the state budget, he would like to deal with public university education by "starving the beast". This in the southern state with arguably the best public university system in the south and one of the best in the country. This platform plank is just so wrong, so outright evil that I can hardly think of a strong enough way to disparage it. They just don't care about anyone but themselves to the extent that they would tear down our citizens' education in the twenty-first century wherein all of our competitor countries are driving their children's education inexorably farther ahead of ours. Shame on them.

Then we come to the inevitable one, "Health Care". Look at it:

We favor a free-market health care system. We recognize the freedom of individuals to determine the level of health insurance they want (if any), the level of health care they want, the care providers they want, the medicines and treatment they will use and all other aspects of their medical care, including end-of-life decisions. People should be free to purchase health insurance across state lines.

There you have a perfect picture of the Libertarian mindset. Everyone can choose their own health care, and they can have as much of the world's most expensive health care as they can afford. All health care should, of course, be provided by for-profit entities so that they can wring the last dollar out of it. (They seem to be overlooking the fact that a huge part of the income for private health care providers comes from government and compulsory employer provided health care plans which would disappear under their platform and the income from health care would probably go down drastically, not up.) These people cannot or will not face the fact that many Americans cannot afford the crappy plans they are putting together. What they do care about is that whatever financial drag the programs they despise cause on their already bloated wealth will disappear. They also ignore the fact that their incomes are generally a result of the good fortune they have of being citizens of this country and participants in its economy. They don't seem to realize that tearing it all down will ultimately beggar them too. It goes without saying that if you can't afford American health care, then you can just screw off and die. It is particularly interesting that they want to preserve the right to buy health insurance across state lines. So far as I know, you can do that now. What you don't see is the right to purchase health insurance across national lines – or medicines. The Medicare and Medicaid systems could save billions if they were permitted to purchase drugs across national lines such as from Canada. We in America are no longer allowed to do that nor are our insurers nor our governments because big pharma got the Congress to forbid it so that they can charge the vastly bloated prices for drugs that they cannot charge anywhere else in the world due to competition.

After the health care tone deafness, we get "Retirement and Income Security". Here we see the death of the Social Security program:

Retirement planning is the responsibility of the individual, not the government. Libertarians would phase out the current government-sponsored Social Security system and transition to a private voluntary system. The proper and most effective source of help for the poor is in the voluntary efforts of private groups and individuals. We believe members of society will become even more charitable and civil society will be strengthened as government reduces ats activity in this realm.

You will note the language "phase out". That is to keep those on Social Security now from automatically voting against them. However, with their programs, it is a certainty that most of us would never be able to afford retirement because we would be totally broke after paying for all of our children's educations and our health care – assuming we were able to pay for them at all – which many of us would not be able to do on their $5.00 per hour wages or even on what is now considered middle income wages. Folks, all other wealthy nations have income security programs like Social Security and welfare and almost all of them are more generous than ours. Civilized nations realize that there is a common responsibility of our people to care for one another. Another problem is that many if not most of us do not have the resolve to save over a lifetime for retirement. That is one reason that Social Security taxes are required and the program is universally available to citizens who have paid anything into the system. Yes, it is true. Many of us need help with long-range planning. That is sad but true. It is also true that Social Security benefits are often not enough to live on except at bare poverty levels. At one time there were pension plans offered by employers. Nowadays there are pretty much only 401(k) plans and other employee contribution plans. This is another way to push the financing and planning for retirement onto the individual, many of whom either can't afford it or won't do it voluntarily. And that is where the rubber meets the road for Libertarians. They absolutely refuse to countenance paying anything for people who could have done better but didn't. Folks, there are among us the weak. We do have a responsibility to help them in my view and the view of the rest of the civilized world. What does that make Libertarians? Uncivilized! This plan will no doubt keep Libertarians from ever winning an election at the federal level. Unfortunately, they have taken over the Republican Party in the Congress and in many state governments and now apparently in the presidency. Their idiocy is creeping into the national dialogue. After all, George W. Bush tried to pass a plan to privatize Social Security already and Paul Ryan is a fan of that approach, although he is far from the only one.

There is one other major issue I see here. They want to leave the needy to the mercy of privately funded charity. We have one of the larger private charity sectors in the world if not the largest. Despite that, it could not possibly pick up the hundreds of billions involved in public care for the needy and helpless. But they want to leave it to those who can afford it to do this. There will be a lot fewer of those folks when they get done. Once they do away with the income tax and there is no more tax deduction for charity, I would be willing to bet that the amount of giving by the 1% would decline and it would not go nearly so much to the needy as to those things that get them recognition such as the arts and entertainment. I am in favor of such donations, but first we need to see to it that our people have basic necessities. Given what we see here and the attitude of the rich which I will outline later, it would be very difficult to see any hope whatever that they would pick up the burden for the needy whom they consider "takers" and "moochers".

Then we have "National Defense":

We support the maintenance of a sufficient military to defend the United States against aggression. The United States should both avoid entangling alliances and abandon its attempts to act as policeman for the world. We oppose any form of compulsory national service.

I wonder how they intend to pay for a national military force without the income tax and the IRS. In any event, it is nice of them to be in favor of defending against "aggression". Does that include international terror?

How would they deal with that? Their program doesn't allow for that at all. In fact, their platform is isolationist and insular. They want us to leave the rest of the world alone and have it leave us alone – except for their export business and the outsourcing of American jobs overseas. Guys, they can't have it both ways. If we are going to be involved in the world, we have to be involved. And in today's world with the ability to be on the other side of the planet overnight, there is no way to sustain insularity. With respect to the opposition to compulsory national service, we are not doing that now, but in the case of need such as a really major war, the government needs that power and if it did not have it, it would create it anyway. Things like this plank in their platform show that they don't think very carefully but rather just put together a list of ideas with no thought at all as to how they would work together as a whole or how they would look in the real world.

Next, we have a plank that will resonate with many members of our citizenry, especially the paranoid part. It is "Internal Security and Individual Rights". It is a mixed bag, and I don't hate all of it. It reads:

The defense of the country requires that we have adequate intelligence to detect and to counter threats to domestic security. This requirement must not take priority over maintaining the civil liberties of our citizens. The Constitution and Bill of Rights shall not be suspended even during time of war. Intelligence agencies that legitimately seek to preserve the security of the nation must be subject to oversight and transparency. We oppose the government's use of secret classification to keep from the public information that it should have, especially that which shows that the government has violated the law.

Well, I thought they didn't want any agencies not required by the constitution. Even so, they want an effective intelligence service but they want it to be transparent. Folks, by its nature, clandestine intelligence work cannot be *transparent.* Further, the more complex are the schemes of international terror and even the cyber capabilities of other advanced nations, the more our intelligence community cannot be small (although I still think it is bloated and works at cross-purposes with itself as it is). It is essential that government be able to classify information, although that is a difficult thing to define or police. And, yes, I think we can all agree that we don't want our government to violate the law and then hide that fact. Unfortunately, it is all very complicated and simplistic statements will not help resolve these issues. With respect to the suspension of any civil liberties during wars, the constitution allows for the suspension specifically of the right to *Habeas Corpus* during rebellion or invasion in Article I Section 9. Otherwise, the constitution doesn't allow the suspension of civil liberties even during war. That didn't stop us from interning our citizens of Japanese descent during World War II and I suspect that we will do what we deem necessary in a major war no matter what our laws might say. (I abhor what was done to our own citizens of Japanese descent and I certainly hope we don't even consider duplicating it for our Muslim citizens.)

The next two sections cannot possibly coexist. Nevertheless, they are there. Let's look at the section entitled "International affairs":

American foreign policy should seek an America at peace with the world. Our foreign policy should emphasize defense against attacks from abroad and enhance the likelihood of peace by avoiding foreign entanglements. We would end the current U. S. policy of foreign intervention, including military and economic aid. We recognize the right of all people to resist tyranny and defend themselves and their rights. We condemn the use of force, and especially the use of terrorism against the innocent, regardless of whether such acts are committed by governments or by political or revolutionary groups.

I agree wholeheartedly with the first sentence. Every government we have ever had would have and did wish to be at peace with the world. So what? The issue is how to do that. So let's look at what they say about that. They want to avoid "foreign entanglements." In prior platforms they have spelled that out more clearly. They want us out of NATO and all similar arrangements. In fact, they want us totally isolated from any agreements that would require us to aid any other nation in cases of aggression against them, which would also mean they would not come to our aid either. They also want us out of the United Nations. They do not want us to provide any military or economic aid to other nations. That means we don't help the needy anywhere else in the world and we don't back up our historic allies such as England and France or other strategic friends such as Japan and Israel. So, if we want a coalition to help us against world terrorism that will not happen. Then we can count on the terrorists to leave us alone, right? After all, they condemn the use of force and terrorism against the innocent. That should take care of it, they condemn it. Would that that worked. If we pulled out of our alliances the effect on world peace, to the extent that it even exists now, would be incalculable. Basically, except for its isolationistic verbiage, this section says nothing in pretty words.

Then this section on international affairs is followed by "Free Trade and Migration". It says:

We support the removal of governmental impediments to free trade. Political freedom and escape from tyranny demand that individuals not be unreasonably constrained by government in the crossing of political boundaries. Economic freedom demands the unrestricted movement of human as well as financial capital across national borders. However, we support control over the entry into our country by foreign nationals who pose a credible threat to security, health or property.

You see, they want to avoid foreign entanglements, but they want free flow of people and finances across national boundaries. How does that work without such treaties as the North American Free Trade Agreement

(NAFTA)? What they want is as many low paid foreign workers in this country as care to come here and the freedom to move their production and their employment to whatever location is the cheapest. They want to export without duties and they want other nations to have the freedom to glut our markets with cheap and perhaps unsafe goods without restraint. After all, they say the consumer should beware. What they want here, besides screwing the average American worker, is incompatible with their position on international affairs. Do they think that other nations will open their borders to us unrestrictedly for commerce when we won't make other types of agreements with them? And what about the unrestricted passage of people into our country? (The Immigration and Naturalization Service (the INS) is one of those agencies which they want to abolish.) How well will that go down with the Trump voters and the rest of the Republican Party? Actually, I kind of like it but it doesn't stand a chance in hell of getting by our voters even though we will vote for so much else that cuts our own throats. And, by the way, without the INS, the FBI and Homeland Security, how do they intend to prevent the passage into our country of those who "pose a credible threat to security, health or property? As a matter of fact, we can't do it well now and less government will be even less able to do it.

The next section is a mixed bag. It is entitled: "Rights and Discrimination". It actually contains some very desirable principles, but as usual, there are thorns in those roses. It says:

Libertarians embrace the concept that all people are born with certain inherent rights. We reject the idea that a natural right can ever impose an obligation upon others to fulfill that "right". We condemn bigotry as irrational and repugnant. Government should neither deny nor abridge any individual's human right based upon sex, wealth, ethnicity, creed, age, national origin, personal habits, political preference or sexual orientation. Members of private organizations retain their rights to set whatever standards of association they deem appropriate, and individuals are free to respond with ostracism, boycotts and other free-market solutions.

There is a good deal of language here about the rights of individuals with which I think even the most left wing of us would agree. But, don't overlook what is hidden among these nice thoughts. For instance, they "reject the idea that a natural right can ever impose an obligation upon others to fulfill that 'right'." What does this mean? It means that one person's "right" to exist with at least a minimum level of food, shelter, clothing and health care is irrelevant to them and not something that can impose any obligation on those of us who are able to help. In other words, the government cannot tax us, for instance, and distribute benefits to those in need. Folks, that is what current rich and civilized nations do! They do not allow any of their citizens to starve or go without health care or shelter. They do, in fact, as the Libertarians and the Republicans seem to hate, "redistribute" wealth so that no one at the bottom is squeezed out. Does this harm those at the top? Do they go without food, shelter, health care or other necessities because of it? Are they deprived of their mansions and their yachts and their private jets because of it? Hell, no. As I have already pointed out, the Koch brothers all but tripled their personal wealth during the "disastrous" economic policies of the Obama administration. They have so much wealth that a billion dollars is pocket change. The wealthy in this country are not harmed, nor will they be harmed if they must give up some to help their fellow citizens. That, of course, is true of all of us. We need to help the needy and only government can do that in a large and organized way. Our government is not doing anywhere near what it should (any level of government) because the right wing is doing all it can to prevent it. I will have more to say later about the need for all of us at any income level who are not in need to contribute and to stop whining about our tax load, which is nowhere near that of most advanced countries. The language about non-abridgement of individual rights is exemplary and, believe it or not, I applaud it. The language about private organizations is another matter. This would mean that government could not forbid businesses open to the public from discriminating against anyone for the reasons they set forth as private rights. If as a hypothetical, some large fast food chain should want to refuse service to gays or blacks or atheists that would be OK. We have come too far to permit this. Government has a legitimate role to play here and the answer is not "ostracism" or "boycott". Those approaches don't work against massive entities and shouldn't have to be resorted to in the world of the public. As for private organizations open only to certain members, that is allowed now. Try to get a woman golfer into the Masters tournament although they have, I hear allowed a woman to become a member of the club.

In the next section (mercifully, the next-to-last substantive one), that is entitled "Representative Government", they say, in part as follows:

We call for an end to any tax-financed subsidies to candidates or parties and the repeal of all laws which restrict voluntary financing of election campaigns. We oppose laws that effectively exclude alternative candidates and parties, deny ballot access, gerrymander districts, or deny the voters their right to consider all legitimate alternatives.

Here you see the Libertarians wanting to clear the way for them to spend as much as they want openly and without super PACs or any other subterfuge mechanism to elect whoever they want to pay for, spending however many hundreds of millions or billions of dollars they please. They want to do away with the presidential campaign fund set up to contribute funds through the government in a public manner. This fund isn't talked about much anymore but it still exists. They want it gone because it gets in their way. Of course, the *Citizens United* case has pretty much allowed them to do what they want anyway. That case is the center of much of the trouble we are now having, although it didn't take *Citizens United* to start us down the road. Let me be as clear as I can: The rich bitches want to buy our government and take it away from the rest of us. They do not want our votes to count for anything if we disagree with them. They have all but achieved that end now. With respect to their position relating to excluding alternative candidates that is aimed at giving them full and equal access to the ballot. Frankly, I can't disagree with that. Of course, there have to be some limitations on what it takes to run for major public offices because if there were not, we would have a ballot so full of wannabes with no chance that the elections would be all but impossible. Other than that, I think every candidate and every legitimate party should be allowed free access to the ballot. So, once again, but not often, I agree with them. On the other hand, I think it is rich that they say they are against gerrymandering because the Republican Party has done a wonderful job of it recently with the help of the money they get from the 1%. (I recognize that gerrymandering has been going on for more than 200 years and all parties that could manage it did it, but it is really hitting its stride now.) As for denying ballot access, that is a deliberate policy of the Republican party which seeks to disenfranchise as many of its opponents, especially the poor and the minorities, as they can. I will later quote some frank admissions on their part to that effect. It is bitterly ironic that these folks would have us believe that they are against denying voter access. What they mean is they want to be sure that all folks who will vote for their agenda have access.

Finally, (yes, finally!) there is the section entitled "Self Determination". It is short:

Whenever any form of government becomes destructive of individual liberty, it is the right of the people to alter or abolish it, and to agree to such new governance as to them shall seem most likely to protect their liberty.

It is hard to disagree with this as a general proposition. It is also all but impossible to do in real life without an uprising of some sort. This may be a veiled reference to Jefferson's famous (and very popular among second amendment proponents) quote: “The tree of liberty must be refreshed from time to time with the blood of patriots and tyrants.” It seems very likely that should the Libertarian supporters be in charge of our government by any means whatever, the freedom of the wolves would be such as to extinguish the voice of the (99%) lambs.

You readers will be glad to know that this completes my review of the Libertarian platform. I hope that as we went along you could see that the intent of the Libertarians is to “free” those who have the wherewithal to ride as roughshod over the rest of us as they want. They wish to be subject to no restraints whatever. If they want to freely manufacture and sell dangerous products, well, let the buyer beware. After all, the buyer “chose to take that risk”. If they want to control our government by buying its representatives and by bombarding the voters with lying propaganda during campaigns, well, that is OK. If they are caught from time to time breaking a law or rule, well, they want the bodies in charge of enforcement to be abolished. They want the courts to protect their “property”, but they will own the judges and most of the lawyers. Perhaps most infamously, they want the freedom to keep us burning their fossil fuels regardless of the fact that it is and will keep on damaging our environment through global warming. If we wait until it is too late (assuming that it is not yet too late), well then we can accept the consequences. After all, we entered into purchase contracts to use their products and we can just live with the consequences or we can migrate … somewhere.

I must admit that until this year I had never read the platform of the Libertarian Party and I suspect most folks still have not done so. If you just watch their presidential and vice-presidential candidates on television (and they do appear there), you will hear them say that they want …” the government out of your pocket and out of your bedroom”. If you just listen to that, you could think they were beneficent fellas (they are fellas) who had the best interests of the public in mind. All of their talk about “individual” freedom in their platform is intended to lead to the same conclusion. It seems highly unlikely they could possibly get elected, so what is going on? Well, many of their leading proponents, such as the Koch brothers (remember, David was their vice-presidential candidate inn 1980), many of their think tanks and organizations such as the Cato Institute, the Heritage Foundation, CEI and AFP as well as many others back the Libertarian positions openly. These people and entities have made it their business to take over the *Republican Party* and infest it with their ideas to the point where if you listen to people like Ted Cruz, Paul Ryan and columnist George Will, you will be hard-pressed to tell the difference between the Libertarian Party and the Republican Party. In fact, Will, one of the most influential columnists in America, a graduate of Oxford universities and Princeton University, has just this year changed his party affiliation from Republican to "unaffiliated" and has said that he is leaning Libertarian. The point is that the Libertarians have infiltrated the Republican Party as I shall explain in detail later. If you Google the Libertarian Party, you will see that it tried to position itself as a real alternative to the Trump Republican candidacy for those who are far right thinkers. No one I know has ever said it, but it would not surprise me to discover a merger of the two parties at some point. Whether that happens or not, the Libertarians already own Congress and many state houses. That is why the Libertarian Party platform matters.

As we go along in this book, I shall identify many individuals and organizations that I identify with the label "enemy" but have not listed so far. In fact, this undertaking is an amalgam of many different subjects which are all interrelated. It is not possible, for me at least, to separate out every subject matter and keep it isolated from others. As a result, it was necessary to try to identify areas of discussion knowing that there would be great overlap no matter how the areas were defined. Thus, even I look at these discussion areas and wonder if they could not have been organized so as to segregate issues better. I couldn't do it, so you will see the overlap I mentioned.

Chapter 2

From Their Own Mouths

When I speak of the enemy, I mean not only those who inhabit the one percent or the corporate powers, but also their instruments. That includes not only their designated organizations and educational bases, but their spokespeople including politicians, academics, media representatives and organizations, authors and so forth. In this section, I will be referring to and discussing things actually said or written by these folks. If you see it coming out of their own mouths, it is easier to understand and believe than it would be for me simply to assert it. In some cases, such as the issue of global warming, some readers will no doubt believe that there either is no global warming or it's just natural or it is caused by humans but is not a big deal or it is a problem but there is nothing we can do about it. As I will show, there is every good reason to understand that these things are not so, but that explanation happens later in the book. If you find yourself agreeing with some of the things I am about to quote, you might try considering the issue again after you finish the book. I would hope by then you might have doubts about it. So, what have they said?

Many of the top one percenters take the view that whatever one is paid is the true measure of one's work or value to society. They almost have to believe that in order to justify what they are being paid because the amounts are so obscene. It also allows them to take the position that if you aren't being paid much, then you simply aren't worth much to society and that's just too bad. This overlooks the fact that many millions of people in America are working hard at whatever jobs they can find but are still below the poverty level and need help just to feed their families and house them. It also overlooks the fact that many of the 1% are just parasites on society who are manipulating the system to get unbelievably wealthy and then look down on those who couldn't see their way to do the same. Almost all of the quotes I will use are from secondary sources. That is, they are originally quoted in these sources. I will give you folks an idea where these quotes came from originally, but if you want the details, I urge you to go to the sources I am quoting from. Please, please, read some of these books.

The first quote comes from Robert Reich's *Saving Capitalism For the Many, Not the Few.* This one is admittedly Reich's characterization of what these enemies say, but it segues right into the real quotes. Mr. Reich says:

What you're paid is simply a measure of what you're worth in the market. If you aren't paid enough to live on, so be it. If others rake in billions, they must be worth it. If millions of people are unemployed or their paychecks are shrinking or they have to work two or three jobs and have no idea what they'll be earning next month, that's unfortunate but it's the outcome of "market forces". (SC 3-4)

This gives you some idea what the "free market" means to the top one percenters. If it benefits them, that is fine. If it does negative things to almost everyone else, that's just too damn bad. Admittedly, this is a conclusion reached and stated by Reich, but I think that after you see some of these quotes you will have no trouble agreeing that Reich is correct.

The next item comes from Ray Dalio, chief of Bridgewater Associates, a Wall Street hedge fund. Hedge funds are Wall Street organizations set up to be free of most regulatory agencies and their oversight. Bridgewater was the largest in the country in 2015 with 155 billion dollars under management. Hedge fund managers usually are paid a percentage of the assets under management, often 1%, plus a percentage that is often 20% of any increase in the value of the funds being managed. In 2012, Mr. Dalio was paid 3.9 billion dollars and he has continued to head the fund. His net worth in 2015 was estimated at 15.5 billion dollars. Just one percent of 155 billion dollars, never mind the percentage for increase in value, is 1.5 billion dollars. What hedge funds do is very complicated and depends on a great deal of savvy in the global financial world. It can be very lucrative but holds the risk of catastrophic losses. When the stock markets, among other financial activities are good, making money with large scale funds is relatively easy and if you are investing tens of billions, you can generate large incomes. These are some of the people who at least used to call themselves "masters of the universe". Mr. Dalio apparently runs an online business-strategy tract called "*Principles*". Hacker and Pierson quote from that tract thus:

Self-interest and society's interests are generally symbiotic. ...Society rewards those who give it what it wants. That is why how much money people have earned is a rough measure of how much they gave society what it wanted. (AA 186)

Have you ever heard the old saw "What's good for General Motors is good for America?" It was attributed to a GM exec but is probably apocryphal. Nevertheless, you see that it echoed here. Realize that hedge funds are not open to the general public. If you ain't already rich, you can't join in the fun. Realize also that these folks mostly don't invest their funds in actual production of things or tangible goods. They usually don't invest in research and development. They invest in complex investment vehicles that may or may not do any of that. They make their money by manipulating money. Note also that Mr. Dalio doesn't say that the amount (he) makes is a measure of the "good" he does society", he says it is a measure of how much they "gave society what it wanted". Just what part of society would that be? Why, it would be the 1%, of course! Mr. Dalio and his hedge fund haven't cured cancer, helped the poor, developed a new wonder drug or done anything else that might actually have benefited society. What then, gives him the hubris to say that his efforts are a fair measure of his real worth to society? The answer is that his efforts have made him rich and therefore powerful and he can say any damn thing he wants. I agree that he can. Not only that, I have no brief against people getting filthy rich. But he and his have to expect that they will be required to give back to a society that made it possible for them to be filthy rich in proportion to their rewards. He doesn't, despite any charitable giving he may undertake. He and his need to be made to do so. How? The answer is at the end of the book. In the meantime, you see the attitude the top of the 1% show toward their right to be our masters.

The next quote comes from Peter G. Peterson. Mr. Peterson was once Secretary of Commerce under President Nixon. He was CEO of Bell and Howell at one time and Lehman Brothers investment bank He founded the investment firm Blackstone and is one of those billionaires who has pledged to leave half his worth to charity. He has a foundation known as the Peter G. Peterson Foundation which is basically involved with raising public awareness about long term fiscal sustainability. He is one of the far-righters and is personally worth more than 2 billion dollars. Back in 1982 he was featured in the *New York Times Magazine* under a title "No more free lunch for the middle class". Therein he advocated steep cuts in retirement and health benefits to make these programs a safety net for the needy rather than insurance protections for the middle class. (AA 190) In his memoir, Peterson complained:

I see an indulgent country living almost entirely in the moment, afflicted with an aggravated case of myopia, and a sense of entitlement, one of my least favorite words." (AA190)

Now, whether Mr. Peterson was talking about retirement and health benefits from an employer or Social Security and Medicare, he is talking about programs that wage earners have paid for with their labor and their taxes. Neither he nor any of the other wolves have done a truly broad and unbiased study of the middle class and the needy and the strictures under which they live, nor do they intend to do that. They just bloviate about the sense of entitlement. The middle class and the working poor are just trying to get along on what they can earn, which is becoming harder and harder to do while the rich get richer and richer. I wonder how they would like to live on what is available to the hard working Americans they like to denigrate. It is true that there are some among those receiving benefits who do feel "entitled" and don't intend to lift a finger to earn those entitlements. If the programs providing those benefits were provided with a decent budget to do it, much of that could be discovered and eliminated from the system. But, I suggest that the number of such people and the benefits they obtain are nothing compared to the billions the U.S. throws away every month on things like the Iraq war and the F-35 fighter program (of which, more later).

Mr. Reich has a chapter in his book entitled "The Rise of the Working Poor". It is well worth reading in full, but I wish to take a couple of quotes out of it. The first comes from remarks made by John Boehner, then Speaker of the House of the U.S. Congress, a Republican, of course. He said in 2014 as follows: the poor have "this idea" that "I really don't have to work. I think I'd rather just sit around." (SC 134) Mr. Reich went on to say, for himself: "The reality is that America's poor work diligently, often more than forty hours a week, sometimes in two or more jobs. Yet they and their families remain poor." (SC 134) As I will dwell on in more detail later, Mr. Boehner is one of those far right Republicans who might just as well be a

Libertarian when it comes to his views. (And yet, he was ousted from his job as Speaker by the ultra-far-right because, as one wag suggested, he was suspected of trying to "commit government.") Listen, those of us who are in the situation of the working poor and the struggling middle class (and I do not claim that I am that poorly off because I am not, but we are all part of the 99%) have to pay attention to this and get rid of the bums with this sort of attitude. America is too rich a society for there to be a "working poor" or a "struggling middle class". So, if you care about this type of attitude in your government, as I will say over and over : learn who they are and get out to vote against these bums!

Next, I would like to quote from the far right-wing Republican senator from Iowa, Joni Ernst retrieved by Hacker and Pierson:

What we have fostered is really a generation of people that rely on the government to provide absolutely everything for them. … We're at the point where the government will just give away anything. (AA 245)

If that were true, why would there even be any working poor or struggling middle class? The Obama administration has been accused of giving away the store. The facts show that is not true. In fact, the Congress has blocked almost every effort to do anything new for the people of this country even though we bailed out Wall Street, the banks, AIG Insurance and General Motors to the tune of hundreds of billions. What we have here is a contempt for the struggling part of the American population by those who are in the 1% and their paid lackeys.

The next quotes come from Mitt Romney. You remember him, ex-governor of Massachusetts who supported a health plan for that state based on a Republican plan put forward back when the Clintons were trying to put together a more inclusive health plan for the country - a health plan on which "Obamacare" was based, but which he denounced as a candidate for president because the wolves backing him didn't want us to have a better health plan for those who couldn't afford one. Mr. Romney, poor thing, is only worth something like 250 million dollars. During his 2012 campaign for president, he said this to an exclusive private fund-raiser crowd:

All right, there are forty-seven percent who … are dependent upon government, who believe they are victims, who believe the government has a responsibility to care for them, who believe that they are entitled to health care, to food, to housing, to you-name-it. That that's an entitlement. And the government should give it to them. And they will vote for this president [Obama] no matter what … These are people who pay no income tax … My job is not to worry about those people. I'll never convince them they should take personal responsibility and care for their lives. (AA 245 – although it was all over the news at the time and is credited with taking him down in the end)

It is pretty hard to be any more insensitive and tone deaf than this, but there are some other quotes to compare with it. What effrontery of the poor in this rich nation to believe they might be "entitled" to health care, to food and to housing! Why can't they just accept that they should go without health care and go without food and go without housing? If they can't get work at more than a minimum wage job at $7.25 per hour or even two such jobs and can't support a family on that amount, then surely, they shouldn't have families … right? Or, maybe they should just shut up and take the cruddy benefits now available and be forever grateful to Mr. Romney and his ilk in government? Do you think I have an attitude problem?

The next Romney quote (there are so many of them) is a statement he made at a campaign event in 2012 in response to a young man who expressed concern about whether he would be able to afford college:

It would be popular for me to stand up and say I'm going to give you government money to pay for your college, but I'm not going to promise that. Don't just go to one that has the highest price. Go to one that has a little lower price, where you can get a good education. And, hopefully you'll find that. And, don't expect the government to forgive the debt that you take on. (AA73)

The short message here from Mr. Romney was: "Screw you, kid." He clearly had no idea how much college costs now nor did he realize that fewer and fewer Americans can afford it without taking on crippling debt which will dog them sometimes for decades. A debt, by the way which, unlike some debts, cannot be discharged in bankruptcy. He said a similar thing on the campaign trail in June 2012 in Virginia:

I think this is a land of opportunity for every single person, every single citizen of this great nation. And I want to make sure that we keep America a land of opportunity, where everyone has a fair shot. They get as much education as they can afford… (Pat Garofolo, Think Progress web site)

This is a pure Libertarian thought. We are all free to have anything we can afford and, if we can't afford it, too bad, even if it is a very important or even critical need. If our richest-in-the-world society takes this view of its population, then we are and deserve to be doomed to become third class. Mitt and his ilk don't recall what the GI bill did for our country's productivity in the mid-twentieth century and beyond. They also don't understand how critical it is for us to have a highly educated populace going deeper into the twenty-first century. Or, maybe, they don't care. Frankly, I don't give a damn which it is, it sucks rotten eggs. If we can afford nearly two trillion dollars and counting for the crappy wars in Afghanistan and Iraq, we can afford to educate our population, not according to their wealth, but according to their ability and hard work. If the Republican Party's slogan, as it appears in a newspaper picture in the Tampa Bay Times, is "you are NOT entitled", then we don't need the bums. This is not just an issue of entitlement attitudes by a few people, it is about our taking care of our people and being competitive in a knowledge-intensive future. Furthermore, the "let them eat cake" attitude (which, in her defense, Marie Antoinette apparently did *not* say) is arrogantly evident in this and the last few utterances quoted. As I have intimated, there are more Romney lovelies, but I want to get on with it.

Another quote along similar lines to the last ones comes from Jeff Greene, who made his fortune betting against subprime mortgages (the instruments that led to the 2008 crash). Speaking at an economic gathering in Davos, Switzerland where he traveled in a private jet, accompanied by two nannies for his children, Greene said:

America's lifestyle expectations are far too high and need to be adjusted so we have less things and a smaller, better existence. (AA 193)

Apparently Mr. Greene, who is a recent richie comparatively, having made his, now feels free to complain that others who aspire to do well should "adjust" their "lifestyle expectations. You know, it would be nice if much of the American population could even think in terms of "lifestyle expectations" rather than getting by from day-to-day and trying to stay out of poverty. What makes these people so dismissive of their fellow human beings? Whatever it is, it is infecting the Republican Party and a few Democratic office holders as well.

Next we turn to Senator Tom Cotton, a recent addition to the Republican Congressional far right-wing from Arkansas. Mr. Cotton was a beneficiary of the almost unlimited pocketbook of the Chamber of Commerce in his campaign. Considering the 2014 farm bill, he opposed it because it didn't cut food stamps enough. About those beneficiaries, he said: "They have steak in their basket, and a brand-new iPhone, and they have a brand-new SUV." This fellow voted to turn Medicare into a voucher program and raise the Social Security retirement age to seventy. He even opposed a resolution to raise the debt ceiling to fund programs already approved and budgeted by Congress, saying that to raise the ceiling would be "cataclysmic" whereas defaulting on the obligations of the government would create only a "short term market correction". (AA 267) This man's grasp on reality is rather like Alice's and he clearly lives in a wonderland of his own making. What arrogance allows him to speak of those who get food stamp benefits the way he did? Has he lived among them himself? Has he done some sort of extensive study of the matter? Why does he so detest the idea that these folks might have just a few of the things so many Americans consider essentials? And how many of them do you suppose have new SUV's? The ones I see in places like Walmart certainly are not driving new SUV's and their carts certainly contain a lot more ground beef and hot dogs than they do steaks. Further, if the U. S. government started defaulting on its obligations, the resulting economic catastrophe would make the recent "Brexit" look like a zephyr compared to a hurricane. He apparently has no grasp on what a horrible effect such an event would have on the world economy. Like it or not, we are the rock on which that economy is based. It was our crazy real estate crash that took down the world economically in 2008 and many countries are still struggling with the aftermath. Finally, it is also interesting that Mr. Cotton, who so detested the failure of the farm bill to cut food stamps enough, had no problem with the bill's huge subsidies for agribusiness. (AA 268) Farm subsidies for enormous agribusiness corporations are just gravy these days and should long since have been terminated. But, oh well, those corporations speak with louder and more wealthy mouths than the 99%.

I have a much longer list of these quotes but I want to switch focus a little bit. Hacker and Pierson speak of Ayn Rand in *American Amnesia* because her book *Atlas Shrugged* has become a favorite of the far right and has led to "Randianism" in both "hard" and "soft" varieties. If you would like to know more about both, please read *American Amnesia,* you will be glad you did. However, for those who haven't read Rand's book or haven't read it recently (it has been fifty years since I read it), I quote from *American Amnesia* on the topic:

The message of *Atlas Shrugged* is simple: Government destroys freedom; only creative capitalists produce wealth; everyone else is a "looter", a "moocher", and "incompetent," feeding on the elite's innovations. In one of Galt's [the protagonist of the book] speeches, he declares: "The man at the top of the intellectual pyramid contributes most to all those below him, but gets nothing except his material payment, receiving no intellectual bonus from others to add to the value of his time. The man at the bottom, who, left to himself, would starve in his hopeless ineptitude, contributes nothing to those above him, but receives the bonus of all their brains." (AA 184)

Don't you love it? This, folks is what many of these scum bags think of the rest of us. The fact that none of them could accomplish a thing without employees, the fact that almost all of the soldiers, sailors, marines and airmen who defend them come from the rest of us, the fact that most of them (not all, but most) have not invented new or better products or services by themselves and the fact that all of us are their fellow humans doesn't mean a thing. That these poor folks do all their marvelous thinking and get nothing but their "material payment" is a real tragedy isn't it? Shall we nominate them for an award? How about "Greediest Stinker Award"? Hacker and Pierson describe it best:

The distinctive core of hard Randianism isn't laissez faire (a very old fancy); it's the division of the world into a persecuted minority that heroically generates prosperity and a freeloading majority that uses government to steal from this small, creative elite. (AA185)

After noting that Rand's book received harsh reviews at the time it was released in 1957 (about the time I read it and was not competent to understand its implications), Hacker and Pierson say:

A half century later, however, the book luxuriated in the embrace of leading political and economic figures, from Fed chair Alan Greenspan to House GOP budget guru, 2012 VP candidate, and current House speaker, Paul Ryan. In 2008, sales of the book reached record highs, and conservative commentators spoke openly about business owners "going Galt." As one *Forbes* column gushed in 2012, "Galt epitomizes all that is glorious of capitalism in its purest form – innovation, self-reliance, and freedom from government interference." (AA185)

Folks, the downfall of the average American started for real in the Reagan administration with the advent of the tax cutting, deregulating and supply siding approach to government. It not only didn't enrich us, it has impoverished more of us and given us the most unequal society among the advanced nations in the world. It gave us the crash of 2008 and is bidding fair to do it again. When will we, the 99% wake up? Do we really want a Congress and a president who feel that way about us to control our destiny? Isn't America big enough to float everyone's boats? We would not be "stealing" from the rich anything they didn't already steal from us. And, never doubt it, they not only want to keep doing it, they want to keep doing it higher, deeper and better.

In a slightly different vein, here are some quotes from our "betters" about the minimum wage, which, by the way, as of this writing is at $7.25 per hour on the federal level. Mr. Reich puts it in perspective rather pungently:

As former congresswoman, Michelle Bachman once put it, if the minimum wage were repealed "we could potentially virtually wipe out unemployment completely because we would be able to offer jobs at whatever level." Theoretically, Bachman is correct. But her point is irrelevant. It is no great feat for an economy to create a large number of very-low-wage jobs. Slavery, after all, was a full-employment system. (SC 136)

Just exactly how could anyone live on $7.25 per hour, even if they worked for 40 hours per week and earned the princely sum of $290 per week? How about something less than $7.25 per hour? Wouldn't the fast food industry just love to pay its workers $5.00 per hour? Or, maybe, $4.00 per hour? Their profits would soar. In the meantime, the employees they depend on would starve or subsist on food stamps and live out of their not-new rat-trap cars. I personally know a woman who makes $3.00 per hour more than minimum wage who helps her adult, but ill children, who cannot feed herself and lives from month-to-month with whichever friend will take her in. This lady is one of the hardest-working people I have ever met and she doesn't deserve what is happening to her. How much worse is it for those who have minimum wage jobs? How about if they were paid even less than current minimum wage? Let me go on.

Jane Mayer has captured a wonderful quote from Richard Fink, (real name, I didn't make it up) who is described as Charles Koch's "grand strategist" and who holds many offices in Koch's many ventures. Fink was addressing one of the gatherings of the one percenters whom the Kochs call their "network" of the truly richest people in the world who are trying to buy the government (successfully, unfortunately). He was addressing the issues related to losing the presidential race in 2012 and what they needed to do to improve their performance. Mayer describes it thus:

The improved pitch, he said, would argue that the free markets were the path to happiness, while big government led to tyranny and fascism. His reasoning went like this: Government programs caused dependency, which in turn caused psychological depression. Historically, he argued, this led to totalitarianism. The minimum wage, he said, provided a good example. It denied the "opportunity for earned success" to 500,000 Americans who, he estimated, would be willing to work for less than the federal minimum standard of $7.25 per hour. Without jobs, they've lost their meaning in life" said Fink. This, he warned, had been "a very big part of the Nazi recruitment in Germany during the '20's. Thus he argued to an audience that included many of the country's billionaires, minimum wage laws could be described a leading to the kinds of conditions that caused "the rise and fall of the Third Reich." (DM 360)

Here you see the cynicism of the wolves. They plan out ways to sell their point of view by lying, distorting history and using scare terms like "totalitarianism" and, of course, the ever-popular Third Reich. We all love to scare folks with Hitler don't we? Mr. Fink rather glossed over the events that closed out the First World War and the crushing burden the allies imposed on the German people. He rather glorified the satisfaction of working for a less than minimum wage job. (He should be required to try it for a few years.) And, in fact, he knew all that, but he was spewing a new sales pitch to make stupid us keep plugging for the (disguised) Libertarian agenda. It is, of course, important to us to see to it that the rich keep getting to screw us and owning the government so that they can't be prevented from doing it. Or, not!

Ms. Mayer also quotes from Charles Koch himself, extracted from an interview in the *Wichita Business Journal* (the Kochs are located in Wichita). Mr. Koch said:

The poor, okay, you have welfare, but you've condemned them to a lifetime of dependency and hopelessness. … We want 'hope and change'. But we want people to have the hope that they can advance on their own merits, rather than the hope that somebody gives them something. (DM 360

Ms. Mayer states that Koch went on in that interview to point out that he had recently promoted his son to the presidency of one of his corporations and how at every step the son had done it on his own. (DM 360) This is about as tone deaf as I can imagine. He wants people to advance on their own merits, regardless, I guess, of whether that is even possible in our economy for many people with all the obstacles we put in the way. He assumes that people who receive welfare don't want to get ahead on their own but instead want someone to give them something. But look, Koch is the original Libertarian. He believes in the freedom of the top 1% to do whatever their money will allow them to do including pay their employees less than a living wage, put out products that are dangerous and rape the environment as they please. Insofar as his son getting ahead on his own, well…

Hacker and Pierson have identified another great quote from the rich that strikes right at their real feeling about their "rights". The speaker is Tom Perkins a wealthy venture capitalist:

Tom Perkins complained, "I don't think people have any idea what the one percent is actually contributing to America." He suggested the problem might be fixed with a change in American voting rules. "You don't get a vote unless you pay a dollar in taxes. If you pay a million dollars, you should get a million votes. How's that?" (AA 188)

Don't you just love it? Look, these people can't get rich without the rest of us working at it too. And it is true that many of the rich got there by pursuing their own genius. The Mark Zuckerbergs Larry Pages and Sergey Brins of the world certainly have a right to speak of the empires they created as a result of their own genius. But, they could not have done it nor could they continue it without their employees. Further, they could not have done it without the society around them which was created by and sustained by the government of the United States. They are entitled to their riches and their plaudits. Having said that, they also have an obligation to help support the system and the people that buoyed them up and the government is the entity to see to it that it happens. Perkins has suggested the best method I have ever heard of to assure that the powerless stay that way permanently. By the way, don't you feel sorry for his feeling unappreciated as a member of the one percent?

By now you may be getting tired of this, but I have a few more that beg to be heard. The next one is the famous "rant" by CNBC commentator Rick Santelli which took place from the Chicago Mercantile Exchange on September 19, 2009 and which is credited with "igniting' the Tea Party. It is recounted by Jane Mayer thus:

What came to be known as Santelli's "rant" started slowly and built as he held forth from the floor of the Chicago Mercantile Exchange. The immediate provocation was the previous guest. Minutes before Santelli appeared, Wilbur Ross Jr. had denounced a proposal Obama had floated the previous day to provide emergency help in restructuring mortgages for millions of homeowners facing foreclosure. Ross, a personal friend of David Koch's, wasn't a disinterested policy analyst. His private equity company, WL Ross & Co., a so-called vulture fund, was heavily involved in servicing mortgages.

Santelli, who tended in general toward tough-guy, free-market pronouncements, excitedly agreed with Ross that the government shouldn't help. "Mr. Ross has nailed it!" he began. He denounced Obama's plan as Cuban-style statism. Stressed homeowners in his view were "losers" who deserved their fate. He objected to the government playing a redistributive role, casting his argument in moral terms. By helping bail out homeowners who had made bad financial bets, he argued, the government was "promoting bad behavior." Critics would later point out that his indignation had not been similarly stirred by the Bush bailouts of the country's largest banks, about which he had grumblingly conceded, "I agree something needs to be done." Yet when Obama proposed help for the overextended underclasses, Santelli looked into the camera and shrieked, "This is America! How many of you people want to pay your neighbor's mortgage that has an extra bathroom, and can't pay their bills? Raise their hand. President Obama, are you listening?" (DM 166)

As you can see, Jane Mayer is well worth reading. Please, please read her book. Anyway, look at this "rant". This bum, who was in favor of taxpayers bailing out the biggest banks in the country to the tune of hundreds of billions of dollars to rescue them from their own "bad financial bets", then was morally outraged that the president had the temerity to suggest that the individual homeowners should also get such help. Folks, the homeowners in these cases had been the victims of a heavily hyped bait and switch con game in which they were enticed and pushed into extending their credit too far without understanding the variable rate mortgage gotchas that would result. And they might never have met that fate so abruptly if the whole scheme had not collapsed when the inevitable happened and the real estate market deflated as it had to do. So, Santelli, who dwelt on the extra bathroom these sinning homeowners had "bet" on as a pejorative label, couldn't see any moral way helping people should happen. It should only happen for the richest banks in America – in fact some of the biggest banks in the world. And yet – and yet - this sentiment ignited the Tea Party. If that is what the Tea Party stands for – and it is – I want nothing to do with it and neither should any intelligent and caring American.

I picked the next goody out of Hacker and Pierson. They refer to a statement made by Mr. James Randall, at the time president of the agribusiness giant Archer Daniels Midland in a private context but exposed during a price-fixing case in the mid 1990's. He said: "We have a saying here ... that penetrates the whole company. It's a saying that our competitors are our friends. Our *customers are the enemy*. (My italics.) (AA90 Please read their book!) You could not have a better statement of what is going on in the big companies than this. The customer is their enemy! That's *us* they are talking about and it is with their competition they intend to screw us by fixing prices. Only government can stop this. No free market answer to this exists. In fact this sort of thing proves that "freeing" the market can only lead to the death of the lambs – us.

If this last one didn't get to you, the next one makes the hair on the back of my neck stand up. This comes from Jane Mayer again. She was speaking of West Virginia University where the Charles Koch Foundation granted nearly a million dollars with the attached string that it got to have a say over what professors it funded. One of the WVU professors edited a 2007 book titled *Unleashing Capitalism: Why Prosperity Stops at the West Virginia Border and How to Fix it.* In this book the argument is made that mine safety and clean water regulations only hurt workers. She quotes from it: "Are workers really better off being safer but making less money? " (DM 90) This professor, Russell Sobel, then went on to advise the West Virginia governor, the cabinet and speak at a joint session of the Senate and the House Finance Committees. Mayer says that the state Republican Party chairman declared Sobel's antiregulatory book the blueprint for its party platform. So, you see, the West Virginia Republican Party didn't (and I suspect still doesn't) give a damn about the safety of its people who work in the mines. They care about the big bucks they get from the coal industry. Now, I suppose some of them may have drunk the Kool-Aid of the Industry that regulation is strangling them, but that is a lie. The industry is richer than Croesus and they can not only afford the regulations, and the needed safety measures, it can afford to pay its workers a living wage and still make a profit. But, the thing that horrifies me about this is the clear signal that they don't care about the safety of their own workers and leave them with the choice of making a little more money if they are willing to stop worrying about things like lung disease, cave-ins and polluted water. (To say nothing of the devastation their mining leaves behind in what at least was some of America's most beautify mountains.)

My last quote in this section is not actually from the mouths of the enemy, but comes from the book *Middle Class Meltdown in America, Causes Consequences and Remedies.* It was written by Kevin T. Leicht, professor and chairman of the Department of Sociology at the University of Iowa and Scott T. Fitzgerald, associate professor and director of graduate studies in the Department of Sociology at the University of North Carolina, Charlotte. If, contrary to the rhetoric thrown around by the right wing and, especially the current Republican Party, you want to know why the middle class is having such a hard time and has been having a harder and harder time since the eighties, read this book! In any event, this quote comes from these authors and epitomizes what I have been talking about as to the attitude of the powerful and the rich toward the rest of us. They say:

Your lifestyle itself is the subject of debunking by the cultural elites. Those who labor diligently at what they do find employers who pay too little, offload most of their risks and expenses onto employees and communities, demand too many working hours, don't follow or violate openly most labor laws, and vote for political parties that glorify images of 1950's "traditional" lifestyles – lifestyles that this very economic system makes it all but impossible to emulate. [And parenthetically was only so great for the white majority at the time.] Employers move production to places where costs are low, offloading expenses for public infrastructure onto their employees, who must pay higher taxes, user fees, and private fees from their limited, non-growing, non-guaranteed paychecks. *These same economic elites attempt to convince their employees that taxes are spent on "undeserving, lazy people" and that still lower taxes will benefit them. Yet tax cut after tax cut, the benefits never come.* (Italics are mine) (MCM 7)

I hope this excursion into the actual words of the 1% and their corporate instruments will give you a taste of what is really going on in the minds of the far right powerful and their demagogue political lackeys. If we understand where they are coming from, we could never want to vote for their positions, even if they make them sound like they are on our side. There is an old saying: "Fool me once, shame on you. Fool me twice, shame on me." These people have been fooling us for three decades. That they have succeeded is our own fault. Thus the question: "How stupid are we?" If I seem to be blaming everyone else, never believe it. Mea culpa, mea culpa. I voted for Reagan not once, but twice. Hell, I even voted for Nixon (who, by the way would have been seen as almost a socialist by today's Republican Party). Not until the last decade have I even begun to wake up. And not until I undertook this book did I realize just how bad it has already been and how much worse it is destined to get if we let it. There are, I should say, tremendously good-hearted rich people. I would cite the Gateses and even Warren Buffett. I am sure there are many others of whom I know nothing. But, those are not the people who want what the far right wants. The far right is the enemy and the party they have co-opted – the Republican Party – is their instrument, although I say again that there are many Democrats who are drinking the Koolaid.

Chapter 3

The Background Story

Next I want to spend a little bit of time talking about the context out of which our present situation arises. This will sound a little bit like a textbook discussion but I will try to keep it from being as boring as that and I will keep it as short as I can. These are things that most of us know or at least knew at one time, because we studied them in school and even, in the case of some of the older of us, we lived through some of this or at least our parents did and told us about them. Those of us who came of age in the 1950's and the 1960's had parents from the so-called "great generation" and they knew these things intimately. But I want to mention again that the 1950's which are being so touted now as a paragon of morality and hard work, of fairness and equality are so touted only by those who either did not live through them or do not remember them. They don't remember the massive bigotry in this country and the last days of outright society-approved discrimination against African Americans. They don't remember the Korean War or the attempted nationalization of the railroads by Harry Truman. They don't remember *The Man with the Golden Arm.* or the beatniks. As for the 1960's, the list is almost endless, but includes Vietnam, race riots, Nixon starting the "war on drugs", or the many other horrors of that decade. Anyway, that's an aside. Let me get on with it. The enemy are now beginning to idealize the late nineteenth and early twentieth century, which had been referred to as the "gilded Age" as being the standard we should once again aspire to creating. This was the heyday of the first generation of industrialist tycoons. They are the people F. Scott Fitzgerald spoke of in his writing. The industrial revolution was in its glory and it is true that a great deal of optimism existed in America. Of, course it co-existed with some of the worst tenements in the world in New York City, the advent of child labor and sweat shops, the advent of the firing of injured employees rather than compensating them, the age of growing and vicious monopolies as the rich elbowed out all competition and the age of the worst wealth inequality ever in our country until recent events overtook that record.

I noted in the beginning of this book that the Libertarians want to do away with central banks and to deregulate banking totally. That is the situation that we were coming out of in the nineteenth century although Andy Jackson set us back badly. The lack of regulation of banking and finance as much as any other factor led to constant economic turmoil. There were regular depressions and recessions in the late nineteenth century. This obviously hurt the poor far worse than the rich, but it is not the poor's story that the current one percenters want to talk about. During the Gilded Age, a robber baron named Jay Gould attempted to corner the gold market aided by public officials in the Grant administration, including Grant's brother. The government averted disaster by selling four million dollars in gold. Gould himself was tipped off by a Treasury official and got out of the market timely. About that, Hacker and Pierson say:

The economic chaos that ensued was a sign of just how unstable the nation's financial system was. Indeed, with the country lacking either deposit insurance or a national bank (abandoned under President Andrew Jackson), financial crises were the norm, not the exception. Major bank panics rocked the nation at least six times between 1873 and 1907. Meanwhile, the country was in a depression or a recession in 1865-67 (featuring a 24 percent decline in business activity), 1869-70 (10 percent), 1873-79 (34 percent), 1882-86 (33 percent), 1887-88 (15 percent), 1890-91 (22 percent), 1893-94 (37 percent), 1895-97 (25 percent), and 1899-1900 (15 percent). (AA 111)

Following this, Hacker and Pierson quote from Leland Stanford (as they say, "yes, the founder of the California University") concerning bribery as follows: "If you have to pay money to have the right thing done, it is only just and fair to do it." (AA 111) Apparently the current apologists for the Gilded Age would like to excuse the bad things by saying that it was only a few bad apples and if the government had stayed out of it, everything would have been alright. If you believe that, as the old saying goes, "I have a bridge I'd like to sell you." The evidence of the last thirty years belies that. Once the enemy were able in the Reagan years and thereafter to deregulate and cut their taxes, they took off and never looked back, thus leading us to become, as I shall set forth shortly, the most unequal nation in the industrialized world. And they want still more. Does this sound like it was likely that the original robber barons would have been cut back by a totally "free" market or would they have kept closing their fists around the economy and government of this country as is happening now? In any event, the "gild" in the Gilded Age was worn only by the very rich.

At the beginning of the twentieth century, the workman (or woman because they were there in the sweat shops) had no control whatever over the working environment. There were no constraints on the employers as to the age of the employee, the hours worked, overtime pay, minimum wages, the ability to bargain with the employer, compensation for injuries on the job, or any other aspect of the work situation. There was no control over the excesses of industry in the dumping of wastes into the environment, banks were free to engage in whatever risky gambit they wished even though they were gambling with other people's money and there was little enough constraint on outright bribery of public officials. (In their defense,

I don't think there is nearly so much outright bribery by the 1% today but that is because they can dump unlimited money into the campaigns of our elected officials and take them on all-expense-paid junkets, etc.) It was the "progressives" at the beginning of the twentieth century who began turning this all around. We all remember about Teddy Roosevelt, the "trust buster". (Although his success in this arena is much overstated.) Perhaps the most successful president in the Progressive mold was Woodrow Wilson. Although a bigot whose racial views are today being excoriated, Wilson still presided over many true accomplishments on behalf of the common American.

I am once again indebted to Hacker and Pierson for what I am about to set forth. In this case, the topic is what Wilson accomplished. He created the Federal Reserve which regulates banking (to some extent). That has helped buffer the twentieth and twenty first centuries from the repeated catastrophes that occurred in the late nineteenth century. Needless to say, the Libertarians hate the Federal Reserve. Wilson backed the graduated income tax (which was legalized by the duly adopted and ratified sixteenth amendment to the constitution in 1913). This freed the federal government from dependence on tariffs for its income and put the wealthy in the position of contributing to the common welfare. Of course the Libertarians and their Republican puppets hate Wilson. He also backed the Clayton Antitrust Act to try to break up the huge monopolies strangling the business of others. His administration established the Federal Trade Commission which the Libertarians especially want to do away with Wilson had been a professor of government at Princeton University. Even then his view was that "The Constitution was not meant to hold the government back to the time of horses and wagons." (AA 13) Hacker and Pierson go on to say:

Ultimately, Wilson's insistence that government and the economy should grow and adapt together is what most enrages today's conservatives. To the outrage of George Will [the columnist I have referred to earlier], "the very virtue of a constitution is that it is not changeable. It exists to prevent change, to embed certain rights so that they cannot easily be taken away. … Gridlock is not an American problem, it is an American achievement. Will wants us to look to another Princetonian for the true nature of American Government: James Madison. "When James Madison and fifty-four other geniuses went to Philadelphia in the sweltering summer of 1787, they did not go there to design an efficient government. That idea would have horrified them." (AA11)

The authors go on to explain, with quotes and some history that Madison went to Philadelphia to design a stronger federal government because the confederation was failing due to the inability of the central government to govern. Madison even wanted a veto by the federal government over state laws, but he failed in that regard. The point is that Madison was not an advocate of a weak or ineffectual central government. For those who doubt that, read *American Amnesia* and some of the sources it cites. Or, go do your own study of the history. If you do that, don't simply read the *Federalist Papers,* read the whole background.

Before I get lost, I have just outlined some of what President Wilson achieved, all things that contributed to a fairer and better run government and economy for all Americans, not just the richest and most powerful. Recent commentary will give you an idea what our present right wing thinks. Again, I cherry pick Hacker and Pierson. Jonah Goldberg, a columnist for the *National Review,* the conservative magazine founded by William F. Buckley, called Wilson, "the 20th Century's first Fascist dictator." (AA 10) Glenn Beck, perhaps the most loathsome right-wing nut and loudmouth, wrote in a recent issue of *American History* magazine that "Wilson is no. 1 on his 'Top Ten Bastards of All Time' lists – ahead of not only Theodore and Franklin Roosevelt, but also Pontius Pilate, Hitler and Pol Pot." "This is the architect who destroyed our faith", Beck said in 2010. "He destroyed our Constitution and he destroyed our founders, okay?" (AA 10) The authors point out that George Will got in on this hate-fest. At a banquet held at the libertarian Cato Institute the same year, he declared that Wilson had "ruined the 20th century." (AA 10)

So, do you want these vindictive and vituperative attitudes to be the ones that prevail over the attempts of our leaders in any age to make the economy and the government responsive to the average American? Are these the voices that speak for the people or for the wealthy and the powerful? Beck, by the way is a paid shill for the right wing. And, yes you can call me a left wing advocate if you want. I actually like the term "progressive" because I like what they accomplished and the Democratic Party clearly adopted the label in the presidential election season of 2016. But, unless I should get lucky and make money on this book, being left wing or liberal or progressive has so far not only not made me any money, it has cost me a lot in small donations to various organizations and campaigns to put my (minor) money where my mouth is. (I wouldn't mind being paid to do this, I must admit. I am not putting Beck down for getting paid, I am just describing what his function is. I am putting him down for being a loudmouth right wing nut.)

As the twentieth century went on, more progressive legislation came along to help ordinary Americans. This included legislation to put an end to child labor, protections for labor unions, unemployment insurance, Social Security, Medicare, Medicaid, various welfare programs such as food stamps, job safety regulation watched over by OSHA, support for educational institutions and many, many more. We all know about the fact that FDR and his administration had a huge impact on the American society and economy with his New Deal and its many programs, but most of us don't know what some of those programs accomplished. Again let me quote from Hacker and Pierson:

The Works Progress Administration built more than a half million miles of road, more than a hundred thousand bridges, more than forty thousand miles of sewers and water mains and more than a thousand airports. (AA116)

In addition, the New Deal accomplished the near complete electrification of the U. S. We take that electrification for granted now, but it was a terrific accomplishment that obviously made Americans a more close-knit country and a healthier and more productive one. In later years, Dwight Eisenhower put the Interstate Highway system into construction (imagine that – a Republican!). That system cost approximately $493 billion in today's dollars, or approximately what the crappy F-35 fighter plane project has cost so far to produce an airplane that is full of bugs, is hideously over budget and is way behind schedule. Which investment do you think has done more for America and will continue to do so?

Let's talk about some other things that the American government has done to benefit the population as a whole. Let me only mention the arming of the allies and then entering into World War Two and helping to win it. Let me only mention the Marshal Plan that helped put Europe back together again after the catastrophe of the war. (And let me not mention the total disaster of Vietnam, which I was "privileged" to take part in, or the total stupidity and, frankly, evilness of the Iraq War with its continuing legacy.) And I will pass over lightly the G.I. Bill which gave us then the most educated population in the world. But notice, these were some of the benefits that our government provided to us. Instead, let me mention government research and development. As Hacker and Pierson say:

In the quarter century after World War II, the United States didn't just lead the world in R&D funding. It owned the field. Well into the 1960's, the federal government spent more than the combined total of all R&D spending by governments *and* businesses outside the United States. The fruits of these investments ranged from radar and GPS, to advanced medical technology, to robotics and the computer systems that figure in nearly every modern technology. Far from crowding out private R&D, moreover, these public investments spurred additional private innovation. The computer pioneers who developed better and smaller systems not only relied on public-fostered breakthroughs in technology; they also also would have found little market for their most profitable products if not for the internet, GPS and other government-sponsored platforms for the digital revolution. (AA 39)

Later, I will discuss just how badly the U. S, stands in government R&D in world rankings today, but suffice it to say, now we are sorry.

Looking at a different area, the American government's investment in medical research has resulted in many and spectacular developments. These were often the result of public-private work of the sort that seems to be anathema to the right wing today. In particular, the National Institutes of Health has been a primary mover on behalf of the government. As Hacker and Pierson say:

The fruits of these early and extensive investments are countless. The MRI (magnetic resonance imaging) emerged from a series of National Science Foundation grants starting in the mid-1950's. The laser, also vital to medical practice as well as consumer electronics and much else, grew out of military-funded research. In drug development, a 1995 investigation by researchers at Massachusetts Institute of Technology (MIT) found that government research had led to eleven of the fourteen most medically significant drugs over the prior quarter century. Another study showed that public funding of research was instrumental in the development of more than 70 percent of the drugs with the greatest therapeutic value introduced between 1965 and 1992. (Most of the rest received public funding and research during their testing in clinical trials.) The same is true of almost all the biggest medical breakthroughs of recent decades: According to a 1997 study of important scientific papers cited in medical industry patents, nearly three-quarters of those funded by American (rather than foreign) sources were financed by the federal government. (AA 55)

Without citation to any special text, let me remind us that it was the U. S. Surgeon General and the government that uncovered the truth about cigarette smoking and did something about it. It was the federal government that did something about seat belts. Both of these things were resisted by industry and big tobacco is still lying to people in other countries about the dangers of smoking. It was the federal government that did something about acid rain and the ozone hole. And it is the far right that has kept the federal government from doing anything very effective about global warming as I will discuss later. Hacker and Pierson, bless them, have some information on tobacco:

In the half century since the 1964 [Surgeon General's] report, cigarette smoking has caused an estimated twenty million premature deaths in the United States. Today about half a million lose their lives each year – one in five annual deaths in the United States – and smoking-related medical costs and lost productivity exceed $300 billion a year. Yet the toll would be far higher were it not for active government. At the time of the surgeon general's report, over four thousand cigarettes were smoked annually for each adult American. [And, since many of them didn't smoke, imagine what the number was for smokers!] In the decades since, following a ban on broadcast ads, rising federal cigarette taxes, increasingly strong warning labels, repeated FDA actions to promote smoking cessation, and a string of settlements between states and tobacco companies (along with various state-level antismoking policies), annual consumption has dwindled to just over a thousand cigarettes per adult. According to a recent careful estimate, efforts to reduce tobacco consumption over the past half century prevented more than eight million premature deaths, extending average life expectancy by a remarkable one and a half to two years. (AA 127-128)

Hacker and Pierson speak extensively about the "mixed economy", meaning an economy composed of a capitalistic market that is regulated and tempered by the government. (My definition, not theirs.) They didn't invent this concept, but I think they speak of it most understandably by the general public (of which I am one). They put forth the position that the mixed economy is what produced the wealth and fairness of the American economy up through the twentieth century and even today, although it has been hobbled substantially by the right wing since 1980. An explosively growing population, economy, technology and global intrusion into our affairs cannot be presided over and tended by a "night watchman" minimalist government pushed by the Kochs and the right wing. It must, in order to provide fairness and even to govern effectively, grow as the country does. Speaking to this issue, they say:

The mixed economy is not about government micromanaging economic decisions. It's about setting up basic rules, institutions, and policies that correct the market's most serious failures. Many such corrections are relatively simple: a tax on carbon emissions, a minimum requirement for bank capital reserves, a disclosure label on cigarettes. Moreover, government has sources of expertise (scientists, statistics, specialized agencies) that become more capable as societies become more complex. Increased complexity and interdependence makes the case for a capable, informed public sector, not for letting markets alone deal with these challenges because markets alone won't.

When the complexity of modern economies, the realities of human cognition, and the imperatives of the profit motive collide, "Let the market decide" is a toxic prescription. Hundreds of billions of dollars and hundreds of thousands of lives are saved in the United States every year because our government has not followed this simplistic bromide. (AA 86)

Please do read American *Amnesia* to properly appreciate what a great education that book provides.

So far, I have just touched upon the great benefits that the government has provided to the people of the U. S. over the past century. Whole volumes of textbooks have been written on the subject. Most of us know about some of this even if not all of it. Has the government often been lumbering and overly laden with red tape? Of course it has. Can we do something about that? Sure we can. But, given the incredibly complex society it governs (at all levels of government), it is inevitable that anything as large as our governments will lumber and will be less efficient than smaller entities. And, given that governing in this country is (or should be if the present right wing will allow it) a matter of compromise solutions, it is also inevitable that many of those solutions will fail to please some of the people. But, government is the only mechanism available to the people of this country by which we can provide fairness for everyone. While our economy should and does and no doubt will continue to produce the massively rich and powerful (which seems to be a standard set for others who would like to follow their example), it also needs to provide for its citizens a basic level of subsistence such that no Americans need be concerned about starvation or compromising their health or that of their children by improper nourishment. No Americans should be excluded from our amazing medical technology. No Americans should be closed out of our public education system and those who have the ability should be allowed to gain all the education available to anyone in this country. After all, we desperately need those educated citizens and workers. No Americans should have to live in an automobile or scrounge for clothes in dumpsters. This country can easily afford for there to be rich people and still assure that no Americans live in want. Further, no Americans should look forward to a degraded environment because the rich and powerful want to make another billion dollars. Our children deserve better of us. After these basic needs are taken care of, then it should be up to each American how hard he or she wishes to work to pursue their own wealth. We can afford it, we should afford it, we must afford it.

Chapter 4

The Legacy of the Past Thirty-Five Years

This will be a long section of this book. This is the description of what the increasing influence of supply-side, free market philosophy in our government, and especially the right wing of our government, has wrought. This encompasses economic inequality, degraded health care, disintegrating infrastructure, increasingly mediocre basic education and increasingly unaffordable higher education. It is a story of an increasingly indebted middle class and the growth of the working poor. It is the story of a nation that once led the world in so many of these categories and can't even look mildly competitive with the rest of the developed world today. And, before I launch into this in detail, let me acknowledge that there are forces in being that affect these things that don't have much of anything to do with our government. These include the increasingly global nature of our world in a day when a person can circumnavigate the world in a day or communicate with someone on the other side of the world instantaneously. Also included is the increasingly technological nature of our industries. Machines and computers have replaced many of the functions once performed by people who had not only held those jobs, but also made a great deal more than minimum wage for doing them. These are problems that our government cannot change. As the functions of so many of our businesses that were performed by semi-skilled workers are displaced, a big chunk of the employment for the middle class is disappearing and will stay gone. This leaves the skilled and highly skilled and educated jobs and the menial service jobs. These trends, along with the trend to leaner structures have also eroded the middle management positions. These factors have had and continue to have an erosive effect on the middle class, squeezing it out into the upper income brackets for those few who go there or into the ranks of the working poor. I say this for two reasons. The first is that it is true and needs to be taken into account in trying to determine what to do about the problem. The second is that the opponents will cite this as the primary reason there is so much inequality and degradation of our society's well-being. It is not the primary reason. The primary reason is the way our government has responded to the problem. The best way to know this is to compare how we are doing compared to the other wealthy nations. My underlying sources set this out in detail. In particular, *American Amnesia. Middle Class Meltdown* and *Saving Capitalism* are very instructive on these problems, although most of the others deal with some aspect of the problem as well. Without further ado, let me count the ways, to borrow the lyrics of an old song.

Economic Inequality

Leicht and Fitzgerald, in *Middle Class Meltdown* have the best introduction to this subject. Before I turn to them, though, let me make one caveat: the problem is not the concern of the middle class alone. Everyone in America is affected to one extent or another. For instance, global warming and pollution are problems for everyone and they are problems that we will leave to all of our descendants, no matter what economic status we hold. The problems of the working poor are certainly different from those of what I would describe as the upper middle class, who are economically sufficient absent health catastrophes or similar life events, but who are not in the upper 1%. And, the upper 1% is only subject to some of these problems if they want to be, for instance, obesity, lack of physical fitness and lack of advanced education. Thus, although I am very much impressed by the analyses of Leicht and Fitzgerald, they are basically dealing with only part of the problem. Nevertheless, I submit that their writing is highly educational in this context. And, to set the context, let me quote their definition of the middle class:

For our purposes, when we speak of the middle class we are referring to Americans who annually earn between $40,000 and $80,000, most of which comes from slaries and wages; who work as upper – or lower level managers, professionals, or small business owners; and who graduated from, or at least attended, a four-year college. (MCM 3)

Although I am not an expert, I would quarrel with the education part of this definition in that there are many people in the middle class economically who don't meet that education requirement. Nevertheless, their definition gives us a base-line for the economic definition of the middle class.

Concerning the economic well-being of the middle class, Leicht and Fitzgerald say this: "*Middle class prosperity in the late twentieth and early twenty-first century is an illusion.* (MCM 4, italics in the original) They set forth in detail why they contend that this is so. Below I quote from the headings of some of their reasons, but will not subject the reader to the details beyond those headings. Details will come as we go along. Here are their reasons:

1. *Good, steady jobs that last longer than a year are hard to come by.*

2. *Companies do not reward employee loyalty.*

3. *It is hard to obtain the economic security on which marriage and "settling down" are based.* Worse, two full-time workers' incomes are needed to support a lifestyle one income used to buy.

4. *Buying a house is increasingly difficult.*

5. *Saving for a rainy day – or any day for that matter – is extremely difficult.*

6. *You may never be able to retire.*

7. *People who work hard and play by the rules are viewed as "suckers".*

8. *Your lifestyle itself is the subject of debunking by cultural elites.*

9. *Your child's education is paid for by student loans.* (MCM 6-7, italics in the original)

The last sentence of paragraph 8 is instructive and it reads as follows:

These same economic elites attempt to convince their employees that taxes are spent on "undeserving, lazy people" and that still lower taxes will benefit them. Yet, tax cut after tax cut, the benefits never come. (MCM 7)

Read through these two quotes and see if they resonate. The authors use an entire book to substantiate their points and if you would like to know all of what they say, please buy their book. It is reasonably inexpensive. If not, I will quote from them extensively. Incidentally, one reason that tax cuts don't help much is that most of them will benefit the middle class to the tune of a couple hundred bucks at the most whereas they all benefit the rich to a much greater degree. That is the reason the rich want tax cuts. Furthermore, tax cuts hamper the agencies of government that regulate the market and industry and for that reason, they are beloved by big corporations and rich people. Let me go on.

With respect to changes in the income status of Americans, Leicht and Fitzgerald say these things, among others:

1. Pursuant to a graph, median (meaning in the middle from top to bottom rather than the average or mean) before-tax family income from 1969 to 2012 (in 2010 dollars) went from $50,000 to approximately $48,000. This means that, although both the overall wealth of the U. S. has increased dramatically and the rich have gotten much richer, the median family has actually lost ground. (MCM 40)

2. "In 2003, over thirty-four million Americans lived below the official poverty line; by 2012 [9 years later!] this number had grown to over forty-six million." (MCM 9)

3. "The American welfare state is also the least generous in the world. In place of extensive income assistance, universal healthcare, and a universal pension system, Americans face a privatized and byzantine system of health insurance, uncertain unemployment benefits, and a tottering Social Security system that doesn't provide much retirement security. Pension plans, where they exist, are becoming less generous and are more dependent on the performance of specific companies at specific times. None of this is the lot of the average member of the middle class of any other industrialized nation in the world." (MCM 7-8)

4. "The combination of job losses, sketchy and unstable opportunities, corporate restructuring, and easy credit have produced am American middle class that is bordering on economic disaster. Bills are paid and appearances are maintained by squandering savings and cannibalizing the future to maintain the present. The American economy moves toward a globalized, knowledge-intensive future, while the American people live in a cultural and consumption fantasyland built on the norms, values, and advice of a prior era. Old cultural ideologies die hard, especially when society is

bombarded with media and political messages that suggest that things are getting better and that you really can own the car or home of your dreams for no money down." (MCM 19)

5. "...about 90 percent of households in bankruptcy are middle class households." (MCM 135)

Leicht and Fitzgerald, of course, go to great lengths to document the proof for their statements, but ask yourselves: "Do these statements ring false to you?" Those authors also document that the average family household is in massively more debt than ever before, mostly as a result of easy credit in purchasing homes and cars as well as easy credit card debt.

Speaking, as I just was, of bankruptcy, there are a couple of interesting things about our present bankruptcy laws. For instance, although corporations can go into bankruptcy easily and cause massive damage when they do it, as when certain airlines went into bankruptcy to relieve themselves of their pension obligations and then came back out of it and went on their merry way, or when Donald Trump took several businesses into bankruptcy and congratulated himself on getting out in time, there are certain entities that cannot relieve their debts in bankruptcy. I quote Robert B. Reich in *Saving Capitalism:*

Big corporations can use bankruptcy to rid themselves of burdensome pension obligations to their employees, for example, while homeowners cannot use bankruptcy to reduce burdensome mortgages, and former students cannot use it to reduce burdensome debts for higher education. (SC 9)

In 2005 President Bush and the Republicans made bankruptcy harder for the average American at the behest of the credit card industry that spent millions and millions lobbying for that result. You see, big money is more important in America than are her people. The extent to which that is true will be explored herein, but the book *Dark Money* by Jane Mayer does a far more exhaustive job of explaining it. Here we see one of the myriad examples of the way that our country is unequal. And, the inequality only works in one direction: in favor of the rich. It is out of control now and if we, the voters, don't call a halt, more of what I am about to show you will happen. As Reich puts it beautifully:

Those who claim to be on the side of freedom while ignoring the growing imbalance of economic and political power in America and other advanced economies are not in fact on the side of freedom. They are on the side of those with power. (SC 15)

So, let's see, what other examples can I share with you of the ill effects we have suffered from the current trends? How about this one from a chart in Reich on page 116; production for a non-supervisory production worker went up 240.9% from 1948 to 2012. Hourly compensation for those workers measured in 2012 dollars went up 7.8%. In other words, although they were producing 240.9% more in 2012 than in 1948, those workers were being paid only 7.8% more. Where did the profits from all that increased productivity go? To the top and to shareholders. That is, the gravy went to the corporate executives and the shareholders of the corporate stock. The employees who produced that increased income got essentially zip. Or, how about this goody:

Starting in the early 1980's, the median household income stopped growing altogether, when adjusted for inflation. In 2013, the typical middle-class household earned $51,939, nearly $4,500 below what it earned before the start of the Great Recession in 2007. [Various authors site the beginning of the recession in 2007 or 2008.] By 2013, the median household was earning less than it did in 1989, nearly a quarter of a century before. Job security also declined as did the percentage of working-age Americans with jobs. In short, much of the American middle-class has become poorer. (SC 115-116)

If you have been feeling that things were not getting better for most folks who work for a living in our industries and businesses, you would be right. The issue, of course, is why that is happening because both major parties claim to have the answer, but one of them is lying to us or, at least, is being duped by those who are controlling this.

How about labor's share of corporate profits? How have they fared? Of course, the answer is obvious, but the numbers are stunning:

Between 2000 and 2014, quarterly corporate after-tax profits rose from $529 billion to $1.6 trillion. This rise didn't reflect increasing returns to capital; it reflected increasing economic power. ...this pushed the stock market to unprecedented heights, thereby enriching investors – most of whom are already in the upper ranks of the nation's wealthy. Meanwhile, labor's share of the economy has dropped. In 2000, labor's share of nonfarm business income was 63 percent. In 2013 it was 57 percent, representing a shift from labor to capital of about $750 billion annually. (SC 83-84)

This type of screw job is not related to computers or globalism or to robots. This is a straightforward refusal of management to compensate labor for its good work.

Well, gee, maybe labor got in on the ownership of capital by way of shares in their employers? Of, course, we know the answer to that, too. As Reich says:

Higher share prices have added substantially to the incomes of the wealth of those at the top. In the bull market that sent stocks soaring from 1994 to 2014 (the downturn from 2008 to 2011 notwithstanding), America's rich hit the jackpot. By 2010, the richest 1 percent of Americans owned 35 percent of the value of American-owned shares, both directly and indirectly through their pension plans. The richest 10 percent owned more than 80 percent. Yet, most Americans did not benefit from the bull market because they were not able to save enough to invest much, if anything, in stocks. The bottom 90 percent owned just 19.2 percent directly or indirectly. In 2014 more than two-thirds of Americans were living from paycheck to paycheck. (SC 92)

The top 1% own more than a third of all the stock in America! The bottom 90% get to share out less than 20%. And that's not the worst statistic by far, as we will see.

At least we have the minimum wage law to provide some protection to workers, right? Of course not. I have already quoted from some of the enemies about their feelings concerning minimum wage laws. They think the minimum wage established by the federal government 0f $7.25 should not only not be raised, but it should be abolished and then there would be lots of jobs available at $5.00 per hour or whatever they think they should pay. Hey, look, the present minimum wage was established in 1996 and inflation has reduced its value below what it was set at then. Well, gee, wouldn't there be people out of work and wouldn't the employers lose money or have to raise prices ruinously if the minimum wage were raised? That, after all, is what the enemy tells us. Mr. Reich has found an interesting example of whether that must happen or not. In Denmark, workers over the age of 18 earn the equivalent of $20 per hour at McDonald's. The result? Big Macs cost 35 cents more in Denmark. You know, if one could be paid $20 per hour working for McDonalds, one could certainly afford even more Big Macs despite the higher price. (You can find this in SC at 137)

Here is an interesting effect the minimum wage in the fast food industry has:

A study … found that 52 percent of fast-food workers were dependent on some form of public assistance, and they received almost $7 billion in support from federal and state governments. That sum is in effect a subsidy the rest of American taxpayers pay the fast-food industry for the industry's failure to pay its workers enough to live on. (SC 137)

In describing the effect of paying workers more, Reich says:

Any wage gains low-paid workers receive will more than likely come out of the profits – which, in turn, will slightly reduce returns to shareholders and the compensation packages of top executives. I do not find this especially troubling. (SC 137)

You know what? I don't find it troubling at all, nor will you when we cover what has happened to executive pay. But, here is a fine example of what I was talking about earlier. Fast food workers are not making enough money to live on as it is. How much better off will they be if the minimum wage is lowered or abolished? Having these jobs is not much of a benefit as it is. By the way, if you have ever sat and watched fast food workers, especially in the kitchens, you will have noticed that they work really hard. Even the counter help are on their feet the entire work shift. These are not lazy people. They are simply being taken advantage of by their employers. And with the decline of labor unions in this country, due to legislation and other factors, there is no place for most of these people to turn for improving their lot.

Well, as of today, surely, we are all better off than we were when the economy tanked in 2008, aren't we? That has not been the trend. In the first six years of recovery from the 2008 recession, the bottom 90%

experienced a drop in their average income. And between 2000 and 2013, the real average hourly wages of young college graduates declined. (SC 117) Between 2010 and 2013, average incomes for the bottom fifth dropped 8% and their average wealth declined 21%. According to a study by Oxfam America, more than half of America's forty-six million users of food pantries and other charitable food programs in 2013 had jobs or were members of working families. (SC 134) So yes, the unemployment rate has declined and the stock market is going great now, but the average American is worse off, not better off than before the recession. Do you suppose that had something to do with the millions of Americans who lost their homes? As we have seen, the opinion among the rich is that it was the homeowners own fault, not that of the crooks who took them for a ride. And although we can bail out their scammers, we would not ethically want to help the homeowners themselves, losers that they were.

We have seen that productivity in the U. S. has increased by almost 250% over the last forty years or so. Corporate profits have been skyrocketing per quarter to $1.6 trillion recently. The stock market has been soaring. Where is all the money going? First let's look at the pay of corporate executives. It is an amazing story. In 1970, the pay of the top CEO's was approximately 35 times that of the average worker. In 2012, the gap was 354 times the pay for top CEO's compared to the average worker. This is the highest pay gap in the world. (MCM 45) Overall, CEO pay climbed by 937 percent between 1978 and 2013 while the pay of the typical worker rose just 10.2 percent. (SC 97) "The share of corporate income devoted to the five highest-paid executives of large public firms went from 5 percent in 1993 to more than 15% in 2013". (SC 98) Not only that, most of that was deductible by the corporation because it was taken in stock options by the executives which then entitled the firm to claim that the payment was "linked to corporate performance". To make matters worse, lately corporations have been plowing revenue into buying back their own stock. That increases its value, thus giving the executives the increased performance they need for their stock options. Then they have the ability to exercise their options when they know beforehand that the buyback is about to happen, thus giving them large holdings of stock that are about to increase in value because the company will be buying back its own stock. This used to be illegal insider trading until John Shad, the Reagan appointed chairman of the SEC, removed these restrictions. So, the corporation gives its executive stock options allowing them to buy stock at a given price. Then the executives exercise the options and buy the stock at the set price, knowing the company is about to enter into a massive stock buy-back. This excites the market and inflates the price of the stock. It can then be sold by the executive at a much greater price than he or she just paid for it. And this isn't insider trading! Not only that, it increases the apparent worth of the corporation. Everybody looks good except – except, this increase in the value of the company is not because it is making better products, or selling more services or has increased its efficiency. No, it is all a manipulation of stock and the market. (And these guys want the stock market "deregulated'???)

How well this has worked for CEO's is set forth in two examples by Mr. Reich. They are stories about IBM and Hewlett-Packard:

IBM, for example, once prided itself on giving its workers lifelong employment and making long-term investments in technologies of the future. But in the 1990's IBM shifted priorities – laying off employees, scrimping on research, borrowing heavily, and using the money to buy back its shares of stock. Between 2000 and 2013 it spent $108 billion buying back its own shares, thereby pumping up share prices even though revenues remained flat. By 2014, IBM showed signs of reaching the end of the game. As its stock price finally began to sink, *The New York Times* said that "all these 'shareholder friendly' maneuvers have been masking an ugly truth: IBM's success in recent years has been tied more to financial engineering than actual performance." Nevertheless, the strategy had paid off for IBM's

CEOs, whose cumulative pay between 2003 and 2012 was $247 million, mostly in stock options and stock awards.

Hewlett-Packard followed a similar formula. It too had a lifelong employment policy, but by the late 1990s was firing employees and from 2004 to 2011 spent $61.4 billion on buybacks – more than its entire income – followed by a $12.7 billion loss in 2012. Between 2003 and 2012, Hewlett-Packard's CEOs received a total of $210 million, more than a third of it in options and awards. (SC 103)

Isn't this fascinating? Two of our supposed high-tech firms diverting billions and billions of dollars into stock buybacks rather than spending it on research and development or on retention of and paying its employees. This had the effect of beggaring the companies in the long run even if it did pump up the stock prices and massively rewarding the CEOs for what looks suspiciously to this layman as fraud. So far as I know, it is not criminal fraud in the sense that it is illegal, but it is certainly a financial lie and instead of enriching the companies themselves and making them more competitive, these financial shenanigans damaged their companies' futures and forced loyal employees out of work. And it was done just to make the companies look good on the stock market and enrich their CEOs (as well as other highly placed executives) to the tune of millions and millions of dollars, money they were paid for actually harming society and their companies. In the meantime the middle class and the working poor were getting worse and worse off.

You would ordinarily think that if a company kept its CEO for an extended time or paid him or her highly, it would be because of their good performance on the company's behalf. But, as Reich sets forth, the opposite seems to be true. In a study by professors at the University of Purdue and Cambridge University of 1500 large companies from 1994 to 2011, they found:

…that 150 companies with the highest-paid CEOs returned about 10 percent *less* to their shareholders than did their industry peers. In fact, the more these CEOs were paid, the worse their companies did. Companies that were the most generous to their CEOs – and whose high-paid CEOs received more of that compensation in stock options – did 15 percent worse than their peer companies on average. … the researchers found that the longer a highly paid CEO was in office, the more the firm underperformed. (SC 103-104)

This tells us that on average these highly paid CEOs not only are not helping their company's performance improve, they are actually holding it back. For what? It looks very much as though it is a scheme to enrich the richest and screw the rest, doesn't it?

Well, at least we know that if the CEOs are really bad, they will be fired and not profit from really bad performance, right? Ah, you are ahead of me. Of course not! For instance, there is Martin Sullivan, during whose tenure at AIG, the insurance giant, the share price dropped by 98% and he left the company with a $47 million payout. In the meantime, the American taxpayers had to pay $180 billion just to keep this "too big to fail" firm in business. Then, there is Thomas E. Preston who lasted just nine months at Viacom before being fired and who departed with a severance payment of $101 million. Next is Michael Jeffries, who was the CEO of Abercrombie & Fitch, whose company's stock price dropped more than 70 percent in 2007, but who received $71.8 million in 2008, including a $6 million retention bonus. Then there is William D. McGuire who was forced to resign as CEO of United Health over a stock options scandal in 2006 but received a pay package worth $286 million. Finally (not because there is no more, but because – why keep this up?) there is Hank McKinnell Jr. who was CEO of Pfizer and presided over a five year decline in the stock market value of the company of $140 billion. He left the company with a payout of nearly $200 million, free lifetime medical coverage and an annual pension of $6.5

million. (SC 103-104) Just exactly what do these people have to do to prevent their going out with up to hundreds of millions? Do you suppose murder would do it? Probably not. And notice this: all these salaries over $1 million are deductible by the corporations. For instance, Howard Schultz, CEO of Starbucks, received $1.5 million in salary for 2013, along with $150 million in stock options and awards. That saved Starbucks $82 million in taxes. (SC 105) Realize here that Starbucks did not spend $150 million on Mr. Schultz, it just gave him stock options that turned out to be worth that much to him on the market. As you can see, this system is rigged at the top and it happens because there is too little regulation of corporations, not too much.

So, what else is happening corporately? It is of interest that the fast food industry, which is one of the largest minimum wage employers, quadrupled the pay of its CEOs to an average of $24 million per year between 2000 and 2013. This happened during the time span including the great recession. But that industry couldn't possibly afford to pay its workers a liviing wage could it? In 2012 Walmart's CEO received $20.7 million. And interestingly, the Walton family (7 people) which owns the lion's share of Walmart stock had wealth in 2012 that exceeded the bottom 40 percent of all American families combined. You are probably aware of the pay rates at Walmart. When the rich complain that increases in minimum wage will cause economic harm and throw people out of work, it is hard to see why that need be so, given the wealth we see here and the fact that these industries cannot survive without service employees. If you have ever shopped at a Walmart, you have probably noticed that the vast majority of their checkout lanes are empty and there are more and more self-checkout counters, and as a result the downsizing of the staff is already happening even though the delays to customers are quite irritating and you would think it might someday matter to the business. Unfortunately, Walmart workers and fast-food workers desperately need the low prices Walmart and fast-food stores can provide because those employees can't get living wages. It is a classic catch-22 situation caused by the game being rigged at the top.

Along the same lines, here are a few more interesting figures. The richest 400 people in the country have more wealth than the bottom 50 percent of Americans. The wealthiest 1 percent own 42 percent of the nation's private assets. The share of wealth owned by the lower half of households has fallen from 3 percent in 1989 to 1 percent today. (SC 161)

As stunning as these compensation figures have been, we are now going to enter the financial sector and we will be able to see some real dollars involved. In 1982, *Forbes* magazine put out its first list of the 400 wealthiest Americans. There were two billionaires on that list and the total worth of all of the 400 was around $225 billion in current dollars. In 2014 all of the 400 were billionaires and 113 billionaires were left off because they didn't make the cut. The total worth then was just short of $2.3 trillion. Of the total, one in twenty-five on the 400 in 1982 were from the financial sector. Thirty years later it was one in five. Now for the really big numbers.

In 2007, the hedge fund Blackstone went public and one of its founders, Mr. Pete Peterson to whom we have referred earlier, walked away with $1.9 billion. Don't be stunned yet. His partner, Steve Schwartzman, got nearly $10 billion in a year that he made a take-home pay of almost $400 million. (AA 181) Now you can be impressed. Let me go on. Also, in 2007 the blog *alpha* put out by the magazine *Institutional Investors* published its annual list of the top twenty-five hedge fund managers' income. The top three made more than $1 billion each. The top twenty-five totaled $14 billion. Better yet for them, most of these hedge fund managers took the bulk of their pay as a share of the investments they oversaw, meaning other people's investments. They were allowed to treat these earnings as "carried interest" and therefore capital gains, subject to a lower tax rate than ordinary "earned income" (which is what you get when you work for a living). In

2014 Blackstone was making $4.3 billion in profits and thanks to the carried interest loophole, paid just 4.3 percent in taxes. (AA 182-183) Attempts by Obama to get that carried interest loophole closed went nowhere in the Republican controlled Congress.

If you are thinking that what you have read so far is awful, let me tell you about the stuff these folks do that is really illegal as opposed to merely outrageous. For instance, in 2014, three banking private equity firms including Kohlberg, Kravis Roberts, the Blackstone Group and TPG agreed to pay the government a combined $325 million to settle accusations that they colluded to drive down the price of corporate takeover targets. Evidence showed that when Blackstone had its eye on a company, Hamilton E. James, its president, wrote to George Roberts at Kohlberg and said: "We would much rather work with you guys than against you. Together we can be unstoppable but in opposition we can cost each other a lot of money." (SC 42) Roberts agreed. For once, the government acted, but consider this: $325 million for these three entities combined would not actually hurt them much. A bigger issue was the Libor scandal. The acronym stands for "London interbank offered rate." The rate is the benchmark for trillions of dollars in loans world-wide. Banks are supposed to report to the manager of Libor (until 2014 Barclay's Bank) the amount of interest they were paying for loans themselves. It turned out, surprise, surprise that banks were lying about those rates either up or down in order to profit from the effect. (SC 42-43) It is obvious that the bigger the scandal, the less likely it is that anyone will go to jail. As I understand it, only one person was convicted in this scam.

Most of us probably thought that insider trading was illegal and, indeed, we saw Martha Stewart go to jail for it. Poor her. She just wasn't rich enough. As Mr. Reich tells us:

But in a world where information spreads almost instantaneously, and in which large amounts of money can be made getting such information a fraction of a second before everyone else, insider trading is difficult to police, let alone define. In 2014, after hedge fund Global Investors made $54 million by shorting Dell Computer stock based on insider information from a Dell employee, Global Investors' co-founder, Anthony Chiasson claimed he didn't know where the tip came from or whether the leaker had benefitted from the leak, and that few traders on Wall Street *ever* know where the inside tips they use come from because confidential information is, according to Chiasson's lawyer, the "coin of the realm in securities markets". Chiasson was convicted nonetheless. But in December 2014, the court of appeals overturned Chiasson's conviction, ruling that Chiasson was so far removed from the leak that he could not possibly have known the source of the information or whether the tipper received a "substantial benefit" in return. The court thereby made official what had been the unofficial law on the Street: it's all about who you know. If for example, the CEO of a company gives his golfing buddy a confidential tip about what the company is about to do, and the buddy tells a hedge fund manager who then makes a fortune off that confidential information, the winnings are perfectly legal.

Because confidential information is the "coin of the realm" on Wall Street, it's likely that a significant portion of what is earned on the Street is based on information unavailable to average investors. Insiders fix the market for their own benefit. What's the chance that Congress will change the law to rein in insider trading? Almost zero as long as the Street continues to provide a significant share of the campaign contributions that members of Congress and the president rely on to get elected. In Europe, by contrast, trading on insider information is illegal. If a trader knows *or has reason to know* that specific information is not yet public, he may not use it. (Italics are mine) (SC 52-53)

The problem here, in case it isn't obvious is that if someone knows that a stock price is about to be affected in either a good way or a bad way before others do, they can invest in that stock massively or dump it massively and that will affect the market and close out others who come later from making a similar profit because the insider trading itself will affect the market price of the stock. Thus, if you hear about it when it becomes public, it is already too late for you to have any advantage on the market. The kind of information we are talking about here is almost always going to be available only to those at the top and in the business – on the Street in other words. And you can be sure that it will be set up so that the person who uses the information will be shielded from knowing whether the leaker was paid for leaking.

As you may know, by law neither individuals nor Medicare are allowed to purchase drugs from foreign sources anymore. Yet Americans pay more for drugs than any other nation on earth. (SC25) We are all familiar with the mark-up on drugs and the fact that the pharmaceutical companies are among the richer enterprises in the country. But here is something that I, at least, did not know. Newly developed drugs get patented. After the patents expire, other manufacturers than the one that developed the drug can then make the drug resulting in what is known as "generic" drugs which are always cheaper than the original name brand. But it turns out that there is a practice among some drug makers to pay off the generic drug companies *not* to produce the drug, thus keeping their monopoly alive. Reich reports that this costs Americans an estimated $3.5 billion per year. The drug companies claim that they need this additional income to pay for research to develop new drugs. Mr. Reich says of this: "perhaps so", but goes on to point out the billions of dollars they spend on advertising every year and their lobbying expenses which in 2013 came to a total of $225 million. (AA 25) Actually, I would not have granted the "perhaps so." The reason drug makers give for their hideous mark-ups is that the money is needed to pay for their research and development costs. If that is so, then they don't need to cheat by paying off generic drug makers. Furthermore, it seems that foreign drug makers can produce drugs more cheaply than we do here. Why is that? And what is all that lobbying about? Could it be to make sure that all their tactics to screw the customer are protected by Congress? Of course it is.

Here is one more tidbit on this subject. The ban on purchasing foreign drugs by consumers is recent. In 2012 Congress authorized U. S. Customs to destroy any medications coming in from foreign sources. Reich, who provided this information, says:

The real reason for the ban is to protect the profits of the U.S. pharmaceutical companies, which lobbied intensely for it. Yet the real threat to the public's health is drugs priced so high that an estimated fifty million Americans – more than a quarter of them with chronic health conditions – did not fill their prescriptions in 2012, according to the National Consumers League. (SC 24)

Imagine the clout the Medicare system could bring to bear if it were permitted to buy drugs from the least expensive sources in the world. Health costs would unquestionably be affected in a very pro-consumer way. Unfortunately, the big pharma companies have seen to it that this is not allowed.

There is another area where what seem to me to be nothing but dirty tricks is affecting the average consumer. It is possible to own a patent on genes. Monsanto, a huge biotech corporation, owns, according to Mr. Reich, more than 90 percent of the key genetic traits of soybeans planted by farmers in the U. S. and 80 percent of the corn. It patented its own genetically modified seeds and an herbicide that would kill weeds but not its genetically modified soy and corn. In itself, this sounds great, but it is what happened then that bears watching. The new seeds and herbicide initially saved farmers time and money. Unfortunately, those seeds produce plants that do not produce their own seeds as they grow. That means the farmers have to buy totally new seed every planting season. Worse yet, if the farmers have any unused Monsanto seeds left over, they have to agree not to save them and replant them in the future. That comes with the purchase agreement. Monsanto also prohibited seed dealers that carry their seeds from carrying anyone else's seeds and bought up most of the small remaining seed companies. This has resulted in most of the commodity crop farmers using Monsanto seeds. This has allowed Monsanto to raise the price on soybean seeds 325 percent on an average acre between 1994 and 2011 and that on corn by 259 percent. I know we have had some inflation, but that is ridiculous. You can bet that increases the cost of the soybeans and the corn. It has also turned Monsanto into a major monopoly. This leaves us with a set of crops with no genetic diversity and when (not, in my opinion, if) the weeds become resistant to the herbicide, we may lose whole crops. (All the data in this paragraph comes from SC 34-35)

You may ask yourselves why, if I am going to rely so heavily on the source books, don't you just read those books. That would be a great question and I would encourage you to do just that. But not enough people are reading those books, successful as they are and if you got far enough in this book to read this paragraph, you are at least benefitting from my reducing the volume of material in those books. You also, of course, get my "inimitable" (in my dreams, maybe?) sarcasm.

Next let's talk about the great recession. This happened because of greed, fraud, corruption and a deregulation of the finance industry that allowed it all. If you haven't seen the movie *The Big Short,* I strongly recommend it. But first a little history. In the late 1970s inflation was raging and the Federal Reserve raised its benchmark interest rates. To soften the blow to Savings and Loans, President Carter and the Congress lifted the interest rate ceiling on the S&Ls which allowed them to pay higher rates but also caused them to seek out riskier investments in order to stay solvent. This eventually led to the collapse of a large percentage of the S&Ls and cost the taxpayers more than $100 billion in bailouts. Then in 1980 President Reagan and his Treasury Secretary, Donald Regan started the deregulation of the financial industry. Mr. Regan was a Wall Street conservative and he designed this deregulation. Within two years Reagan and Regan, working with a willing Congress, eliminated many of the rules that had restrained the financial industry for more than fifty years. Gone were most of the restrictions on S&Ls. Gone were most of the rules that stabilized the mortgage market (watch this one). For the first time, the federal government allowed companies to buy back their own shares to raise stock prices. For the first time, the federal government allowed the pooling of mortgages into so-called mortgage-backed securities. (Think Lehman Brothers) And for the first time, corporate raiders started taking on established companies, financing buyouts with massive amounts of new borrowing. (AA 176-177) Along the way, things like the dot-com bust and Enron happened. And then in the early to middle 2000s decade, lenders went into the run-up to the great recession by opening up the sub-prime mortgage market. The country was inundated with massive advertisement pushes urging homebuyers to access cheap loans to purchase far more expensive homes than they should have purchased or even for some of them to purchase homes when any prudent lender would have known that they couldn't afford it. The trick was the variable rate mortgage and the balloon payment. These gadgets allowed the purchase of homes with low payments and sometimes no down payments. The problem was that they would get to the time for the allowed variation in interest rates or the balloon payments and the homeowners couldn't afford them. This led to more and more foreclosures. In the meantime, the lenders would sell these mortgages to other, larger institutions. They would get bundled together in the mortgage backed security market and sold in huge lots to other lenders, including Fannie Mae, Freddie Mac and large financial investors such as Lehman Brothers. These were seen as safe investments because they were backed by so many mortgages on real property. Unfortunately, huge swaths of those mortgages were subprime. That is, they were based on loans to people who did not qualify for such loans in more rational times. This meant that many of them were likely to result in defaults on the underlying loans. When this happened in massive numbers, the sky fell on that scheme and it fell on the American economy, rippling out to the world.

We all know what went on in America. We had the worst economic conditions since the great depression. We the taxpayers had to bail out big banks, big insurance companies and automobile manufacturers. Worse yet, by 2014 more than five million people lost their homes and another two million were near foreclosure. (SC 63) To say "they lost their homes" is to gloss over the wrenching effect this had on the people involved, their loved ones and other creditors, the disruption of whole communities and the immediate growth of the carrion industry including enormous growth in foreclosure law firms on a huge (and sometimes less than honest) basis, real estate deals by big money buyers, con men and women playing with the unwary and just general deterioration of our society for a long time as thousands of families were homeless.. It is only in 2016 that we were even beginning to see some small part of the increase in our economy reaching down beyond the top one percent. (In the meantime, you may have noticed that "fast loan" lenders who promise no closing costs and easy approval for home loans are once again infesting the airwaves.) I have already pointed out how the wealth and income during the recovery until 2016 has been so badly distributed. Just today, August 31, 2016, as I write these words, the *Tampa Bay Times* is carrying an article about the "hollowing out" of the middle class on a world-wide basis and the concern that in our economy this will soon result in less purchasing by consumers of homes and automobiles as well as major appliances and other big ticket items. That would, of course, slow the economy and put it into another downward slide. To this writer it seems inevitable that we will see such a slide within the next two to three years. It also seems likely that this would not be happening nearly so badly had Wall Street not caused the whole thing by its outrageous behavior in the first place.

It has to be said that we the general populace did indeed contribute to our own downfall here. Even though I call the folks who bought into these subprime mortgages victims, and they were, it should have been obvious to anyone who was being careful that what was on offer had hidden traps. Certainly, anyone who was stretching themselves to buy a home with payments at the limits of what they could afford should have noticed that the lender could increase their payments with variable rates or balloon payments. Unfortunately, as we all know, those who offer such deals do not encourage buyers to read the huge, complex documents involved which are usually in the tiniest print they could find. Further, the sophisticated sellers of almost everything these days know about the psychology of their market. Hacker and Pierson refer to the work of Daniel Kahneman, a Nobel Laureate who has written on the subject of "behavioral economics" in a book called *Thinking, Fast and Slow.* This field deals with the issue that the buyers and sellers in our economy often do not work from an even playing field in which both sides understand perfectly the nature and details of their deals. Hacker and Pierson summarize some of the principal points thus:

1. We are easily distracted by shiny objects and thus vulnerable to being "primed" to attend to particular aspects of a choice situation – and even to things that actually have nothing to do with it.

2. We are overconfident, typically expecting our own experience to be better than average, and cocky about our ability to exercise self-discipline down the road.

3. We are biased toward avoiding losses rather than achieving gains.

4. We are very bad at assessing risks. We are overly concerned about vivid things that are extraordinarily improbable (such as terrorist attacks) and we are lousy at drawing the important distinctions between things that are truly rare and those that are merely unlikely.

5. We are prone to inertia. Once we've made a choice, we are highly resistant to changing it, even if the stakes are big, the basis for the initial choice was flimsy, and we're exposed to new information that should lead us to change our minds. (AA 81)

The foregoing are conclusions reached by scientists in studying the problem. If you put the foregoing characteristics into the context of a hard push by a seller of something we truly want to have such as a new home or car or other big ticket item, the push to keep up with our peers, the complexity of the paperwork involved and, the misrepresentations or minimizing of risks by the sellers, it is no wonder so many of us get caught up in purchases we shouldn't have made. That is well known to big sellers and they push it to the limit and even beyond as when they may be outright lying to us. As I will set out later, it certainly is up to each of us to do better in making choices and paying the full price for those choices. And, some of the more important choices we do and will make have to do with our political leaders. That, after all, is what this book is truly about.

As I have intimated before, one of our problems economically has to do with the strategy of supply side economics in which we aim at enabling the market to produce more by deregulating it and letting the increased production result in more salaries, more purchasing and a more robust economy for everyone. (If I have it right, and I think I do, at least for my purposes here.) We have been pursuing that type of approach since Reagan, even through the two terms of two Democratic presidents because the real control has been in Congress which, after all, has control of the purse and the law. I cannot begin to explain the effect of supply-side economics better than Leicht and Fitzgerald have done it, so here it is:

While interpretations vary on what happened next, the statistics are not in dispute: the political and economic consequences of supply-side economics have been far-reaching.

1. Since the 1980s, income inequality increased substantially, more so than during any other peacetime era in America's history.

2. The federal government ran record deficits, borrowing more money in the eight years of the Reagan administration than in the history of the U. S. federal government from 1776 to 1980.

3. Tax rates were lowered and tax cuts passed. Federal revenues did not rise fast enough to meet expenditures. [Which was supposed to be one result of the economic benefits of supply-side economics.]

4. The administration had trouble finding domestic program spending cuts that would allow the budget to balance without appearing to be insensitive to the needs of the poor. (Most government spending does not go to help the poor anyway - …)

5. Public infrastructure such as roads, airports, bridges, and dams, began to fall into disrepair as appropriations for their maintenance were trimmed or eliminated.

6. Individual state governments passed "supply-side packages" of their own in an attempt to match the federal government at reducing tax rates to increase revenues. This shift in tax burdens hit the middle-class especially hard.

7. The deregulation of industry included the financial sector – banks and investments – led to a rash of corporate takeover activity and other unproductive pursuits that were substitutes for saving and investment in actual business enterprise.

8. The same deregulation ushered in the era of easy credit: cars and other consumer items could be purchased with "no money down". …Credit cards became much more widely available and the debts accumulated started to grow as middle class consumers attempted to maintain their lifestyles.

9. The economy never fully recovered until the first Bush administration and then only tentatively. When Bill Clinton took office in 1992, supply-side economics were replaced by a focus on deficit reduction as a federal government priority. The administration of George W. Bush faced record federal deficits – around $458 billion in 2008 as the recession began, $1.4 trillion in 2009 …

10. Tax cutting and business incentives stimulated new lobbying groups in Washington, all of whom look for special favors for their particular industry or product. …

11. The political claim that low taxes stimulate economic growth became entrenched in the American political landscape. State and local governments began to compete for footloose and mobile businesses seeking favorable tax treatment and the best economic deals to locate in specific places. The epidemic of tax cutting left state and local governments with reduced revenues, spawning further cuts in public services. …

12. The view that investors and capitalists don't respond to incentives has been put to the test and found wanting. Not only do they respond to incentives, the incentives produce a new financial elite that does more to manipulate the system to its advantage.

13. Foreign competition has led to changes within American companies that have cost the economy hundreds of thousands of jobs. (MCM 38-39)

It seems to me that thirty years of tax cuts and deregulation, which is still the panacea of the Republican Party (and the Libertarian Party, by the way) has well and truly proven the total worthlessness of that approach. Not only has it beggared the public sector, it has led to economic disaster after disaster, culminating in the great recession and heading in that direction again. If we still buy the supply-side baloney, we deserve what we will truly get and in short order. (I will suggest better approaches later in the book.)

A few more words on what has resulted and we will move on to other subjects. Hacker and Pierson have this to say about our infrastructure:

American infrastructure is no longer the envy of the world. The World Economic Forum, the Davos-based center of business-oriented thinking, ranks the United States fifteenth in the quality of railway structures, sixteenth in the quality of roads, and ninth in transportation infrastructure. The American Society of Civil Engineers estimates that the United States would have to spend $3.6 trillion more than currently budgeted just to bring our infrastructure up to acceptable levels by 2020. China and India are spending almost 10 percent of GDP on infrastructure; Europe around 5 percent. Even Mexico spends just over 3 percent. The United States has not broken 3 percent since the mid-1970s. (AA 41)

These authors also point out that they often traveled from Boston to Washington DC on the fastest train in the US, the Amtrak Acela and it took seven hours. China has a similar length route that takes two hours on their high-speed rail network. Finally, they spend some time on the old and overtaxed electrical grid in this country. We have experienced some major blackouts already and if we don't do something, we can expect more and worse. Not only that, but there is a large transmission loss of power along the lines just because they are in such poor repair. This loss costs a lot of money and adds 150 million tons of carbon dioxide to the air making up for the transmission loss. (AA 41)

So where does this leave us? Despite their decreasing income and their increasing productivity, Americans now work more hours than anyone else in the industrialized world except for South Korea. (MCM 63) We are in more and more consumer debt. Where did all the growth go? It went to the very top. "When it comes to inequality, the United States once looked relatively similar to other rich countries. Today it's the most unequal rich nation in the world by a large margin. (AA 36) And as I have quoted before, the U. S. is the least generous welfare state (and we are and should be a welfare state; after all, our constitution adjures Congress to care for the general welfare) in the world. (MCM 8) Although there are global and technological bases for some of what is happening to us, those forces aren't causing the havoc in other advanced countries that they are in ours. Further, we have the largest economy in the world right now (China may fix that soon) and we can do way better than we are now if we curb the wolves and act responsibly toward all our citizens.

Chapter 5

Unhealthy and Poorly Educated

Coming out of the nineteenth century and coming out of World War II, we were the best educated and healthiest country in the world. The general education of our whole population gave us a head start over all other industrialized nations. With the GI bill and inexpensive state universities, we were able to mobilize our population and spurt into the space age, create the computer age, cure or treat many illnesses that had been resistant before such as polio, heart disease, diabetes and many others. We were the tallest country in the world. When I went to Vietnam in 1963, we towered over the indigenous population and I am only (or at least used to be) five feet, nine inches tall. Our health care system could provide the best care in the world (albeit, not so evenly as it should have). None of these things is true anymore.

This will be a short section because it doesn't take long to state the unfortunate facts. Included in this section will be some overlap with other sections and I will also discuss the question of Americans' "wellbeing" as an issue related to health. For a comparison of these issues in greater detail, see *American Amnesia.* What you will see is that our current measures of health and education are misleading because we are still working off the older population who stood higher in these measures than do younger Americans. This means that our relative standings compared to other advanced nations is skewed by an age cohort (such as mine) which is slowly dying off.

Speaking of the comment by George Will that Woodrow Wilson ruined the twentieth century, Hacker and Pierson say:

The century that Will thinks Wilson ruined brought greater increase in human prosperity – measured not just by income, but also by life expectancy and education and much else – than the entirety of human history. (AA13)

The twentieth century is often referred to (at least by Americans) as the "American Century". We are all aware of that characterization, I think, and it is not a bad one when measured by almost any standard. We think of ourselves as exceptional as a nation. Yet, as Hacker and Pierson say:

Over the last decade or so, a growing body of evidence has shown that the United States is indeed exceptional, just not always in a good way. In a range of areas – human health, high-quality education, economic opportunity, broad-based income gains – we are losing the significant lead over other democracies that our successful mixed economy produced. (AA 12)

So what are the facts today? Let us see.

Regarding height, Hacker and Pierson say this:

While people know that height is a strong predictor of individual achievement (test scores, occupational prestige, pay), it is also a revealing marker of population health. Height has a lot to do with genes, but height differences across nations seems to be caused mostly by social conditions such as income, nutrition, health coverage, and social cohesion. Indeed, one reason for the correlation between height and achievement is that kids whose mothers are healthy during pregnancy and who grow up with sufficient food, medical care and family support tend to be taller adults. An average US white girl born in the early 1910s could expect to reach around five foot three; an average white girl born in the late 1950s could expect to exceed five foot five. Evolution just doesn't happen that fast.

So it's striking that Americans are no longer the tallest people in the world. Not even close. Once three inches taller than residents of the Old World, on average, Americans are now about three inches shorter. The average Dutch height for men is six foot one, and for women, five foot eight – versus five foot nine for American men and five foot five for American women. (AA 25)

And,

Older Americans are roughly on par with their counterparts abroad; younger Americans are substantially shorter. The United States is the richest populous nation in the world. Nevertheless, its young are roughly as tall as the young in Portugal, which has a per capita gross domestic product (GDP) less than half ours. (AA 26)

So, we don't tower over people any more. That is a real and measurable effect of our slowly becoming less healthy and less well-off in the general sense.

Well, how about life expectancy? We live longer than others don't we? Naw. Would that it were so. Going to my favorite authors on this subject, Hacker and Pierson say:

Take life expectancy at birth – the easiest statistic to track, since death records are generally reliable and consistent across nations. The National Academies study [*U. S. Health in International Perspective: Shorter Lives, Poorer Health*] looked at seventeen rich nations. Among these, the United States ranked seventeenth for men in 2011 (life expectancy: 76.3 years, a full 4.2 years shorter than the top-ranking nation). It ranked an equally dismal seventeenth for women (81.1 years, 4.8 years shorter than the top-ranking nation). The United States is home to about 163 million women and 158 million men, so ranking in the middle teens rather than the top translates into 1.45 *billion* fewer years of life. (AA 30)

In case it slipped past you, the figures above mean that of the seventeen rich countries in the comparison, we were *dead last* for both men and women. We are not taller and we don't live longer anymore. Why is that, do you suppose? Could it be that our health care system is failing a large part of our population? Could it be that the working poor and the destitute aren't able to eat as well as those who have more money? And, of course, there is that fact that we deliberately eat too much and too much of the wrong food. (You may have noticed that the fast food industry is unhappy with any government efforts directed to this problem – such as the effort of New York to ban huge soft drink portions – and fights them consistently. After all, it's our own fault if we eat too much of the wrong food even if they advertise the hell out of it, especially to the young.)

There are more statistics and they are just as bad. A study found that American whites between forty five and fifty four were dying at higher rates in 2013 than they had been in 1999. But every other rich country experienced no such drop. The numbers mean that if this drop had not occurred and the death rates had remained as they were, a half million earlier deaths would have been avoided. Worse yet (worse??!!) the trend was most devastating for whites with a high school diploma or less. In 2013 there were 736 deaths per 100,000 people in this group, up from 601 deaths per 100,000 in 1999. By comparison, in Canada (where there is universal health care), the death rate for people in this group fell from around 300 per 100,000 in 1999 to just under 249 per 100,000 in 2013. Only among whites with a college degree did the death rates fall substantially over this period. In 2013, white adults in the forty five to fifty four year old age group with no more than a high school diploma were more than four times as likely to die as those with a college degree. (All facts in this paragraph from AA 30-31)

There are many ways to measure differences to try to learn how folks are doing. Another comparison that seems almost surreal is a comparison of the death rate for American women between the ages of fifteen and fifty. Four in one hundred American women will die between those ages. For other rich nations, that figure is two per one hundred and, on average, the death rate in this group fell below four per one hundred forty years ago. In other words, we are a full generation behind other rich nations. (AA 31)

What does this mean to me? I am not an expert, but I have to think that the absence of universal health care in this country has a large effect on these numbers. And let me ring a bell I have rung before. Americans pay more for drugs than the citizens of any other nation on earth. It is estimated that fifty million Americans per year fail to fill their prescriptions because they cannot afford them. (SC 24-25) In a universal health care system, this would not occur. Even our American Medicare and Medicaid systems do not alleviate this problem entirely because they do not cover much and sometimes none of drug costs.

There are many other aspects to this conundrum of falling health care quality in the U. S. I have already alluded to the fall of expenditures by the government in non-defense spending research and development (R&D). Here is a really frightening thought:

We are not talking just about dollars and cents. We are talking about lives. Consider one chilling example: drug resistant infections. As America's breakthroughs in antibiotics recede into the past, bacteria are evolving to defeat current antibiotics. For more and more infections, we are plunging back into the pre-antibiotic era. In the United States alone, two million people are sickened and tens of thousands die each year from drug-resistant infections – mostly because private companies see little incentive to invest in the necessary research, and the federal government has failed to step in. Though federal funding for the National Institutes of Health ramped up in the mid-1990s, it has fallen precipitously since, cutting the share of young scientists with NIH grants in half, in roughly six years. As one medical professor lamented recently: "In my daily work in both a university medical school, and a public hospital, it's a rare month that some bright young person doesn't tell me they are quitting science because it's too hard to get funded ….A decade or two from now, when an antibiotic-resistant bacteria or a new strain of bird flu is ravaging humanity that generation will no longer be around to lead the scientific charge on humanity's behalf. (AA 40)

This is a very real threat. How many people have had a brush either personally or through a family member or friend with methicillin-resistant staphylococcus (MRSA) in a hospital already? The fallback drug Vancomycin is failing more and more frequently. And, if flu doesn't seem such a problem, remember the great flu epidemic of 1919. More than twenty million people were estimated to have died in that one and it has been suspected that the number was actually much higher than that, but figures from less advanced nations are suspect to say the least. If you think that our more advanced medicine would prevent this kind of result, think again. We don't have a drug to cure viral illness, much less a drug to cure the flu. And the flu can kill the youngest and the healthiest among us. That is what happened in 1919.

So, what are we doing about these problems? Well, in the decade before 2015, the budget for the NIH was cut by $5 billion after inflation, resulting in a loss of almost a fifth of its budget. Even worse, the Centers for Disease Control, (CDC) had its budget for disaster preparedness cut in half. (AA 327) These are the agencies intended to keep America healthy in a health crisis. Someone in Congress doesn't care.

Well, how are we doing in taking care of our kids? What is their level of well-being? Again, Hacker and Pierson know:

Again it's the youngest of the young who are most disadvantaged. The United Nations Children's Fund (UNICEF) has compiled a composite index of "material well-being" of children in developed countries which takes into account various measures of childhood poverty and material deprivation (lack of access to regular meals, for example). In the most recent reports, the United States ranked twenty-sixth out of twenty-nine developed nations. First in the standings was the Netherlands, where soon-to-be-giants are born. UNICEF has produced its index since the early 2000s. The United States was one of five nations that were below average at that time yet failed to improve kids' material well-being in the following decade. The other four were Greece, Hungary, Italy and Spain.

"Prediction is very difficult." The physicist, Niels Bohr reportedly said, "especially about the future." But today's young are the clearest vision of the future we have. If they are falling behind – unhealthier than young people in other rich countries, less well educated, more likely to be economically marginalized – we face grim prospects. (AA 38)

I have treated well-being as part of health, but as you can see, economic condition, which I have already talked about and education, which is next are also involved in well-being. These comparative issues and economic factors bearing on health are conspiring (if inanimate conditions can do that) to make our children poorer and sicker than the preceding generation and maybe the preceding several generations if we don't do something about this. And who else can do it? If not us, then who? It is we every-day Americans who must rise up, like generations before us and do something!

Before I leave health care, one other thing. A word about the Affordable Care Act, otherwise known as Obamacare. The program is widely despised by Republicans who have tried several times to repeal it or defund it. They have even threatened to shut the government down over raising the federal deficit limit even though the funds needed had already been approved by Congress in the budget. So far twenty million people have obtained coverage through this program who did not have it before. The Congressional Budget Office says that it will actually reduce the deficit over time. The provision for a public program that was a part of the bill initially was knocked out of it before it passed, so the insurance coverage under the program comes from private insurance carriers. All complaints about the program appear to be unfounded. It has been hated by the Republicans because they did not want to see the Obama administration have a single success, as I will discuss later. They also hated the tax provisions aimed at the rich in the ACA. Not to worry, "President" Trump and the current Congress will mess this benefit up and deprive many of coverage as they are trying to do as I write this.

As promised, the next issue is education. Once world leaders in education and especially university level education, we are no longer leading. True, we do still get students in our better universities from all over the world, but those universities, especially the public ones, are steadily being eroded by lack of financial support. North Carolina, as an example, had one of the very best public university systems in the country. As I set forth later in the section "The Rape of North Carolina", recent Republican activists have taken over the state government from top to bottom and, in the words of big money man Art Pope, have begun to "starve the beast". In my state of Florida, support for the state university system from state funds has declined drastically such that when I attended the University of Florida in the 1950's there was no tuition and only a registration fee, to the point that now the university system is out of reach of a large portion of the population economically. When our current (Republican) governor, Rick Scott first took office one of the first things he did was to cut funding for universities (although that has been slightly reversed since then). As we saw in the platform of the Libertarian Party, they would like to eliminate all publicly funded schooling at every level. Let's examine some data.

Although we were once the world leaders in education, the United States is now mediocre in international education rankings. We would look even worse if we hadn't done so well in the past. Among young adults, the United States now ranks twentieth out of twenty-seven OECD (Organization for Economic Cooperation and Development) nations in the share of that group expected to finish high school. (AA 32-333) The OECD includes such heavyweights as Estonia, the Czech Republic, Greece, Chile, Hungary, Iceland, Latvia and Mexico. There are other issues here affecting the education picture. As Hacker and Pierson say:

In the United States – which incarcerates roughly ten times as high a share of the population (eight in a thousand versus fewer than one in a thousand in most advanced industrial democracies) – it makes a real difference, especially for demographic groups with the highest rates of incarceration. Indeed, the high school dropout rate for young black men is more than 40 percent higher when we include in our count the incarcerated, wiping out all the apparent gains in their high school completion since the late 1980s. Here again, conventional indicators present an overly sunny picture of our relative performance.

The big story, however, is our relative decline in higher education. The United States has many of the finest institutions of higher education in the world. The problem is that the share of young people getting a degree is rising much more slowly in the United States than in other OECD nations. One reason is the erosion of public support through federal grants and state universities, leaving students and their families much more reliant on loans. Once without peer, the United States has fallen to nineteenth in college completion in the OECD, and the gap in completion between higher-income and lower-income students has widened. Older Americans are the most educated in the world. Younger Americans, not even close. (AA 33)

At every level the US is falling behind. This is a reflection of our unwillingness to provide the funding and the special programs needed to solve these problems. In large part, this is a reflection of the tax cutting plans of the supply-siders. It would, however, be disingenuous of me to overlook the fact that there is more to the problem than money. As we have been learning lately, there is a real lack of insistence in our school systems on the need for all students to study STEM (science, technology, engineering and mathematics) subjects. There has been too lenient a standard for progressing through the school system without learning the required material. But on the other hand, we need to see to it that those who have problems with the more rigorous studies get help and are encouraged to do well in these areas. We also need more alternative paths for those who are not cut out for this curriculum. This would include beefing up support for community colleges and technical schools where subjects such as welding, plumbing, dental hygiene, LPN diplomas and similar studies could be pursued with hope of real employment opportunities after school. I agree all this is true, but the big problem is the lack of real commitment on the part of our politicians to give proper precedence to education and to find ways to fund it. In most states (like Florida), education is funded largely at the local level through property taxes. This means that school systems in poorer counties or school districts have far less funding than those in more prosperous areas. This is just another way to leave the poor behind, which we seem to be so good at in this country. Most OECD nations either invest equally in all students or invest more in the disadvantaged. The US is in a small group doing the opposite. (AA 35)

How are our schools doing in basic education comparatively? Not so well, as I am sure you probably know. In an OECD assessment in 2011 and 2012 of adult skill levels, the US was average in reading and close to the bottom in math and ability to work with computer technology. Hacker and Pierson say;

In all countries, the young are better at math and working with digital technology than the old. But improvements in test scores from one generation to the next are much smaller in the United States than in other rich countries. Older Americans are close to the international average for older adults. Younger Americans, while scoring slightly higher, are years behind their international peers. So, again, American math scores are improving – barely. But they are improving far faster in other nations. The same is true of other skills measured by the OECD: The United States falls further and further in the rankings as you move down the age ladder. (AA 34)

It is the same picture everywhere we look. Older Americans are better educated comparatively than younger ones and the trend is continuing. In the face of the fact that we are living in a rapidly more sophisticated world requiring more and more high-level education to cope, we don't seem to want to compete. That is a fearful predictor of how we will be competing in the global economy in the future. And the problem will devolve on our kids and grandkids – one which we will bequeath them if we don't do something about it soon.

In analyzing the state of health, education and well-being in this country, we don't get a rosy picture. We are certainly not a third world nation nor are we heading toward that status, but we are certainly heading toward being second-rate. We need universal health care for all citizens. We could get to that result without the government owning the hospitals and employing the physicians as some other countries do. But we can't get there unless we are committed to the result. This means getting a handle on outrageous costs in the health care system such as the incredible cost of drugs and the uneven and ridiculous differences in the cost of medical care across the country.

We need a major improvement in our efforts at education. Our goal must be the education of every American to the highest level of his or her abilities with a much stronger emphasis on teaching our young the technical and high-level service fields that the future will reward. We will need those doctors, nurses, scientists, high-level craftsmen and others trained by our schools more and more, not less and less.

The bottom line here is that the inequalities that have crept into our economy and the outsize power they have produced in a small minority of Americans is detrimental to the future of our country in the many ways I have outlined. But, the picture has other dimensions that are frightening as well and I shall set them forth next.

Chapter 6

The Rape of North Carolina

I am sure that many would quarrel with my description of what has happened to North Carolina as rape, but I stick by the label. The state is a textbook example of what happens when the extreme right wing gets its hands on the levers of government and this happened to North Carolina in a sudden and overwhelming way. The things that have happened there since the election of 2012 warm the cockles of people like Art Pope and the Koch brothers as well as all good Libertarians everywhere. Before I launch into the story, let me say that these things are happening in many parts of the country but more gradually than they have happened to the Tar Heel state. I could recite many of these things that have also happened to Florida where I live and in Wisconsin. However, they are a part of the playbook of the extreme right and they are happening everywhere to some extent or other. The shame of it in North Carolina is that it immediately began the degradation of a good public school system and an outstanding university system. Of course, it may be more important that it started the immediate degradation of benefits for the needy resulting in a loss of health insurance benefits for half a million residents and many other losses as set forth below.

At the outset, let me recommend that anyone interested in this topic read the section in Jane Mayer's book *Dark Money* for details. There is also a paper prepared by Edward B. Fiske, who previously was the education editor for the New York Times and presently is a consultant on education matters and Helen F. Ladd, the Edgar Thompson Professor of Public Policy and professor of economics at Duke University entitled *What's Up with Education in North Carolina?* This paper is available online.

Prior to the 2012 election, Republicans had gained a majority in the state assembly. They then were able to gerrymander the Congressional districts to eliminate the majority Democratic makeup of the congressional delegation. With the help of millions from Mr. Pope, Koch brothers entities and others, they were able to hold on to a majority of the state supreme court which, when faced with the complaint that the districting had been unfair, sustained it. This resulted in a reduction of Democrats in their congressional delegation from 7 out of 13 to 4 out of 13 by 2010. But that is only a small measure of what happened in 2012.

In the state assembly, the Republican majority was increased to veto-proof majorities in both houses and a Republican governor was elected putting the state in complete Republican control for the first time since Reconstruction. It was due in large part to a huge influx of right wing money from the Koch entities to Art Pope's various entities and others. Pat McCrory, the new Republican governor, immediately appointed Art Pope to be the state budget director. Finally, finally, Mr. Pope had his hands on the financial controls of the state government and this Libertarian-oriented gentleman set out to show the world, along with his state assembly, what the far right was really all about. I will set it forth, but before I do, let me say that all these facts and much of the wording come from Mayer, Fiske and Ladd.

As Mayer says:

Within a few months, the legislature had overhauled the state's tax code from top to bottom. On almost every issue, the legislature followed the right-wing playbook that had originated in two think tanks, the John Locke Foundation and the Civitas Institute, which were founded by Pope and largely funded by the Pope family's $150 million John William Pope Foundation. …A good bit of the remainder came from tobacco companies and two Koch family foundations. (DM 338)

The think tanks in question were 501(c)(3) organizations which put them in the same category as churches, universities and public charities. However, they wrote model legislation, touted it to legislators and bragged about their clout with the general assembly. As Mayer says:

Pope was proud of the achievement [of the think tanks], telling the conservative Philanthropy Roundtable, "In a generation, we've shifted the public-policy debate in North Carolina from the center-left to the center-right. (DM 339)

I have to say, Pope is understating his accomplishment. What he and the Republican legislature accomplished was to move the state so far to the right that it couldn't be seen from the middle with a telescope. From my perspective, he should have been proud of the result because he was a big winner. Unfortunately, the state of North Carolina was the big loser. Let me count the ways.

Again. From Mayer:

The legislature slashed taxes on corporations and the wealthy while cutting benefits and services for the middle class and the poor. It also gutted environmental programs, sharply limited women's access to abortions, backed a constitutional ban on gay marriage, and legalized concealed guns in bars and on playgrounds and school campuses. It also erected cumbersome new bureaucratic barriers to voting. Like the poll taxes and literacy tests of the segregated past, the new hurdles, critics said, were designed to discourage poor and minority voters who leaned Democratic. The election law expert Richard Hasen declared, "I've never seen a package of what I would call suppressive voting measures like this." The historian Dan T. Carter, who specializes in southern history and the University of South Carolina, noted that when friends around the country asked if things in North Carolina were as bad as they looked from the outside, he was forced to answer, "No, it's worse – a lot worse." (DM 339)

Providing a little more detail, Fiske and Ladd said:

The General Assembly cut corporate and individual tax rates, replaced the 91-year old graduated income tax with a 5.8 percent flat rate, and extended the range of goods and services subject to the sales tax. The N. C. Budget and Tax Center estimated that these changes will eventually cost the state $1billion per year – with 75 percent of the tax savings going to the top five percent of taxpayers.

With the pending tax reforms a given, legislators began enacting a social agenda rooted not in mainstream Republican values but in those of the Tea Party and the Koch Brothers. Gov. McCrory announced that the state would turn down Federal funds to extend Medicaid even though doing so would cost North Carolina hundreds of millions of Federal dollars and deprive 500,000 state residents of health care. Republican leaders also declined to extend unemployment benefits at the end of the year, despite the fact that at 9.2 percent, the state's unemployment rate was fifth highest in the country. ("What's up with Education Policy in North Carolina" – henceforth What's Up- 3)

Some of the other things the legislature did were just perfect in defining how far right they were, as Fiske and Ladd say:

Some new legislation borders on the comical, including the law outlawing the use of Sharia law in a state where Muslims make up less than a quarter of one percent of the population. The lawmakers also saw fit to require the teaching of cursive writing and the memorization of the multiplication tables in primary schools. Fortunately, a proposal to make Christianity the official state religion never gained traction. (What's Up 3)

Going back to taxes, the legislature eliminated the estate tax, which would probably benefit just 23 estates because the estate tax law already exempted the first $5.25 million of inheritance from taxation, but which was projected to cost the state $300 million in its first five years. Ask yourselves, who was the intended beneficiary of this move? Not the average citizen, for sure. In fact, taking that money out of the budget, just meant that losses had to be made up from things like sales taxes which are considered regressive taxes because no matter how poor you may be, you will pay those taxes day in and day out. Of course, the major way the legislature handled the loss of tax revenues was to make cuts in various programs that benefited the public.

To explain the cuts, I turn to Mayer, who, herself, simply summarized:

So, for savings, the legislators turned to the one institution that had distinguished North Carolina from many other southern states – its celebrated public education systems.

The assault was systematic. They authorized vouchers for private schools while putting the public school budget in a vise and squeezing. They eliminated teachers' assistants and reduced teacher pay from the twenty-first highest in the country to forty-sixth. They abolished incentives for teachers to earn higher degrees and reduced funding for a successful program for at-risk preschoolers. Voters had overwhelmingly preferred to avoid these cuts by extending a temporary one-penny sales tax to sustain education funding, but the legislators, many of whom had signed a no-tax pledge promoted by Americans for Prosperity [a Koch funded entity], made the cuts anyway.

North Carolina's esteemed state university system also took a hit. Ideological warfare infused the fight. Pope's network had waged a long campaign to slash spending, with employees of the John William Pope Center for Higher Education Policy, another Pope-created nonprofit accusing the university system of becoming a "niche for radicals," describing the public funding as a "boondoggle," and demanding that the legislature "starve the beast." The center dug up professors' voting records in an effort to prove political bias. Once the Republican majority took over the legislature, it quickly imposed severe cuts that were projected to cause tuition hikes, faculty layoffs, and fewer scholarships, even though the state's constitution required that higher education be made "as free as practical" to all residents. …

At the same time that Pope's network fought to cut university budgets, he offered to privately fund academic programs in subjects he favored, like Western civilization and free-market economics. A $500,000 gift that Pope made to North Carolina State University for instance, funded lectures by conservatives. "I'm pretty sure we would not invite Paul Krugman" [a world famous economist, recipient of a Nobel prize in economics, previously a professor at MIT, professor at other acclaimed universities and an op–ed columnist, but a liberal] a professor who picked the speakers and was affiliated with the John Locke Foundation, he acknowledged. Some saw Pope's donations as a bid to buy academic control. "It's sad and blatant," said Cat Warren, an English professor at North Carolina State. Pope, she said, "succeeds in getting higher education defunded and then uses those cutbacks as a way to increase leverage and influence over course content."

The John Locke Foundation also sponsored the North Carolina History Project, which aimed to reorient the state's teaching of its history by providing online lesson plans for high school teachers that downplayed the roles of social movements and government while celebrating what it called the "personal creation of wealth." In a similar vein Republicans in the state senate passed a bill requiring North Carolina high school students to study conservative principles as part of American history in order to graduate in 2015. The bill stressed the "constitutional limitations on government power to tax and spend." (DM 341-342)

That is admittedly a long quote, but it contains a multitude of important points. For instance, the Republican legislature's refusal to accept a tax voted by the public to avoid cuts to the school budget. Why? Because they promised Americans for Prosperity not to raise taxes! And who the hell is AFP to dictate to the people of North Carolina? They are right wing nuts, that's who. Or, how about Mr. Pope's ambition to cut university funding, to "starve the beast" because he thinks it is a "niche for radicals"? And having his "Center for Higher Education" dig up the voting record of professors? Does he give a damn whether the students of North Carolina universities get an education or not? It would not seem so. In fact given his efforts to control the course content of the universities and sway it to the far right, he seems only to be interested in propaganda. It all stinks of the McCarthy era doesn't it? But even Senator McCarthy couldn't buy anticommunist coursework at public universities. And the requirements imposed by the legislature to teach the limits on the power of government to tax and spend as a requirement for high school students to graduate! The far right has been seeping into the university system for decades. The Kochs have been behind this as have several other wolves. Things like the Cato Institute and the Heritage Foundation have been turning out "scholars" steeped in the far right and supply side economic tripe. Even scarier are things like the Mercator Institute at George Mason University in Virginia, an excrescence on the university system of the state of Virginia. But, none of this has captured the curriculum of a university system itself quite like Art Pope in North Carolina.

But, surely, at heart Mr. Pope must wish the people of his state of North Carolina well, even if I and others disagree with his politics? Surely he wants the best for "his" people? Don't you believe it. Relying on Jane Mayer again (what a genius that lady is), get this:

Pope, who credited a summer program run by the Cato Institute [!!] for first exposing him to free-market theories, argued that the country's growing economic inequality was not a worry because "wealth creation and wealth destruction is constantly happening." All Americans, he said, had a fair chance at success. Citing Michael Jordan and Mick Jagger as examples, he asked, "Why should they be deprived of that money – why is that unfair?" He noted "I'm not envious of the wealth that Bill Gates has," and added, "America does not have an aristocracy or plutocracy." (DM 343)

There is more to come, but consider this. Remember that Mr. Pope was born into wealth. He had all the tools to do whatever he wanted. I am not about to claim he didn't increase his wealth and work hard, I just want it clear that he had the wealth and the power at birth, making him one of the elite to begin with. He got turned onto free-market principles by the Libertarian Cato Institute! A fine example of the success of their propaganda machine, but they were preaching to the (rich) choir with Mr. Pope. Then he says that wealth inequality is no problem because everyone has a fair chance in America. Well, no Mr. Pope, they don't. Those born into poverty are overwhelmingly likely to stay there. Those born with disabilities or lack of real talent don't get ahead by and large (unless they were born rich and manage to stay that way). And, Michael Jordan? Really? That man was born with incredible talent and brains. He made it work. How many poor kids shooting hoops and playing for their high school basketball teams have a hope in hell of duplicating that success? Not many (like a handful total). And Mick Jagger – a Brit??? What does he have to do with the problem of wealth inequality in the US? Ah, but let us go on. It gets so much more enlightening.

Quoting again from Mayer about Art Pope:

The poor, he argued, were largely the victims of their own bad choices. "Really, when you look at the lowest income, most of that is just simply a factor of age and marriage, If you're young and single – and God forbid if you're young and a single parent, and don't have a high school education – then your earnings will be low, and you'll be in the bottom twenty percent." (DM 343)

To borrow a line from the movie, *Good Will Hunting,* "How do you like them apples?" The man is in a position to screw millions of people and he believes this kind of crap. Yes, single parenthood is a limiting factor and lack of a high school diploma is also. But what about all the poor people of whom these things are not true (ignoring the fact that many of those with no high school diploma couldn't stay to get one because they had to help support their family and those single parents who are trying mightily to raise their child(ren) and be good citizens)? He just doesn't want anyone to rock his (golden) boat. But, Mayer is not through, bless her.

She goes on to say:

The constellation of nonprofit groups supported by Pope's fortune echoed this tough-luck message. For instance, a researcher at the Civitas Institute asserted that the poor in America lived better than "the picture most liberals like to paint." The researcher, Bob Luebke cited a Heritage Foundation study showing that the poor often had shelter, a refrigerator and cable television. "The media obsession with pervasive homelessness also appears a myth," he declared. John Hood, a bright young protégé of Pope's who moved from the John Locke Foundation to become head of the John William Pope Foundation in 2015, stressed that "the true extent of poverty in North Carolina and around the country is woefully overestimated." Where poverty did exist, he asserted, it resulted from "self-destructive behavior." (DM 343)

Well hell, thank you all very much, you one percenters. The poor "often had shelter", did they? I suppose that means, even to Mr. Luebke, that they sometimes didn't have shelter. And, isn't shelter the second need right after food? But we shouldn't be concerned about the poor because they "often have shelter", you boob? Not only do they often have shelter, they also often have a refrigerator! Be still, my heart. A refrigerator! You try living without one, sonny. And, worst of all, the poor have cable television. Well, by all means, let's cut them off from all help if they have cable television. Mr. Luebke, have you ever walked into the poor neighborhoods of your city? Can you honestly tell anyone that you think people should have to live that way – especially in the richest nation on earth? The media "obsession" with homelessness is a myth? Did you do a large-scale study to say that? And don't cite the Heritage Foundation to me. I mean a real scientific study. No, you did not. I didn't either, but I support a local charity in my city of Tampa and I can tell you that homelessness is a big problem for families in our area. I worked in downtown Tampa for decades and I can tell you that the homeless are there every day. Not only that, since the 2008 great recession fostered by the thieving rich bastards on Wall Street, there are a lot more homeless in our area. And then there is the "bright protégé". Mr. Hood. You know what, I don't doubt that he has intelligence and probably education, but he has no heart and no common sense. North Carolina is not a well-to-do state. It is full of pockets of poverty. If he hasn't seen them, he hasn't looked. And if he hasn't looked, he has no business bloviating about the lack of poverty. Finally, he knows from his omniscience that those who are poor are so as a result of "self-destructive behavior". Hey you know what, I bet there are such people. But, to label a whole segment of the population (yes, Mr. Hood, a *large* segment) that way on no factual basis whatever is what your right wing psychosis is all about. Yay for the rich, they worked hard and earned every penny and boo for the rest because they were not dedicated enough to getting rich –oh, and by the way, screw them. If I have my way, the bottom 99 percent might yet do the screwing.

The right wing of the Republican Party and the rich people and entities behind it consider North Carolina an example of how they want the rest of the country to look. If this little excursion into what that actually means didn't discourage you, stay tuned because it only gets worse.

Chapter 7

Global Warming

This topic never fails to puzzle me. The facts about global warming are all available on the internet, not to mention in books and articles in the media and magazines. The science of climate change is relatively advanced now and actually has been for decades. The planet is warming up and it is being caused by the burning of fossil fuels. That releases the greenhouse gas CO2 into the atmosphere. That results in warming our climate globally. The temperature rise over the last fifty years has been more extreme and far faster than any similar change in our climate for as long as we can document. This doesn't mean that the planet hasn't been warmer at other times. It was warmer when dinosaurs walked the earth. But it appears clear that the current increase is faster than any we can document and the current global average temperatures are the highest in thousands of years. There have been vociferous attacks on the science of global warming by the vested interests in the fossil fuel industry, using the media and a set of pet experts who feel free to dispute every bit of the science. However, the cold, hard facts remain. I will deal with the dissenters (commonly referred to as global warming "deniers") in some detail later. As of this writing in August of 2016. The average global temperature for this year to date is 1.05 degrees

Celsius above the global average for the twentieth century according to the National Oceanic and Atmospheric Administration (NOAA). The year has set records every month. We know from direct measurements at the Mauna Loa Observatory in Hawaii that the CO_2 content of the atmosphere has risen from approximately 310 parts per million (ppm) in 1958 to 404.39 ppm in July 2016. (This is known as the Keeling curve after Charles Keeling who first started it.) From indirect measurements (Such as ice cores), we know that the CO_2 content had been fairly stable for millennia at about 280 ppm until the beginning of the industrial revolution. The current rate of increase in CO_2 is greater than was expected based on past data, primarily due to the rapid progress of China and India into the advanced world economy. This is not to blame the problem on China and India. England is the first and longest culprit and the US is the biggest culprit. In past decades, it was hoped to arrest the CO_2 content growth at 350ppm, but that doesn't seem very likely now. (See 350.org) It was hoped that temperature rise could be capped at two degrees centigrade, but that does not seem likely any more.

A brief recap of what this is all about seems in order. CO_2 is referred to as a "greenhouse" gas because it can cause warming in the atmosphere. The analogy to a greenhouse is not really accurate, but the name has stuck. What happens in the atmosphere is that heat is radiated from the sun into the atmosphere down to the ground. The earth radiates some of this heat back toward the sky. Greenhouse gases absorb this radiation and hold it in the lower atmosphere like a blanket. This results in heat that would otherwise escape into space being held where it can warm the earth . There is nothing strange about this concept. It has been known to science for more than a century. It is the mechanism that has turned Venus into a literal hell with surface temperatures hot enough to melt lead. The reason our CO_2 has been increasing is the burning of fossil fuels. Coal is the worst culprit, but oil and gas also have the effect. Any activity that burns fossil fuels will emit CO_2. This includes power plants, industrial plants and, yes, automobiles burning gasoline and trucks burning diesel fuel. The measurement of increase in CO2 is in the billions of tons annually. And the rate of increase in atmospheric CO2 is accelerating. Just to keep things interesting, methane is also a greenhouse gas and a more potent one than CO2. Methane is released in the extraction of fossil fuels, especially natural gas, as in the fracking process. (And yes, billions of cows farting are a significant contributor as well, but I don't intend to pursue that issue now.) There are also enormous quantities of methane trapped in ice and under the sea that could be released by glo0bal warming. However, I will keep this simple and deal with the number one problem, CO2. The most current estimate of potential temperature increase by the turn of the century is as much as six degrees Celsius, or 10.8 degrees Fahrenheit. That much increase will convert our planetary environment into a very different place. That would probably make it a hostile place for human habitation. The point is that we are currently and rapidly turning the earth into a place that will kill many if not most of us, not to mention what we will do to ourselves as we all strive to keep or obtain more favorable situations in terms of habitat, food, water, disease and many other factors. Presently there is great resistance in this country to recognizing the problem or, horrors, changing our ways in order to mitigate and hopefully relieve the problem over time. If we keep on the way we are now, our grandchildren and their children will have every right to hate us, those of them who survive.

I have said that these are hard facts. Despite that, the sense of a large proportion of Americans is that these facts are not true. They believe that the warming we are currently experiencing is natural and the weather will correct over time as a part of a natural ebb and flow of temperature. They believe that the scientists who are trying vainly to alert them to the danger are liars who have some nefarious ambition to make money by getting grants from governments and also trying to impose some international control over the US. They even believe that the scientists are guilty of a great "hoax" and have an ambition to do away with the free market economy. My wife and I are friends with two lovely couples who have college educations and work or worked in professions including teaching, newspaper editing, securities trading and library science. These are some of the more solid and caring Americans you could imagine. However, they all believe that there is no global warming problem, despite the facts that can be cited to them. Frankly, they frighten me to death with their attitudes because they prove how horribly effective the fossil fuel industry, Wall Street and manufacturing industries along with their allies such as the Chamber of Commerce and their tools such as the Heritage Foundation, the Cato Institute and many others have been able to achieve in sowing lies and disinformation in order to preserve the enormously profitable status quo for them. They have convinced tens of millions of intelligent Americans that : 1) there is no global warming problem and 2) those who say otherwise are simply advocating steps that would cost Americans millions of jobs and economic hardship for their own (imagined) profit. Look at it. Are scientists usually rich? Are oil and gas moguls rich? Is Exxon-Mobil rich? Is big industry rich? Which side has the money to buy politicians? Which side owns almost all of the mass media? Well, I will go into more detail below. Just understand this: the 2016 Republican Party platform (more on it later) not only discounts the world's climate scientists, it advocates, as Sarah Palin once famously said, "Drill, baby, drill". The Party encourages drilling on all the coastal waters, the public lands and everywhere possible to have the reserves, not for now, but in hand for later. Frankly, if we burn all the oil, gas and coal we already have under development, our fate is cast even without more and more development.

Let me say again what I will repeatedly say: I am not a climate scientist any more than I am an economist or social scientist. I rely for the facts on several of the books I have referred to, including Mann's *Hockey Stick,* Oreskes and Conway's *Merchants of Doubt* and Klein's *This Changes*

Everything. I am also deriving information from online sources from NASA, NOAA and others as I cite them. For those who would doubt the truthfulness of these facts, I urge you to read these sources before doubting them.

I know that Mann, especially, is hated by the right wing and they have done everything in their power to smear and discredit him. Despite these efforts, every scientific challenge to his work has been rebutted definitively by such sources as the National Academy of Sciences, other climate scientists and various University investigations. The reason the right really hates Dr. Mann is that he and his collaborators came up with the graph referred to as the "hockey stick" which is a visual representation of their climate model for the past 1000 years showing that the warming that has taken place in the last half of the twentieth century is the hottest the earth's climate has been in this time frame. The point here is that what our global climate is today for heat is not a normal part of any cycle that has occurred in the past millennium. That goes toward refuting the argument that the current heating is natural and not caused by humans. Dr. Mann didn't call it the hockey stick; that label got hung on it by others. It is called that because the graph is fairly smooth through most of its length until the late twentieth century when it curves upward rather like a hockey stick laid on its back. The thing about that is that Dr. Mann and his team are only one of literally thousands of scientists and teams of scientists who have reached the same and even more extended results. Dr. Mann just got unfortunate enough to have been the lead author on this very graphic representation of the result which was picked up and featured in a report of the Intergovernmental Panel on Climate Change (the IPCC), of which more later. If you actually read his book, you will see the truth laid out well. It is also covered in the other two books to which I just referred. Dr. Mann's book will also tell you just how vicious and brainless the attacks on him and climate scientists generally have been. The "official" smears have led some not-so-well- hinged people to do things like threaten the life of Dr. Mann and his family and even send him an envelope containing a white powder at his University office. If you go online, you will readily come across a blog saying horrible things about Dr. Mann and accusing him of claiming to have received a Nobel Prize, which he did not receive. Dr. Mann has not made that claim. However, a Nobel peace prize was awarded to Al Gore and the IPCC jointly and Dr. Mann, among many other lead authors of the relevant IPCC report each received plaques from the Nobel Committee recognizing their contribution and Dr. Mann has talked about that in his speeches and his writing. In any event, if you are dubious about the scientists and think they are lying for some nefarious reason, read the stuff I am citing to you.

Now a little narrative about the recent history of the climate change "debate". I put the word debate in quotation marks because there is no scientific debate about global warming any more. The science has been clear that global warming is happening and it is caused in large part by humans (it is anthropogenic). How quickly it will proceed in the future and exactly what all the ramifications will be is not so clear, but the fact that people are warming the earth past its recent (geologically) history is a settled issue among scientists who are trained in climate science and currently doing research in it. The so-called "experts" who argue otherwise don't have either the credentials or the actual scientific research to back them up. So, let me be clear: there *is no scientific debate about whether humans are heating the earth's climate by burning fossil fuels.* There *is* uncertainty about how fast and to what extent we will see the changes. However, increased temperature, glacier melt and rising sea levels are already apparent. There have also been a number of violent storms and forest fires that *might* be related to climate change such as superstorm Sandy and flooding taking place in Louisiana as I write this sentence, but in truth, scientists can only say that we will experience more such extreme weather as we further heat the earth but cannot and will not say that they can know whether any particular weather event is related to global warming. What

I will say, as a mere layman, is that increasing CO2 levels are peculiar to the industrial age in the recent (geologically) past and it is continuing and even accelerating. We know CO2 is a greenhouse gas. Therefore it is inarguable that the CO2 we have been and are pumping into the atmosphere can only continue to heat us up. It is possible that the last few years of increasing temperatures will give way to a period in which there is not so much warming. It is also possible that there will be no such let-up. But either way, over time the climb will be inexorable as CO2 concentrations in the atmosphere continue to rise. Because we absolutely *know* this is so, how can we in good conscience keep doing what we are doing?

Now the history part. A great summary of the early history of the climate change science is contained in *Merchants of Doubt.* The later history is well set forth in *The Hockey stick* with interesting comments on it in *This Changes Everything.* However, going back to the nineteenth century, as Oreskes and Conway tell us, an Irish scientist named John Tyndall first discovered that CO2 traps heat and keeps it from escaping into space. Then in the twentieth century Swedish geochemist Svante Arrhenius concluded that CO2 released into the atmosphere by burning fossil fuels could alter the earth's climate. In the 1950's Charles Keeling received funding to measure CO2 systematically leading to the Keeling curve. His funding was arranged by Roger Revelle, then Director of the Scripps Institution of Oceanography. In 1965, Dr. Revelle was asked by the President's Science Advisory Committee to write a summary of the potential impacts of carbon dioxide-induced warming. (All from DM 170) Thus, we have interest by the president's Science Advisory Committee as early as 1965 in the issue of carbon dioxide caused global warming. Dr. Revelle's report went to President Johnson, who mentioned it in a Special Message to Congress later in 1965. Among other things, he said:

This generation has altered the composition of the atmosphere on a global scale through … a steady increase in carbon dioxide from the burning of fossil fuels. (DM 171)

There you have it, a presidential recognition of the problem in 1965! Unfortunately, given the other problems Lyndon Johnson had, to include things like Vietnam and the civil rights issues, he did nothing further on the problem.

In 1977 the Department of Energy asked the Jasons, an independent committee of elite scientists who were mostly physicists to review the DOE research programs related to CO2. They rendered a report in which they said, in part,

The Sahelian [an area of Africa south of the Sahara in which a near-decade-long drought occurred in the 70's] drought and the Soviet grain failure … illustrate the fragility of the world's crop-producing capacity, particularly in those marginal areas where small alterations in temperature and precipitation can bring about major changes in total productivity. (MD 171)

The Jasons went on to develop a climate model which showed that doubling the CO2 concentration from its pre-industrial level would result in an increase in average surface temperature of 2.4 degrees Celsius. They also thought that there might be an even greater increase in temperature at the poles by up to 10 to 12 degrees Celsius. (DM 171) Now, these were early days in climate modeling with respect to available computer power and I am not suggesting these numbers are correct, but insofar as average global surface temperatures are involved, the Jasons appear to have been pretty good. But remember, this was 1977 to 1979 (the time it took the Jasons to do their climate models). Thus, an independent committee of elite physicists, asked by the government (the DOE) to weigh in, had confirmed at that time that global warming was real and that it could have devastating effects on our crop yields. This all occurred before the major fights erupted over the existence of anthropogenic climate change. Still, nothing in particular was done about this by the government.

Concerned that the Jasons were mostly physicists with only one with a professional interest in climate change, President Carter's science advisor, Frank Press, asked the National Academy of Sciences president, Philip Handler to empanel a review of the Jasons study. Handler turned to MIT professor Jule Charney to review the Jasons report. Professor Charney was one of the ground-breaking founders of the science of modern numerical atmosphere modeling. Charney went beyond the simple review of what the Jasons had done. Leading climate modelers Syukuro Manabe from the Geophysical Fluid Dynamics Laboratory and James E. Hansen (who would become a significant player in the later climate change controversies) from the Goddard Institute for Space Studies were selected to present the results of the work of the Charney study, which was more complex and advanced than the Jasons study. Their results were basically the same as the Jasons' study. They concluded that doubling CO2 would lead to warming of three degrees Celsius plus or minus 1.5 degrees, or an increase of from 1.5 degrees to 4.5 degrees. This study took into effect the limiting factors that might decrease global warming such as low clouds and ocean heat absorption. Thus, they didn't fail to consider this as so many others would be accused of doing (almost never accurately). Their final conclusion was:

If carbon dioxide continues to increase, the study group finds no reason to doubt that climate changes will result and no reason to believe that these changes will be negligible. (MD 173)

Thus, no matter what climate change deniers may say today, this conclusion was reached decades ago and no serious climate scientist since then has done a rigorous research study that contradicts the conclusion. A few have argued with the figures, but none I have seen dispute the bottom line: we humans are altering the global climate by burning fossil fuels and increasing the CO2 content of the atmosphere. Incidentally, I suppose I should say that CO2 is a natural part of the atmosphere and it is part of what keeps the world as habitable as it is. It is just that one can have too much of a good thing. Also I should say as you will see if you read *Merchants of Doubt,* I am lifting much of this right out of it. So read *Merchants of Doubt,* please!

Before the Charney study was even published, the White House Office of Science and Technology asked the National Academy of Sciences for more information, including when this warming would occur. The response was a letter. This time, rather than a full panel of scientists, the panel included as chairman Dr. Thomas Schelling, a noted economist who won a Nobel prize for his work in game theory, Dr. Revelle, Bill Nierenberg, a true scientist who would become one of the premier climate change deniers and who would not do any real research or modeling of his own and McGeorge Bundy, national security advisor to presidents Kennedy and Johnson. Thus, the only real climate scientist on this panel was Dr. Revelle. The letter was written by Dr. Schelling. He dwelt on the uncertainties, not only scientific ones but the potential costs. He said policy makers should do nothing yet but fund more research. He argued that climate change would only change the distribution of climatic zones on earth (as though this in itself would not cause wide-spread hardships and conflicts). As Oreskes and Conway say, "This suggested the idea that climate skeptics would echo for the next three decades: that we should continue to burn fossil fuels without restriction and deal with the consequences through migration and adaptation." (MD 175)

Schelling went on to say that past human migrations "to and throughout the new world subjected large numbers of people – together with their livestock, food crops and culture – to drastically changed climate. (MD 175)

Schelling recognized that these migrations took place on an Earth with fewer national boundaries, if any, but nevertheless advocated adaptation as the best response. We had time, he said and during that time, the cost of fossil fuel would go up and usage would go down. The slowing rate of fossil fuel use would make adaptation to climate change easier and might permit more absorption of CO2 into carbon sinks. It would also permit conversion to alternate energy sources at a lower cumulative carbon dioxide concentration and it would *be likely that the sooner we begin the transition from fossil fuels the easier the transition would be.* (My italics) Schelling went on to say all this would happen naturally as market forces kicked in, so there was no need for regulation now. (MD 175) This would be the most negative report of any sort (and notice that this letter did not report any new research or climate modeling) from the National Academy of Sciences and it came out in 1980. Two of the members were not scientists, one being an economist and the other a politician. But more importantly, of the conclusions stated by the letter report *every single one of them was or turned out to be wrong except that the earlier we started conversion, the easier it would have been to accomplish.* Although fossil fuel prices did go up, that did not reduce the use of those fuels. Usage has and continues to increase, not decline. Atmospheric carbon dioxide has increased markedly. Therefore, there was no conversion to alternate energy sources at lower cumulative CO2 concentrations. And, manifestly, the "market forces" have done nothing but exacerbate the problem by their massive campaign to deny the problem in the first place. The market will not "cure" any problem if it is making a satisfactory profit doing what it is doing and it will not give up any asset without a major fight. We cannot depend on the so-called "free market" because it is only free to predators.

There are a couple of wonderful quotes from Naomi Klein's book that help understand why even non-fossil fuel companies are against doing anything to reverse the increase of CO2. One concerns a quote she unearthed from Raytheon Company:

And, in a moment of candor, the weapons giant Raytheon explained, "Expanded business opportunities are likely to arise as consumer behavior and needs change in response to climate change." Those opportunities include not just more demand for the company's privatized disaster response services but also "demand for its military products and services as security concerns may arise as results of droughts, floods, and storm events occur as a result of climate change." This is worth remembering whenever doubts creep in about the urgency of this crisis: the private militia is already mobilizing. ((TCE 9)

Here you see a huge weapons company recognizing that there will be upheavals and crises resulting from climate change that will bring big new markets for not only lifesaving efforts such as disaster response services (for a profit), but an increasing need for weapons as those who have suffered battle with those who still have viable economies. In other words, there will be world-wide warfare between those who are drowning from sea level rise, those whose crops are devastated, those whose populace is dying in the tens or hundreds of thousands from heat stroke (which is beginning to happen today in India and other countries), those who are suffering the ravages of newly mutated bacterial and viral illnesses and other unknown results of climate change. We will all need more weapons! The super-rich will want to set up their own redoubts protected by these new private militias provided by such as Raytheon. *This* is what the free market will give us.

A second quote from Klein follows the one above and she nails it again:

Droughts and floods create all kinds of business opportunities besides a growing demand for men with guns. Between 2008 and 2010, at least 261 patents were filed related to growing "climate-ready " crops – seeds supposedly able to withstand extreme weather conditions; of these patents close to 80 percent were controlled by six agribusiness giants, including Monsanto and Syngenta. Superstorm Sandy, meanwhile, has been a windfall for New Jersy real estate developers who have received millions for new construction in lightly damaged areas, while it continues to be a nightmare for those living in hard-hit public housing, much as the aftermath of Hurricane Katrina played out in New Orleans. (TCE 9)

Those are other ways to profit from climate change and, by the way, I am not saying that either Katrina or Sandy were necessarily related to climate change; they are just examples of what will become more common as climate changes. But, I digress. Back to the unfolding story of the climate change fiasco.

The next National Academy of Sciences study was a result of an amendment to the 1978 National Climate Act authorizing the study, thanks to Senator Abraham Ribicoff. The Carbon Dioxide Assessment Committee was chaired by William Nierenberg, a physicist who was director of the Scripps Institution of Oceanography from 1965 to 1986. He also was a co-founder of the George C. Marshall Institute in 1984, an organization that would become a vociferous opponent of the climate change scientists. Also on this committee were Thomas Schelling from the previous report, an economist and another economist, William Nordhaus from Yale. There were also a number of actual climate scientists. The results were five chapters of the report written by the scientists and two by the economists. The scientists agreed that climate change was occurring as a result of the accretion of CO2 in the atmosphere from burning fossil fuels. The exact results and timing of those results were not clear and, to some extent, they are not clear today. But, that it was happening and presented a real threat was agreed to by the scientists. None of them suggested that we should wait and see. Unfortunately, the executive summary or synthesis of the report was controlled by the economists. Thus, this National Academy of

Sciences report was a mixed bag and the naysayers were allowed to have the upper hand over the scientists. This would not happen again, but it caused a problem at the time.

Interestingly, Nordhaus, in his chapter acknowledged that there was widespread agreement that anthropogenic carbon dioxide emissions have been rising steadily, primarily due to burning fossil fuels. However, the non-scientists focused on the uncertainties of the results. They thought CO2 would double by 2065 but agreed that there was a 27 percent chance that it would happen by 2050 and could happen in the first fifty years of the century. They thought the most effective action would be a large permanent carbon tax but felt it would be hard to implement and enforce. They went on to say:

> Whether the imponderable side-effects on society – on coastlines and agriculture, on life in high latitudes, on human health, and simply the unforeseen – will in the end prove more costly than a stringent abatement of greenhouse gases, we do not now know. (MD 179)

Thus, even the economists on this committee recognized the long-term results of climate change but they reduced the problem to a matter of economics, even though they recognized that the exact timing and results of climate change could well be worse or happen sooner than they thought.

Schelling, for his part,

> …insisted that it was a mistake to assume a "preference for … dealing with causes rather than symptoms … It would be wrong to commit ourselves to the principle that if fossil fuels and carbon dioxide are where the problem arises, that it must also be where the solution lies." It might be best just to treat the symptoms through deliberate weather modification or to adapt. (MD 179)

Basically, Schelling was projecting that the problem would not arise in current lifetimes.

The synthesis followed the position laid out by Schelling and Nordhaus. It did not disagree with the scientific facts, but it rejected those facts as a problem. As Oreskes and Conway say about the synthesis and quote from it:

"Viewed in terms of energy, global pollution, and worldwide environmental damage, the CO2 problem appears intractable." The synthesis explained, but "viewed as a problem of changes in local environmental factors – rainfall, river flow, sea level – the myriad of individual incremental problems take their place among the other stresses to which nations and individuals adapt." [Got that? Stop looking at the forest and concentrate on the trees and let nations and individuals "adapt".]

Some climatic effects – like serious sea level rise – might make some areas of the world uninhabitable, but this could be addressed through migration. Nierenberg stressed that people had often migrated in the past and when they did they often had to adapt to new climates. [Note he isn't saying they moved to get away from bad climates.] (MD 180) (Although I have cited to *Merchants of Doubt* several times when quoting it, I need to acknowledge that the facts and many of the points I am making come from that same source.)

So there you have it, although this National Academy of Sciences report acknowledged that climate change would result from humanity's burning of fossil fuel, and even that the results might come sooner than they calculated, the recommendation of the economists and chairman Nierenberg was to do nothing and "adapt" as well as "migrate". It would be OK for humanity to have to adapt to this change and it would be OK for areas of the world to become uninhabitable and for the people there to migrate. To where they might migrate in the political and human affairs climate of our world was not and has never been addressed. We know from the Syrian and other refugee problems that "migrating in this world today is all but impossible. (To give some credit, Nordhaus, Schelling and Nierenberg didn't know how tough the human and geopolitical climate would become. On the other hand, that is exactly why a "wait and see" attitude is a terrible idea).

At the time that the Academy committee was working on this, the EPA prepared two reports, both of which concluded that global warming would be serious and the nation should take immediate action to reduce coal use. White House science advisor George Keyworth used the Academy report to refute them. In a report to Ed Meese, Keyworth wrote:

The Science Advisor has discredited the EPA reports ... and cited the NAS report as the best current assessment of the CO2 issue. The press seems to have discounted the EPA alarmism and has taken the conservative NAS position as the wisest." (MD 182)

Oreskes and Conway quoted a *New York Times* reporter thus: "The Academy found that since there is no politically or economically realistic way of heading off the greenhouse effect, strategies must be prepared to adapt to a "high temperature" world. (MD 182)

Thus did two economist and a physicist who was not trained in climate science subvert the work of the NAS scientists and once more provide the politicians with a credible sounding out for doing nothing even though it was based on the recommendation that we should just "adapt" and "migrate"

In 1988, one of the hottest and driest years on record then, James Hansen, a groundbreaking climate scientist to whom I have referred previously, testified before the Senate Committee on Energy and Natural Resources. He said, among other things that the evidence then showed an increase in the global temperature of approximately one degree Fahrenheit. He also said; "The global warming is now large enough that we can ascribe with a high degree of confidence a cause-and-effect relationship to the greenhouse effect." (MD 184) Then Vice President and future president George H. W. Bush was so impressed by it all that he even said that when president he would counter the greenhouse effect with the "White House effect." Needless to say, that never happened.

1988 was also important to climate science because the Intergovernmental Panel on Climate Change was created under the aegis of the United Nations. The IPCC has become the premiere entity on the issue of climate change and has become anathema to the far right and the Republican Party at the same time. It was established by the UN's World Meteorological Organization and the United Nations Environment Programme and later approved by the UN General Assembly. It was set up at the request of member nations. The function of the IPCC has been to assess the current state of climate science and report on it. It does not do original research. Instead, it reviews and assesses the literature and research that has been done, using peer reviewed articles, some non-peer reviewed material and some other sources. The Panels are made up of climate scientists, economists and other experts from all over the world. During its existence there have been thousands of scientists involved. None of these scientists is paid for this work. Three areas are assessed by working groups. The first group deals with the state of climate science (and is the one that generates the most hostile feedback), the second deals with potential environmental and socio-economic impacts and the third deals with possible responses to the problems. For each group there are two directing authors who have had various titles, a number of lead authors and then various numbers of experts who contribute to the assessments, provide content and assist in the work product of the group. There are several levels of review of the work and a final review by reviewers from the participating governments. Thus, the final product is not simply the work of scientists, but also has the imprimatur of the representatives of the governments (political members) themselves. The United States has had political participants at every assessment. Thus, before the assessments are released, The US government has the opportunity to have approval of the work product. To date there have been five reports. The first was released in 1990, the second, a supplemental report for the Earth Climate Conference in Rio de Janeiro, the third in 1995, the fourth in 2007 and the fifth in 2014. From the outset. The US government has been hostile to the reports. This is a direct result of right-wing efforts as I set forth below.

The first chair for the 1988 review was Bert Bolin, who felt that Hansen's data had not been satisfactorily reviewed and thus was not an automatic fan of the conclusions reached by Hansen. The first IPCC report, as stated, came out in 1990. In 1989, three men, Robert Jastrow, Fred Seitz and Bill Nierenberg wrote a paper that was published as a small book claiming that the source of global warming was the sun and the sun only, drawing on data from Hansen's work. These were big name scientists, although not climate scientists, and they were affiliated with the George C. Marshall Institute, a notorious right wing think tank that had been formed to fight in favor of Reagan's SDI ("star wars") initiative. This paper, however was intended to derail the climate change discussion. These three authors cherry-picked Hansen's work which had identified three major factors in climate change including the sun, volcanic ash in the atmosphere and CO2 as well as other greenhouse gases. Because they were well-connected, the authors had access to governmental ears and made presentations that comvinced the administration and the Congress that there was no global warming caused by humans. In 1990, the first IPCC assessment came out. The executive summary stated that they were certain that greenhouse gases resulting fron human activity had increased and that warming had occurred as a result. They predicted "a rate of increase of global mean temperature during the next [twenty-first] century of about .3degrees C per decade: this is greater than seen over the past 10,000 years." (MD 189) By the time the IPCC report was released, Jastrow *et. al.*. had won that round so far as credibility with the government was concerned. In October 1992 Bill Nierenberg took his dog and pony show to the World Petroleum Congress in Buenos Aires. In attacking the IPCC (to this *disinterested* group?) he claimed that global temperatures would increase at most by 1 degree C by the end of the twenty-first century based on a straight linear projection of twentieth-century warming. He didn't mention that the greenhouse gas emissions were increasing exponentially, not linearly, nor that the oceans had been soaking up heat and holding back atmospheric warming but that there would come a time when that no longer happened as the oceans heated and that would accelerate atmospheric warming. The point is that the warming over the twenty-first century would not (and has not been) linear. In fact, Nierenberg's one degree C warming by the end of the twenty-first century has already arrived. The global warming deniers would continue on this lying track from that day to this. I don't intend to document all of them. Read the books I am citing to for much greater detail. What I will do is skim over a few high points.

The second IPCC report would become a major battleground. Benjamin Santer, whom I have mentioned before, was chosen as the "convening lead author" for the part one analysis of the climate science. He had been taken on at the Lawrence Livermore National Laboratory in the Program for Climate Model, Diagnosis and Intercomparison, having obtained his PhD and studied at the Max Planck institute in Germany. He had become interested in the idea of "fingerprinting". He and a number of collaborators had studied the vertical variation in temperature and had concluded that the "fingerprint" of greenhouse gas warming appeared. That is, the atmosphere was warming in the lower area and cooling above. This is what would be expected if greenhouse gases were absorbing heat and holding it, thus causing the atmosphere above to receive less of the heat being radiated back into the atmosphere from the ground than it would have received otherwise.

That is what Santer's group found was happening. They wrote an article and had submitted it to *Nature* for publication, but it had not come out yet when the IPCC was considering it among many other papers.

In the meantime, Congressional Republicans held a set of hearings on global warming in what Oreskes and Conway describe as a "preemptive strike". The star witness against the IPCC proceedings was Patrick J. Michaels, who was indeed a climate scientist and had done modeling on relating climate to crop yields. However, as time went on he became more involved with industry defense of scientific issues, including the ozone depletion question. In the early 1990's he had worked as a consultant to the Western Fuels Association – a coal mining industry group – to promote the idea that burning fossil fuels would lead to higher crop yields as increased atmospheric CO2 would increase photosynthesis and therefore increase agricultural productivity. (MD 203) Michaels testified that based on his own analysis, the IPCC climate models overstated the global warming from greenhouse gases and could not be trusted. He had picked on a particular IPCC study, and it turned out that he had misunderstood what that study intended and, based on information from other scientists, Michaels simply didn't know what he was doing. Nonetheless, he was beloved of the Congressional Republicans who obviously didn't have the scientific training to know what Michaels was all about (or did know and liked it?).

While this was going on, the IPCC groups continued their work. A fight erupted between the scientists and the Saudi delegates (political) as to the wording of the central conclusion of the part one group. The sentence in question was "The balance of evidence suggests that there is a __________ human influence on global climate." The fight was over what adjective went in the blank. The scientists wanted "appreciable". The Saudis didn't want that. They eventually agreed on "discernible" so that the sentence then read: "The balance of evidence suggests that there is a *discernible* human influence on global climate." Note that there was *agreement* on this sentence even by the oil rich Saudis!

Later in the editing process, the report of the part one group was divested by Santer of the second summary at the close of the report to make it conform to all the other sections which had a summary only at the beginning. This was something Santer was told to do, not something he did on his own. He also insisted that there be a discussion of uncertainties in the science and almost six pages on that subject were included in the final product. Later Santer would be viciously attacked by various right wing sources for "removing material from the report and others would state blatantly falsely that the report ignored the uncertainties in some issues. The attacks eventually moved from the science as a target to the scientists personally. (The preceding information about IPCC 2 was lifted from MD 200-205, but any errors in my text are my fault and cannot be attributed to Oreskes and Conway.)

The third IPCC assessment report involved Michael Mann as a lead author in part one. This is when the hockey stick got into that report and was featured in it. That resulted in an assault on Mann by the oil and gas interests, the Republican Party, the scribbling columnists, talk radio and so forth. It was he who received the white powder in an envelope at his office resulting in clearing the area. I do not intend to go through the story. I strongly urge the reader to read his book *The Hockey Stick and the Climate Wars*. I will note that I consider the man a hero because, unlike most nerds, he had and has the guts to stand up on his hind legs and call a spade a spade. You might also Google his name and see the filth that infests the internet about him. Again I ask you to consider: what do scientists gain from this fight? Are they really submitting themselves to this abuse in order to get rich? If so, they are doing a crappy job of it. Where is the money? Follow the money. Charles Koch, Exxon Mobil. The coal industry. The automobile industry. Monsanto. Etcetera. That's where the money is. Who owns the right-wing political establishment? These entities, that's who. Who owns the right-wing media? These guys do. Who pours billions over time into lobbying Congress? These dudes do it. If you want to know who is David here and who is Goliath, just follow the money.

Brief follow-up. There have been a fourth and a fifth IPCC assessment report. Look them up. The fifth assessment, completed in 2014 concluded, among other things, the following;

1. Warming of the climate system is unequivocal. And since the 1950's, many of the observed changes are unprecedented over decades to millennia.

2. Atmospheric concentrations of carbon dioxide, methane and nitrous oxide have increased to level unprecedented in at least the last 800,000 years.

3. Human influence on the climate system is clear. It is extremely likely (95-100% probability) that human influence was the dominant cause of global warming between 1951 2010.

4. Increasing magnitudes of global warming increase the likelihood of severe, pervasive and irreversible impacts.

5. Without new policies to mitigate climate change, projections suggest an increase in global mean temperatures in 2100 of 3.7 to 7.8 degrees C relative to pre-industrial levels (median values: the range is 2.5 to 7.9 degrees C including climate uncertainty). (Cribbed word for word from the Wikipedia article on the IPCC, a very scholarly and easily understood article and I commend the author and thank him or her.)

It is worth noting that 16 National Academies of Science approved the IPCC third report. Not only that, but the US National Research Council. The research arm of the American National Academy of Sciences reported in 2001 that it "generally agreed" with the assessment of the part one report and called the full report of part one an "admirable summary of research activities in climate science". (Again lifted from the Wikipedia article circa August 29, 2016) The Council made similar observations on IPCC Assessment number four.

The number of attacks on climate science by the right wing are far too numerous to even know about. Report after bogus report by "scientists" and many who are just lawyers or lobbyists or right wing think tanks have been written. A White House advisor for several years rewrote and altered scientific reports so as to misrepresent and misquote them. That didn't change the science but it changed what happened in Congress and in the administrations. To this very day nothing very significant has been done to control greenhouse gases as is evident by the accelerating growth in atmospheric CO2. A carbon tax has never been seriously considered. A cap and trade agreement has been considered and rejected, even though it was once offered by the Republicans. Progress on alternative energy development has been slow and hindered as much as possible by the fossil fuel industries. I know that you, reader, have seen hybrid cars on the street and all- electric cars are no longer novelties. Honda is coming out with a hydrogen fuel cell powered car. But it is all far too little. The CO2 level tells us that and so do the current world temperatures.

I leave the subject of global warming with a few items. The first is an article I pulled from the *Tampa Bay Times* dated May 3, 2016. It reports that the town of Ile de Jean Charles, Louisiana is being evacuated due to sea level rise and the inhabitants are being assisted by a federal program to help the relocation which is part of an allocation of $1 billion to aid communities in 13 states adapt to climate change. Another is an article from the same paper dated April 30, 2016 reporting that a third of the world's coral is at risk from climate related bleaching. The third is a column which appeared in the same paper by George Will under the title "Gangster Government for Your Own Good." Therein he rails against the climate change scientists and the government's adoption of their conclusions and he says, among other things, that there was a "…2001 National Academy of Sciences study which said: 'Because there is considerable uncertainty in current understanding of how the climate system varies naturally and reacts to emissions of greenhouse gases and aerosols, current estimates of the magnitude of future warming should be regarded as tentative and subject to future adjustments (either upward or downward).'" What Mr. Will conveniently forgot to mention is that very NAS report did agree that climate change was occurring. He also forgot to mention the what the subsequent reports of the US National Research Council arm of the NAS have subsequently said. He also conveniently forgot to mention the recent increases in temperature by 1 degree C. This dude is too smart not to know this stuff, so I can only conclude he is deliberately setting out to mislead. Finally, I suggest to the reader that you surf the net for reports of sea level rise in places like Miami Beach, and England among other places (not to mention the vulnerability of Manhattan).

If the current generations of Americans let this happen to their progeny, we will deserve the label of the "despoilers', the label of the "greediest" generations", the scorn and even the hatred of our posterity. We know what the risk is. Admittedly it is still not clear how bad it will get, but it is already happening and if we don't think it is worth the money or the trouble or the inconvenience to minimize that risk, then we are everything those labels convey.

Chapter 8

How Did It Get This Way?

The current situation as discussed so far in this book did not get this way overnight. An amazing amount of money and effort went into getting us to where we are today. While I despise where we are now and don't feel much better about the people who got us here and keep us here, I have to admit that I am amazed and impressed by what they have accomplished. The books that I have been relying on for the facts I cite are replete with myriad details on this subject. In particular, I recommend *American Amnesia* and *Dark Money* for this history in detail. However, I will set forth some of it and then recommend that the readers review this history in more detail not only in the books I cite, but the many others that they cite. It will be an eye-opening experience.

I have already alluded to the Gilded Age of the late nineteenth and early twentieth centuries in which the early multi-millionaire industrialists in the railroad business, the oil business and many others rose into prominence resulting from the industrial age itself. These folks eventually became so powerful and so disdainful of the common good that the progressives arose and the government of the US, led by such as Teddy Roosevelt and Woodrow Wilson, made the changes in government policy that reined them in and gave the common folks a break. This included such things as child labor laws, rules about disposal of industrial wastes, unemployment benefits, labor laws and, following the great depression, regulation of high finance and banking. Following the Second World War, a period of prosperity and development took place in this country culminating in things like the civil liberties legislation and the EPA (created on Richard Nixon's watch). But, beginning in the 1950's, a strengthening opposition to progressive agendas began to arise. Of course, the industrialists and other moneyed interests never did give up and such entities as the Liberty League were created to try to oppose the FDR juggernaut in older eras. As Jane Mayer says, speaking of the later Tea Party:

The scale was unusual, but history had shown that similar reactionary forces had attacked virtually every Democratic President since Franklin Roosevelt. Earlier business-funded right-wing movements from the Liberty League to the John Birch Society to Scaife's Arkansas Project, all had cast Democratic presidents as traitors, usurpers, and threats to the Constitution. (DM 167)

Speaking of the John Birch Society, it was founded in 1958 by a number of businessmen including Robert Welch, who was the driving force and, among others, Fred Koch, the father of Charles and David Koch, of whom I will have a great deal to say. To my surprise (showing my ignorance), the John Birch Society survives to this day, but the end of the Cold War has certainly muted it. Originally the Society was a strong-voiced anti-communist organization. However, it was also in favor of decreasing the size and power of the US government and keeps that aim today. Charles and David Koch were exposed to the Society in their youth. They were also exposed to their father's strong right-wing views about the government and the wonders of the "free market". They have a brother named William, but he has long been estranged from them and has sued them successfully on occasion. As a result, I will have no more to say about William. There was also a brother Fred who is not relevant to this discussion either. It is Charles and David who are of interest in this saga. They turned Koch Industries, a family corporation that was making many millions of dollars per year into one that now makes more than $100 billion per year. They also received the wisdom of the right wing from their father. They were not the first rich men to start the revolution to the right that has taken place in this country, but they are at the apex of the movement now and are therefore of interest for that reason. But, with respect to the John Birch Society, it espoused and still espouses many of the aims of the right wing as to the free market and government.

While both Charles and David Koch have been and are forces in the right wing, Charles is perhaps more verbal about it and is the more driven of the two. Apparently from early in life, Charles was driven to be in control. Eventually he achieved this aim with respect to Koch Industries, which he and David wrested from their siblings. Charles Doherty, a Libertarian chronicler, said that Charles and David agreed on everything and Charles wanted to "tear the government out at the root." (DM 53)

Later clashes with unionized workers at the Pine Bend Refinery and with the expanding regulatory state strengthened his resolve. "Only the governments and the courts remained as sources of authority," Coppin [Clayton Coppin, a researcher first hired by the company and then hired by William] writes, and if enacted, Charles's Libertarian policies would eliminate these. … He was driven by some deeper urge to smash the one thing left in the world that could discipline him: the government." (DM 54)

Charles told the Wichita Rotary Club (the Kochs are from Wichita and they and their company, Koch Industries, are still based there) in the 1970's that government's only legitimate role was to "serve as a night watchman, to protect individuals and property from outside threat, including fraud. That is the maximum." (DM 88)

The brothers (henceforth meaning only Charles and David) became early advocates of the Libertarian Party. David was the Party's vice-presidential candidate in 1980. The Party was soundly and roundly defeated then as it has been ever since (although it made a slightly stronger showing in 2016). They quickly realized that a direct approach to politics would not succeed and turned to the long-range policy that helped in large part to get us to where we are today. As Jane Mayer says:

...during the next three decades, they contributed well over $100 million, much of it undisclosed, to dozens of seemingly independent organizations aimed at advancing their radical ideas. Their front groups demonized the American government, casting it as the enemy rather than the democratic representative of its citizens. They defined liberty as its absence and the unfettered accumulation of enormous private wealth as America's purpose. Cumulatively, the many-tentacled ideological machine they built came to be known as the Kochtopus. (DM 88)

Several years later, Richard Fink, a man who became the chief political lieutenant to Charles, laid out the method for the course the Koch's would take. Again as Jane Mayer says, Fink drew up a plan:

Called "The Structure of Social Change," it approached the manufacture of political change like any other product. As Fink later described it in a talk, it laid out a three-phase take-over of American politics. The first phase required "an investment in intellectuals whose ideas would serve as the "raw products." The second required an investment in think tanks that would turn the ideas into marketable policies. And the third phase required the subsidization of "citizens groups" that would, along with "special interests" pressure elected officials to implement the policies. It was in essence a libertarian production line, waiting only to be bought, assembled and switched on. (DM 142)

This plan, funded with a fortune that by today has left each brother worth about $48 billion, has also left them as the single strongest political force on the right in this country today, and some say, the owners of the Republican Party.

Was their motivation really greed and self-interest? They certainly deny that. However, as you observe what they did over the years and what they said, it is hard to draw any other conclusion As Fink later said to a group of wealthy donors at a Koch conference:

"We want to decrease regulations. Why? It's because we can make more profit, okay? Yeah and cut government spending so we don't have to pay so much taxes. There's truth in that." (DM 358)

It needs to be said that the Kochs were not the first to have some of these ideas nor were they the first to start implementing these approaches. They were simply the most successful and are today the foremost among the right wing. A few others certainly deserve mention here. You can find out about many others in the underlying books.

Another of these right-wing benefactors was Richard Mellon Scaife, a scion of the Mellon banking fortune along with interests in Alcoa and Gulf Oil. Jane Mayer says that he estimated he had spent approximately $620 million, adjusted for inflation, over a period from 1950 to 2000 on influencing American public affairs. His giving mainly worked through foundations he set up. These included the Carthage Foundation. It was named that allegedly because he and other conservatives thought the US was trending toward a fall like that of ancient Carthage and it was his intent to save the country from the clutches of liberals. Then there was the Sarah Scaife foundation which gave away the bulk of this money and the Scaife Family Foundation which, as best I can tell, spent more of its money on true philanthropy. Then in 1975 Scaife established the Heritage foundation which was not a funding source particularly, but one of the first and most renowned right wing think tanks. Between then and 1998, donations from Scaife sources to the Heritage Foundation totaled $23 million. If you Google Heritage, you will find that it is still a very active right wing think tank and has produced a massive volume of literature and publications. It is one of the ways that the right wing has been able to create and propagate its philosophy and "educate" young Americans and others about its agenda. As a practical matter, in and of itself the Heritage Foundation is and always has been a perfectly legitimate and reasonable method for the right wing to spread its ideas if it didn't have the habit of ignoring, the facts and spreading the slant. I will have more to say about these think tanks as we go along, but they fit neatly into the Fink three stage plan that the Kochs developed. Richard Scaife was a mainstay of the conservative right wing and a strong funder of it. He is given credit by many on the right, and I believe rightly so, for being one of their angels. A great deal can and probably should be said about him in this context, but this book is not intended to go into the kind of detail you can find in the ones I have been citing.

Another of the great voices and purses on the right was John M. Olin through his John M. Olin Foundation. That foundation was particularly effective in inserting the conservative dogma into the educational system of the country, which will be detailed a little more in the section on education. The foundation spent itself out of existence in 2005 as designed. About it, Jane Mayer says:

By the time the John M. Olin Foundation spent itself out of existence in 2005, as called for in the founder's will, it had spent about half of its total assets of $370 million bankrolling the promotion of free-market ideology and other conservative ideas on the country's campuses. In doing so, it molded and credentialed a whole new generation of conservative graduates and professors. (DM 94)

As I have said, I will deal with what the Olin Foundation did under the section concerning education.

When the Olin Foundation closed down, the director, Michael Joyce moved to the Lynde and Harry Bradley Foundation that had just become flush with funds totaling over $290 million. About that foundation, under the direction of Joyce, Mayer says:

> During the next fifteen years, The Bradley Foundation would give away $280 million to his favorite conservative causes. … At least two-thirds of its grants, according to one analysis, financed conservative intellectual activity. It paid for some six hundred graduate and postgraduate fellowships, right-wing think tanks, conservative journals, activists fighting Communism abroad, and its own publishing house, Encounter Books. Continuing the strategic emphasis on prestigious schools, the foundation gave both Harvard and Yale $5.5 million during its first decade under Joyce's management. It was an activist force on the secondary-school level, too. The Bradley Foundation virtually drove the early national "school choice" movement, waging all-out assault on teachers unions and traditional public schools. In an effort to "wean" Americans from government, the foundation militated for parents to be able to use public funds to send children to private and parochial schools. (DM 113)

These were not the only founders and funders of right wing efforts. This is just a short list of some famous ones

In August of 1971 a famous memorandum was written by Lewis Powell, then a corporate attorney, but shortly to become a justice of the US Supreme court. It was written for the Chamber of Commerce. About that memo, Hacker and Pierson say:

In August 1971 a top corporate lawyer named Lewis Powell wrote a now-famous memo to business leaders warning that the "American economic system is under broad attack" Just two months later, Richard Nixon would nominate Powell to the Supreme Court. Powell's memo, which did not become public until after he was confirmed, argued that corporate America needed to fight back with every weapon in its arsenal: "It is essential that spokesmen for the enterprise system – at all levels and at every opportunity – be far more aggressive … There should not be the slightest hesitation to press vigorously in all political arenas for support of the enterprise system. Nor should there be reluctance to penalize politically those who oppose it.

Powell's memo ended up being circulated widely, influencing important figures on the right, from beer magnate Joseph Coors to Charles Koch. Yet he had prepared it specifically for top Chamber officials. (AA 214)

As stated by Hacker and Pierson, that memo would resound in the ears of the right and has been given credit for mobilizing many of them.

Speaking of the effect of Powell's memo, Charles Koch was one of the people affected by it. As Mayer says:

Not long after echoing Powell's call to arms, Charles too set up a think tank, transforming his private foundation into the Cato Institute. The name paid homage to the nom-de-plume used by the authors of a series of pro-liberty letters during the American colonial period. Its start-up funding, according to one account, dwarfed even Scaife's early contributions to the Heritage Foundation, with Charles giving an estimated $10 to $20 million of tax-deductible donations to the nation's first libertarian think tank during its first three years. (DM 87)

One need not guess that Cato is a libertarian think tank. Log on to its web site and you will see that it proudly proclaims that. I suppose it is time for me to again say that in and of itself, there is nothing wrong in any way with the right wing or any other group or entity having a think tank or taking any other effort to make its ideas and goals public and accepted by the public. My problem with them is that only the rich can afford to do this sort of thing and the rest of us are letting them take over our political structure and advance ideas and policies that hurt the majority of Americans and our very environment as well. In other words, this is my own poor effort to write a Powell memo for the progressive side, or, to be less obscure, for the left and liberal side of things which is the side trying to help average Americans. And if you have read the section on the Libertarian Party platform earlier in this book, you know very well that libertarianism is no friend of the middle class or the working poor, much less the disadvantaged and the poor. In any event, the Cato Institute is, in my opinion, along with the Heritage Foundation, one of the top think tanks in America with many famous names having been and presently being associated with it. Like the Heritage Foundation, it does not hesitate to take the Powell approach to any issue. And as we have seen in the environmental fights, these think tanks are more than ready to hire mouthpieces who have no real credentials to speak propaganda, as they have been designed to do.

Almost from the first, the think tanks have had an outsized effect on this country. For instance, only six years after it was founded, the Heritage foundation accomplished the almost unthinkable. Mayer tells us:

Once elected, Reagan embraced the Heritage Foundation's phone-book-sized policy playbook, *Mandate for Leadership,* and distributed a copy to every member of Congress. His administration soon delivered an impressive number of items on its wish list. Heritage had laid out 1,270 specific policy proposals. According to Feulner, [Edwin who, along with Paul Weyrich was instrumental in getting the Heritage idea going] the Reagan administration adopted 61 percent of them. (DM 90)

According to Mayer, by the early 1980's backers of the Heritage Foundation, included Amoco, Amway, Boeing, Chase Manhattan Bank, Chevron, Dow Chemical, Exxon, General Electric, General Motors, Mesa Petroleum, Mobil Oil, Pfizer, Philip Morris, Proctor & Gamble, R. J. Reynolds, Searle, Sears, Roebuck, SmithKline Beckman, Union Carbide and Union Pacific. (DM 88-89) Do you suppose that they were interested in the welfare of the general public or their bottom line? Also according to Mayer, for years, Heritage Foundation staff were the only outside folks allowed to regularly caucus with Republican members of Congress. (DM 89)

Speaking of Paul Weyrich, he became a famous name in American politics, but not as a politician. He was an organizer and thinker. He helped found the American Legislative Exchange Council (ALEC) which prepares conservative legislative bills that more and more are being picked up by state legislators and enacted into state law. We saw that in the North Carolina debacle. ALEC is almost frightening in the success it has had and is having in affecting the law of the several states. Along with Jerry Falwell, Weyrich also founded the Moral Majority that thankfully was not so successful in its agendas and went defunct in the 80's. However, as Mayer says, "Weyrich was particularly adept at capitalizing on white anger over desegregation." (DM 90)

Another right-wing organization founded by Charles Koch was called Citizens for a Sound Economy. Although the name sounds like it is a true grassroots outfit, it never was. It was, as so many of these groups were, a deceptively named instrument to advance the political agenda of the Kochs. It and many other organizations like it have been labeled "Astroturf", playing off the "grassroots" terminology. Over the next couple decades, with the backing of many industrial companies, CSE advocated many of the Kochs priorities and those of its donors. But active and successful as CSE became, it was nothing compared to the success of the two entities that came out of internal dissent in CSE resulting in the creation of both Americans for

Prosperity, the Koch's amazing political juggernaut and Freedom Works, formed by Dick Armey, former Republican House Majority leader from Texas who had been chairman of CSE. Freedom Works would go on to become an enormous conduit for dark money in future years. Mayer has many details about how all this worked.

With the various rich and aggressive organizations created by the wealthy folks I have named and many others, the right wing became more and more potent in American thinking which was the first step in the plan to take over American political power. They never had a better run than they did in the administration of Ronald Reagan until George W. Bush came along. Not only did the Heritage Foundation playbook get adopted by the president of the US, but the supply side economics of the right was instituted by Mr. Reagan. Since that time, the supply side point of view has dominated economic policy even when Democrats have held the government. The mantras of tax cuts, deregulation and smaller government have prevailed through any small deviations that could be made by President Clinton and President Obama. That economic philosophy has resulted in the enormous economic inequality in this country today and has contributed to the inability of the government to rectify that inequality. There is a great deal more to how we got where we are today and those steps are at least hinted at in the next chapters.

Chapter 9

Motivations

What motivates these folks is really not complicated. They are driven people. And no matter whether they started out in the top one percent or got there by their own efforts, they did in fact achieve much of their success on their own. Individually there is much to admire in all of them. Many, probably most of them, believe that they are acting in the greater good although they tend to define the greater good as whatever benefits them. That is as kind as I intend to be to them because the fact is that they are motivated by greed first and foremost. The greed is for money, power and self-aggrandizement. Some, such as the outright multibillionaires, are less interested in being known to the general public. Others, such as the politicians, are after fame to go with power, not that they shun money either, as, for instance, Bill and Hillary Clinton. (See, I don't always pick on Republicans.) For that matter, greed and drive are necessary for the leaders of the pack. The question is: Do those leaders care about the rest of us or not? Do they care about the world of which they are the custodians while driving the bus? My answer to those question is: not really, no matter how much they might protest to the contrary. Below I will set out a few examples of the evidence on which I base my conclusions, although, I will say their behavior about such things as tobacco, the ozone hole and global warming is in itself the best indicator. All of the examples I am about to cite come from Jane Mayer, although the foundation of her facts is cited in her book and much of it is available in public records. Further, I will only be talking about the Kochs and the Olin

Corporation. However, whether you are talking about the Coors folks, the Amway founders or any other of these oligarchs, the same kind of story can be found.

In one of the more famous and egregious pollution cases during the twentieth century, the Olin Corporation poisoned a whole town that is still to this day poisoned. The town is Saltville, Virginia. Saltville was basically a company town. Olin's chemical plant there used mercury in its manufacturing processes and spilled tons of that material over the years into the nearby North Fork and Holston Rivers as well as an open sediment pond. Although this happened in the mid-twentieth century, the danger of mercury was well known even then. The company actually ceased operation in Saltville in 1972 shortly after the creation of the EPA and the state of Virginia's enactment new standards that the company said it couldn't meet, although Mayer doubts their motives because the company had been having trouble competing with other manufacturers of their product and was having union problems at Saltville. In any case, Saltville became one of the first environmental superfunds and to this day Saltville is a "ghost town" and the few remaining residents tell stories of how they used to play with mercury as children. No one had been warning them or their parents about the dangers. Many residents of the town became ill and birth defects were high while the plant operated. (DM 95-97)

In 1970, the U. S. Interior Department charged the Olin Corporation with dumping 26.6 pounds of mercury per day into the Niagara River. Subsequently the Justice Department charged the Olin Corporation with dumping sixty six thousand tons of chemical waste, including mercury into a landfill in Niagara Falls New York and with falsifying records about that. As Mayer says:

Eventually, the Olin Corporation and three of its former corporate officers were convicted of falsifying records in the dumping case, after which the presiding judge imposed the maximum available fine of $70,000 on the company. (DM 96)

The various representatives of the Olin Foundation deny that the clashes with regulatory agencies concerning the company's bad behavior motivated the actions of the Foundation later, but the evidence makes it hard to credit that. In any event, Mayer says:

> It was, however, against a backdrop of serious clashes with the increasingly robust regulatory state that John Olin directed his lawyer to enlist his fortune in the battle to defend corporate America. As he put it, "My greatest ambition now is to see free enterprise re-established in this country. Business and the public must be awakened to the creeping stranglehold that socialism has gained here since World War II." (DM 100)

Let me remind everyone at this point that "socialism" is that system in which the government owns the means of production. That is not happening in America and it never has been. The term is used as a pejorative. It used to be frightening in a vague way because the USSR (the Union of Soviet *Socialist* Republics) was a socialist state as was China, although, goodness knows what China's system is today. In the USSR, the government planned out all production and consumption and put out a "five year plan" concerning the economic activity of the Union (although those five year plans had a way of being issued more frequently than every five years and more irregularly). The regulation of business activities to protect public interest is not, let me say it again, *is not* socialism. Let me get off that hobby horse (for the moment). When Mr. Olin complained of socialism, he was complaining about being reined in by government with respect to his corporate activities that harmed the public and in some cases constituted crimes. Such corporate behavior had absolutely nothing but money as a goal.

Next, the Kochs. Consider the approach advocated by Charles;

In 1978. For instance, he wrote an impassioned call to arms in the *Libertarian Review* arguing, "We should *not* cave in the moment a regulator sets foot on our doorstep ... Do not cooperate voluntarily; instead, resist wherever and to whatever extent you legally can. And do so in the name of *justice.* (Italics in original) (DM 123)

Charles Koch had disparaged government regulations as "socialistic." From his standpoint, the regulatory state that had grown out of the Progressive Era was an illegitimate encroachment on free enterprise and a roadblock to initiative and profitability. (DM121)

What can we make of this? I submit what is clear is that Charles Koch believed and, as we will see, believes to this day, that he and his company are sovereign in every way and it is wrong for the government to stand in his way no matter how rotten what he is doing may be.

For instance, there is the story of Donald "Bull" Carlson, a Koch employee and the absolutely shabby way he was treated after being poisoned by his job. Read that one in Mayer if you are curious about the details, but it is certainly a rotten way to treat a loyal employee.

In April of 1996 a Koch employee named Sally Barnes-Soliz reported to the government regulators that a Koch plant in Corpus Christi, Texas, which she had investigated as a Koch employee at the request of the company, had been pumping fifteen times the legal limit of benzene, a toxic pollutant, into the atmosphere. Worse, she reported that the company had then disregarded her calculation and falsely reported to the Texas authorities a level of benzene emission 1/149th of the amount she had calculated. As a result, In September of 2000, Koch Industries was charged with covering up the discharge of ninety-one metric tons of benzene. Eventually Koch Industries plead guilty to one count of felony concealment of information and charges against individual managers were dropped. The prosecutor who headed the environmental crimes section of the Justice Department at the time, David Uhlmann, described it as a guilty plea to "an orchestrated scheme to conceal benzene emissions – a known carcinogen" – from regulators and the community. He added that, "Environmental crimes are almost always by economics and arrogance and in the Koch case there was a healthy dose of both." (DM 123 – 125)

Then there is this case:

In 1995, the Justice Department sued Koch Industries for lying about leaking millions of gallons of oil from its pipelines and storage facilities in six different states. Federal investigators documented over three hundred oil spills during the previous five years, including one 100,000-gallon crude oil spill that left a twelve-mile-long slick in the bay off Corpus Christi, not far from where the Koch refinery was located. ... On January 13, 2000, OConnell's [the prosecutor] division at the Justice Department prevailed. Koch Industries agreed to pay a $30 million fine, which was the biggest in history at that point, for violations of the Clean Water Act. M 126 and 127)

Notice that Koch Industries is "pleading guilty" or "agreeing to pay" here, so that we have their own admissions to the wrongdoing.

Then there is the case involving a newly graduated high school student, Danielle Smalley, in Lively Texas who was incinerated when starting her automobile ignited a leak of butane gas from a Koch Industries pipeline. That pipeline was known by Koch Industries to be leaky and had been taken out of service for that reason, but for reasons of profit then put back into service. After a long lawsuit by the girl's parents in which Koch Industries denied all responsibility, a jury returned a verdict against Koch on October 21 1999, in which it found the company not just negligent but guilty of malice and awarded $296 million. (DM 128-130)

Yet another sterling example is the American Native oil scam. The Senate started an investigation into allegations that Koch Oil had stolen tens of millions of gallons worth of crude oil from Indians and others. The committee investigating compelled Charles Koch to be deposed under oath at company headquarters in Wichita. "One committee official recalled him as 'quietly enraged' by the government intrusion." (DM 130) Under oath, Charles Koch admitted that the company had taken $31 million worth of crude oil over a three-year period from Indian lands but claimed it was an accident because oil measurement is "a very uncertain art." The evidence gathered by the committee showed that none of the other companies buying oil from the Indians had substantial problems with oil measurement. Mayer says that the other companies had actually ratted Koch out because they felt it was cheating. In 1989, the Senate released a scathing report accusing Koch Oil of "a widespread and sophisticated scheme to steal crude oil from Indians and others through fraudulent mis-measuring". (DM 130-131)

In late 1999, a whistle-blower lawsuit filed by Bill Koch, an ousted brother, went to trial in Tulsa, Oklahoma on charges that Koch Industries engaged in a "deliberate pattern of fraud" regarding claims made to the government for sale of petroleum. Many Koch employees testified. On December 27, 1999, the jury found Koch Industries guilty of making 24,587 [!!] false claims to the government. In the end, that case was settled for $25 million. (DM 137-138) But consider the enormous and obviously persistent effort to steal from the government!

Despite self-serving pontifications over the years from the Kochs about their concern for the free market system in America and their concern for the interests of this country we get one other goody cited by Mayer (remembering that I have not listed them all). Based on a report by *Bloomberg Markets,* Koch Industries helped Iran build what became the largest methanol plant in the world in the midst of a US government trade embargo on Iran. Koch Industries acknowledged that it had helped Iran build the plant, but claimed that the deal had been structured in a strictly legal way, by relying on foreign subsidiaries. Mayer says the company subsequently fired the employee who ratted it out. (DM 140) Of interest to the reader might be the older history of the Koch family business in Mayer's book. They made a fortune doing business with Nazi Germany before American entry into the war. The patriotism of the Kochs is certainly open to severe question based on this foreign adventuring, not to mention stealing from the US government.

Mayer quotes from Charles Koch in his book *The Science of Success* as to his thinking about regulation:

> We were caught unprepared for the rapid increase in regulation. … While business was becoming increasingly regulated, we kept thinking and acting as if we lived in a pure market economy. (DM 138)

There you have it in Koch's own words. What a "pure market economy" means to him is an economy in which, if you are big enough and rich enough, you can lie, steal, defraud and trample on anyone smaller than you are. Take heed, readers! This is the meaning of the "free market" to all the wolves who prate about it. It means the freedom to do just as they damn well please and to hell with everyone too small or too weak to stop them. And they want that "too small and too weak" description to include the federal government and all the state and local governments that aim to get in their way. Read the Libertarian Party platform again in light of all this information. If the governments are too weak, especially the federal government, to stop these folks from steamrolling the rest of us, they will damn well do it and it will be our own fault. If we would wake up, understand it and vote the right wing out of office, the governments will be able to protect the little guys and make our society more equal and there will be more real freedom for everyone. After all, those who are one percenters will still be one percenters even then. If they aren't, it will be because they couldn't figure out how to make all that money work for them in a different milieu. Too damn bad.

One final note in this chapter, having to do with motivation that relates to aims and aspirations. These are again from Mayer. The first comes from the William Simon (a one-time Treasury Secretary under Nixon and Ford and Olin's chosen president of his foundation) work which Mayer describes as his "1978 manifesto". He argued against the regulatory state, which he described as being backed by the "New Despots", which included from his point of view, "college-educated idealists" (whoa, bad group there), who claimed to be working for "the well-being of 'consumers,' the 'environment,' 'minorities,' and other *nonmaterial* (italics mine) causes in order to "expand the police powers of the state over American producers. Quoting from fellow right winger Irving Kristol, he charged that these usurpers (whom he had just described) wanted "the power to shape our civilization." That power, Olin said, should belong exclusively to "the free market". There is the aspiration: the power to shape civilization should belong to the free market. That is, the market empowering the wolves. It is imperative, I say, that the "free market" not be allowed to attain any such goal. If it does, we, the 99 percent are well and truly screwed. (All from DM 101)

The second quote concerns the public relations efforts of the right wing following the 2012 election which, at the national level, was a bitter disappointment to them. This quote comes from a talk by Arthur Brooks, the president of the right wing think tank the American Enterprise Institute (AEI). He was speaking at the March, 2013 annual Conservative Political Action Conference in reference to the loss to Obama in 2012. As Mayer says about Brooks and his speech:

"There's only one thing you need to know," Brooks said about 2012. "I know it makes you sick to your stomach," he added. But one statistic, he said explained why the conservatives had lost: only a third of the public agreed with the statement that Republicans "care about people like you." Further, only 38 percent believed that they cared about the poor. ... as the Kochs assessed the damage after 2012 and began planning their next moves, they embraced Brooks advice. They then launched what was essentially the best public relations campaign that money could buy. Underlying it all was the simple point that Brooks had stressed. If the "1 percent" wanted to win control of America, they needed to *rebrand* themselves as champions of the other "99 percent." (Italics mine) (DM 354-355)

And there you have it. Put starkly. They want control of America. This tiny minority of ruthless oligarchs want control of America and they want the power to shape civilization. They have proven they want nothing to do with openness or empathy or concern for their fellow Americans (unless those Americans are part of the 1 percent and only to the extent that they aren't competing against that other 1 percenter). They will disguise their obvious predatory ways by "rebranding" themselves as the good guys. (See Trump, Donald.)

A very poignant example of this effort has cropped up here in the Tampa Bay area in the last few days. The enormous phosphate and potash company Mosaic has been advertising heavily in this media market about what great stewards they are of the environment, never mind that their pollution record belies that. But in the *Tampa Bay Times* for September 17, 2016 (the day I am writing this sentence) it is reported that a 45 foot wide sinkhole has opened up in one of their gypsum stacks at a phosphate mine in Polk County Florida. The stack had a standing pond above it and is dumping hundreds of millions of gallons of contaminated water into a hole over 300 feet deep and into the Florida West Coast aquifer. It is apparently expected to take months to close that hole. And, by the way, this area is a warren of soft underground sandstone and clay where sinkholes are prevalent and cause one of the most notoriously common property damage insurance claim problems in Florida. There was apparently a plastic liner as protection for the environment from the enormous weight of this mountainous gypsum stack and its ponds. But, if you watched the TV ads, you would think that Mosaic was the best possible steward of the environment imaginable. If we believe the conservatives of the right wing that they now care for us all, then their propaganda campaign has succeeded and we deserve what we get. After all, we know they do not intend to change their operations or their goals, they just intend to "rebrand" themselves as the friends of us all.

Chapter 10

Invading Education

It was an early part of the right wing playbook to enter the educational institutions and wrench them from their perceived left wing slant (which they probably had) and pour money into professorships, fellowships, curricula, school newspapers and the hearts and minds of the next generation of college educated thinkers. They would create from the whole cloth a right wing slant in our educational institutions. Frankly, it was a brilliant idea and it has been carried out with astonishing success over the last few decades. This was part of the long game, but it has come to fruition and is part of the present American social picture. It is also why so many educated Americans think that the right wing is our friend. Borrowing heavily from Mayer, but not in the detail she provides and you folks should read, I will set forth herein a few examples of what has been done.

One of the first and most effective of the big money players in this arena was John Olin, through his foundation. As Mayer says, Olin:

… embarked on a radical new course. He began to fund an ambitious offensive to reorient the political slant of American higher education to the right. His foundation aimed at the country's most elite schools, the

Ivy League and its peers, cognizant that these schools were the incubators of those who would hold future power. If these young cadres could be trained to think more like him, then he and other donors could help secure the country's political future. It was an attempted takeover, but instead of waging it with bandoliers and rifles, he chose money as his weapon. (DM 93)

As you see, the intent was to affect the opinions of those who would come to hold power. It was not, at that point, as it would come to be, at the level below University.

As Mayer goes on to say:

By the time that the John M. Olin Foundation spent itself out of existence in 2005, it had spent about half of its total assets of $370 million bankrolling the promotion of free-market ideology and other conservative ideas on the country's campuses. In doing so, it molded and credentialed a whole new generation of conservative graduates and professors. (DM 93-94)

They succeeded in a big way. Here are some of the things they did. Michael Joyce, a fierce and deeply conservative activist became executive director of the Olin Foundation and was joined by James Piereson, who had been a professor at the University of Pennsylvania. Mayer says that, "Having closely observed America's academic intelligentsia, Piereson concluded that the foundation needed to 'penetrate' the most prestigious institutions, 'because they were emulated by other colleges and universities of lesser stature'." (DM 103) They established the idea of "beachheads" in academia. However, they did not want their efforts recognized for what they were and, as Piereson suggested, they should not label their programs in terms that were ideological but define them by areas of study such as the John M. Olin Fellowships in Military History, or name them after an important historical figure such as the James Madison Programs in American

Ideals and Institutions at Princeton University. (DM 104) That institution was started up with $525,000 of Olin Foundation money.

The Olin Foundation also diversified its efforts by supporting media efforts such as William F. Buckley's television show *Firing Line* and went into books as well. Thus, it supported Dinesh D'Souza's book *Illiberal Education* which blasted "political correctness" such as rules requiring sensitivity to women and minorities, calling that the overreaching of liberal thought. The foundation funded professors at leading schools such as Harvey C. Mansfield and Samuel P. Huntington at Harvard. It donated $3.3 million to Mansfield's Program on Constitutional Government at Harvard which emphasized a conservative interpretation of American government. It also donated $8.4 million to Huntington's John M. Olin Institute for Strategic Studies which inculcated a hawkish approach to foreign policy and national security. As Mayer says,

In all, by the time it closed its doors in 2005, the Olin Foundation had supported eleven separate programs at Harvard, burnishing the foundation's name and ideas and proving that even the best-endowed American University would allow an outside, ideological group to build "beachheads," so long as the project was properly packaged and funded. (DM 105)

If it comes from Harvard, it must be right! In more ways than one it seems.

The foundation would back works that were not peer reviewed and that sometimes got into trouble. For instance, it funded the book *More Guns, Less Crime* by John R. Lott, Jr. then an Olin Fellow at the University of Chicago. In that book he argued that more guns made America safer and legalization of concealed weapons would make citizens safer. But according to Adam Winkler, who wrote the book *Gunfight,* Lott claimed that the source of information for his book was "national surveys" and then revised that to one survey which he and a research assistant had conducted but also said that the data had been lost in a computer crash and thus he could not share it with anyone. It also backed the book by David Brock *Real Anita Hill* which excoriated the woman who testified against the confirmation of Supreme Court Justice Clarence Thomas, a strong right winger. Brock later recanted and admitted that he had been wrong and had not had proper factual basis for the book's slurs.

Dear to my retired lawyer heart is the program advocated by the Olin Foundation referred to as the "Law and Economics" discipline. This strongly right wing approach to law was at first only a fringe idea supported by libertarians. But, after the foundation spent an estimated $68 million underwriting it in the law schools, things changed. The foundation underwrote 83 percent of the costs for all Law and Economics programs in American law schools between the years 1985 and 1989. It put $10 million into Harvard, $7 million into Yale and Chicago and over two million into other schools such as Columbia, Cornell, Georgetown and the University of Virginia. Mayer says:

"Law and Economics stresses the need to analyze laws, including government regulations, not just for their fairness but also for their economic impact. [Think economic impact on the rich] Its proponents describe it in apolitical terms such as as bringing "efficiency" and "clarity" to the law rather than on fuzzy, hard to quantify concepts such as social justice."

Piereson [of the foundation], however, admitted that the beauty of the program was that it was a stealth political attack and that the country's best law schools didn't grasp this and therefore didn't block the ideological punch it packed. "I saw it as a way into the law schools – I probably shouldn't confess that," he told *The New York Times* in 2005. "Economic analysis tends to have conservatizing effects." In a later interview with the political scientist, Steven M. Teles, he added that he would have preferred to fund a conservative constitutional law program, but had the foundation tried such a direct political challenge, it probably would have been barred entry into America's best law schools. "If you said to a dean that you wanted to fund conservative constitutional law, he would reject the idea out of hand. But if you said you wanted to support Law and Economics, he would be much more open to the idea," he concluded. "Law and Economics is neutral, but it has a philosophical thrust in the direction of free markets and limited government. That is, like many disciplines, it seems neutral, but it isn't in fact. (DM 107-108)

Thus this lovely Law and Economics propaganda sneaked on little mouse feet into American legal thinking. And let me say that I have no quarrel with the idea that government *should* consider the economic impact of laws and regulations it enacts, but that cannot be the only criterion, nor should it be the driver. This particular program is self-professedly intended as propaganda and stealth propaganda at that. It also demonstrates the power of money. These law school deans and faculties are, by definition, not stupid. However, given the economics of higher education, money can blind even smart people into making mistakes.

Speaking of Law and Economics, the foundation also funded seminars for judges on that topic at swanky facilities. These seminars were initiated by Henry Mann, dean of the law school at George Mason University in Virginia, which he was trying to transform into a hub of libertarian jurisprudence according to Mayer. The judges got a two-week-long, all-expenses-paid immersion training in Law and Economics in settings such as the Ocean Reef Club in Key Largo, Florida. Mayer goes on to say,

They soon became popular free vacations for the judges, a cross between Maoist cultural reeducation camps and Club Med. After a few hours of learning why environmental and labor laws were anathema, or why, as Manne argued, insider trading laws did more harm than good, the judges broke for swimming, and delightful dinners with their hosts. (DM 109-110)

Eventually 660 judges went to these seminars. By one estimate, 40 percent of the federal judiciary attended one including future Supreme Court Justices Ruth Bader Ginsburg and Clarence Thomas.

Yet another creation of the Olin Foundation was the Federalist Society, an organization of conservative law students. Funding has also been provided by organizations tied to Scaife and the Kochs among others. It eventually became a powerful professional network of 42,000 right-leaning lawyers with chapters at 150 law schools. All the conservative members of the US Supreme Court are members as are former vice president Dick Cheney, former attorneys general Edwin Meese and John Ashcroft and numerous members of the federal bench. (DM 110) Speaking as a recovering lawyer, I gotta tell you that it is no wonder our courts have headed to the right for years and years.

Finally, the Olin Foundation supported what was called the Collegiate Network, which constituted a string of right wing newspapers on college campuses. Famous among those was *The Dartmouth Review.* That is the paper that published a send-up of "Ebonics" shaming blacks for coming to Dartmouth and not doing well scholastically. It also hosted a feast of lobster and champagne to mock a student fast against global hunger, blasted students who erected shantytowns to protest South African apartheid and published transcripts of secret meetings of the Dartmouth gay student association. Out of that incubator came D'Souza, the conservative radio host Laura Ingraham, ABC correspondent Johnathan Karl and Mark Thiessen, an online columnist for *The Washington Post.* Once right wing figures become more well-known and famous, they usually try to hide the kind of cruelty that they were steeped in at *The Dartmouth Review,* but it is there in their background. Of course, not all take that approach, witness Rush Limbaugh and Glenn Beck, neither of whom holds a college degree and both of whom are multi-millionaires but both of whom like to take the low road. Sorry about the digression, but I couldn't help it.

Next, we consider the efforts of the Lynde and Harry Bradley Foundation on educational funding. In the mid 1980's that foundation suddenly became huge due to a corporate merger and enlisted the services of Michael Joyce from the Olin Foundation. They got a tiger. Mayer says that Joyce considered himself a righteous combatant in an ideological war and over the next fifteen years, the foundation would give $280 million to his favorite conservative causes. It paid for six hundred graduate and post-graduate fellowships, right wing think tanks, conservative journals, activists fighting Communism abroad and set up its own publishing house known as Encounter Books. It gave Harvard and Yale $5.5 million each in its first decade under Joyce. Mayer says,

"The Bradley Foundation virtually drove the early national "school choice" movement, waging an all-out assault on teachers' unions and traditional public schools. In an effort to "wean" Americans from government, the foundation militated for parents to be able to use public funds to send their children to private and parochial schools. (DM 113)

This effort by the right is directed toward the Libertarian goal of doing away with public schools entirely. As I have pointed out before, the intent is to make the parents responsible for the cost of their children's education and to see to it that all money spent on education goes into private coffers. This, of course would indeed take the government out of control of education and also see to it that more than half of our population couldn't afford education for their children. It would also inject a great deal more religious indoctrination into schools. As you can probably tell, I am adamantly against the spending of public funds on private schools and against closing a large part of the populace out of educational opportunities. It is a formula for destroying the place of the US in the advanced nations because we could no longer compete. It is also just plain cruel. By the way, Florida is a leader in this nonsense and we have some lengthy experience with this school choice business. Our so-called "charter schools" haven't distinguished themselves in any way educationally. Those private schools in Tampa (and we have several of them) which are of the traditional "preparatory school" bent are hideously expensive, but they are also first rate educationally. That is what folks think they may be getting with our charter schools, but the results prove that to be folly.

Joyce supported, among others, the authors Herrnstein and Murray who wrote *The Bell Curve* in which they correlated almost all success in life to intelligence and, among other things, attributed less intelligence to blacks. (DM 113) Almost all scientists who have reviewed the book have been critical of it and it seems to be full of biases. It also provides seemingly intelligent backing for those bigots who wish to attribute inferiority to blacks and others. This is a fairly common approach to science for the right-wing literature.

The assets of the Bradley Foundation reached $630 million by 2012. It has continued to finance attacks on public schools. It has also supported what Mayer calls "conservative beachheads" in thirty-five different colleges and universities, including Harvard, Princeton and Stanford. (DM 118) Beyond that, the Foundation now awards annual Bradley Prizes at a fancy event in Washington DC in the amount of $25.000. Among the winners have been George Will, he of the right-wing columns who has become a trustee of the foundation. Also receiving such an award was Roger Ailes, the then president of Fox News, subsequently fired for alleged sexual harassment of female employees, thus demonstrating the love of the right for that network.

In the mid-1980's the Kochs began their move into the higher education system. They began to focus on George Mason University, a part of the university system of the state of Virginia. Fink, working on the Koch's behalf, had started an Austrian economics program which finally settled at George Mason and became known as the Mercatus Center. This economic system is related to the supply side theories. Mercatus is a think tank supported entirely by outside donations, but is embedded at George Mason. It has touted itself as, "the world's premier university source for market-oriented ideas – bridging the gap between academic ideas and real-world problems." According to Mayer, financial records show that the Koch family foundations donated over $30 million to the school, much of it going to the Mercatus Center. Further, she says that *The Washington Post* described Mercatus as a "staunchly anti-regulatory center funded by Koch Industries Inc." Clayton Coppin, who taught history at George Mason and compiled a confidential study of Charles Koch's political activities for Bill Koch (admittedly the relationship between Charles and Bill at the time was distinctly adversarial), stated that Mercatus is "a lobbying group disguised as a disinterested academic program." The arrangement, according to Coppin had financial advantages for the Kochs, because it enabled Charles "to have a tax deduction for financing a group, which for all practical purposes is a lobbying group for his corporate interest." (DM 150)

Also at George Mason and sharing a building with the Mercatur Center was the Institute for Humane Studies chaired and principally funded by Charles Koch. The founder was F. A. "Baldy" Harper who had in the past written essays calling taxes "theft", welfare "immoral" and labor unions "slavery" and opposing court ordered remedies to racial segregation. Charles eulogized Harper, saying of him, "Of all the teachers of liberty, none was as well-beloved as Baldly, for it was he who taught the teachers and, in teaching, taught them humility and gentleness." (DM 150) Please, folks, there is nothing gentle about the right wing and the quotes from Harper don't portray humility or gentleness. Neither is there anything in the evidence about Charles Koch's personality to show any concern for gentleness or humility. Charles kept his finger on the Institute for Humane studies and, unsatisfied with the pace of progress, required that applicants to the Institute write essays that would be judged in terms of how often the applicant mentioned Ayn Rand and Milton Friedman. Students were tested at the end of each week for ideological improvement. Koch also had a summer internship program at the Institute with paid fellowship placing students in like-minded nonprofit groups where they could join the libertarian network. (DM 150)

In the meantime, the economics department at George Mason became an incubator for the supply-side tax cuts in the Reagan administration that hugely advantaged the rich. A star faculty member was James Buchanan who categorized elected officials and public servants as just another greedy, self-aggrandizing private interest group, a view popular with antigovernment libertarians. Julian Sanchez, a fellow at the Cato Institute, soon exalted George Mason as a "libertarian mecca", saying, "It may well be the most heavily libertarian-staffed institution of higher education in the country." (DM 150-151)

Fellows of the Mercatus, which is located just across the Potomac from Washington frequently have testified before Congress as "independent" experts. As Mayer says,

By 2004, *The Wall Street Journal* dubbed it "the most important think tank you've never heard of" and noted that fourteen of the twenty-three regulations that George W. Bush placed on a "hit list" had been suggested by Mercatus scholars. (DM 153)

- Ridiculous positions have been taken by Mercatus scholars and bought by courts whose jurists have attended one of the Koch's all-expenses-paid seminars. For example, Susan Dudley, an economist, who became a top official at the Center, produced an argument against a move by the EPA to reduce surface ozone emissions to the effect that the EPA had not considered that smog blocked the sun and therefore reduced cases of skin cancer. This was bought by the DC Circuit Court. Fortunately, the Supreme Court overruled that decision. (DM 153-154) But think of the audacity!

Smog is good and we should take that into consideration when deciding about pollution. Wow.

According to Mayer,

By 2015, according to an internal list, the Charles Koch Foundation was subsidizing pro-business, anti-regulatory, and anti-tax programs in 307 different institutions of higher education in America and had plans to move into 18 more. The schools ranged from cash-hungry West Virginia University to Brown University, where the Kochs, in the tradition of the Olin Foundation, established an Ivy League "beachhead." …Charles Koch's foundation gave additional funds to Brown to support faculty research and postdoctoral candidates in such topics as why bank deregulation is good for the poor. …

At West Virginia University, the Charles Koch Foundation's donation of $965,000 to create the Center For Free Enterprise came with some strings attached. The foundation required the school to give it a say over the professors it funded in violation of traditional standards of academic independence. The Kochs' investment had an outsized impact in the small, poor state where coal, in which the Kochs had a financial interest, ruled. One of the WVU professors approved for funding, Russell Sobel, edited a 2007 book called *Unleashing Capitalism: Why Prosperity Stops at the West Virginia Border and How to Fix It,* arguing that mine safety and clean water regulations only hurt workers. "Are workers really better off being safer but making less income?' it asked. (DM 155)

The reader may recall that Sobel was subsequently invited to brief the state governor, cabinet and a joint session of the Senate and House Finance Committees and and the state Republican Party chairman declared that the book would be the blueprint for its party platform. I still find that absolutely stunning, You, Mr. Miner, may have either safety or you may have a more decent wage, but you can't have both and wouldn't you really be better off being in danger of your life and making a few bucks more? How brain dead does any politician have to be to endorse such an approach for his or her own people?

Again, from Mayer:

John David, an economics professor at West Virginia University Tech, who witnessed the school's transformation, wrote in a scathing newspaper column that it had become clear that "entire academic areas at universities can be bought just like politicians. The difference is that universities are supposed to permit open dialogue and exchange of ideas and not be places for the indoctrination of innocent students with dictated propaganda prescribed by outside special interests." (DM 156)

By 2014, the Koch foundations alone were funding pro-corporate programs at 283 four-year colleges and Universities. According to Mayer, a Koch foundation grant to Florida State University gave it a say on faculty hires. (Gasp, my own state!) An undergraduate student named Jerry Funt complained about the introductory economics course. He said "We learned that Keynes was bad, the free-market was better, that sweatshop labor wasn't so bad, and that the hands-off regulations in China were better than those in the US." Their textbook had been written by my favorite guy, Russell Sobel. Funt said it argued that "climate change wasn't bad, wasn't caused by humans and isn't a big issue." The textbook had been given an "F" by an environmental group. When critics complained, the Kochs defended their purchase of influence over public universities as merely providing "fresh" college thinking. (DM 365)

Perhaps the most egregious example, however, of Koch influence on education comes from the Topeka school system. Charles Koch had devised a program called the Young Entrepreneurs Academy. The financially pressed Topeka school system signed an agreement with that organization to teach students, among other things, that Franklin Roosevelt didn't alleviate the depression, minimum wage laws and public assistance hurt the poor, lower pay for women was not discriminatory, and the government, rather than business, caused the 2008 recession. The program, which was aimed at low-income areas, also paid students to take additional courses online. (DM 365) I cannot believe it has come to this, but I suppose I should. These bums are aiming this poison at the people who are too young and too poor to understand how badly it hurts their own interests and, to the extent that they buy it, takes them out of the voting groups that could actually do something to help them. This, folks, is the very essence of evil.

Ryan Stowers, a vice president of the Charles Koch Foundation, speaking at a Koch conference of their dark money funding network said some interesting things about their educational efforts. Mayer says:

A breakthrough, Stowers related, was the creation of some two dozen privately funded academic centers, the flagship of which was the Mercatus Center at George Mason University. As a 2015 report by one of the nonprofits connected to Art Pope explained, private academic centers within colleges and universities were ideal devices by which rich conservatives could replace the faculty's views with their own. "Money talks loudly on college campuses," it noted. As an example, the report profiled the trailblazing record of John Allison, the former Cato Institute chairman, who had overseen grants to sixty-three colleges when running the BB&T bank. All of these programs were required to teach his favorite philosopher, the celebrator of self-interest, Ayn Rand. (DM 364)

Jane Mayer has many more facts and great quotes from these folks and I commend them to you, but I am through with the education section of this book. It is not hard to look at the numbers here and understand that these efforts by the rich have turned out literally millions of young people indoctrinated with their poison. This is especially so if those young have been indoctrinated with it since high school. The right has literally convinced huge swaths of the population that the interests of big business are their interests and if the government would only set these folks free, why then, everyone would benefit. Those indoctrinated don't seem to know despite all the evidence, and who can blame them with this "education" floating around in their minds, that – *freedom for wolves is death to lambs.* And, folks, we are almost all lambs.

Chapter 11

The Money Machine

The Kochs, the Scaifes, the Bradleys and others like them have spent decades perfecting the ways to pour money into the think tanks, the educational systems, the media and all the other types of enterprises they could devise to turn the thinking in this country into their world-view. They have succeeded beyond any expectations those watching them might have formed. In this section we will take a look at the current mechanisms by which the right wing pours money into our political system. Some of these mechanisms have been alluded to in prior sections as they relate to specific instances, but here the emphasis is on the funding itself. In the next section we will look at some of the results.

Before the *Citizens United* case, about which more later, there were a number of ways the right wing (and anyone else who had the money) could donate funds toward their conservative aims without it being attributable to them. As an example, there is the Donors Trust and its affiliate Donors Capital Fund. Donors Trust is a 501(c)(3) organization, meaning that the IRS considers it a charitable organization. It may receive funds without making their source public. Thus, big money interests can put funds into them without the source being publicly known. The Fund will then transfer those funds to a particular use or organization that can openly support a cause or interest without the ultimate donor being known. Donors Trust was formed in 1999. Between 1999 and 2015, it redistributed some $750 million to various conservative causes under its own name. This permitted the donors to have a tax-deductible donation which would be spent on various conservative causes to which, if they had been donated directly by a right-wing foundation such as the Charles G. Koch Foundation, would have been publicly known. This is not illegal and it is a mechanism available to anyone with enough money to make it work. But that is the rub, isn't it? Who has the money? There actually is a similar liberal fund called the Tides Foundation, but it is only one such organization and it is woefully outspent. The point here is that this is a stealth mechanism for conservatives to expend millions without it being known to us folks who is doing it and getting a tax deduction to boot. (See DM 206)

Mayer outlines that between 1998 and 2008 the Charles G. Koch Charitable Foundation made more than $48 million in tax deductible grants to groups promoting his political views. Another Koch entity, the Claude R. Lambe Charitable Foundation made more than $28 million in tax deductible grants. During those same years, Koch Industries spent more than $50 million on lobbying and KochPAC spent $8 million on political campaigns as well as the Kochs and their families spending millions on political campaigns. (See DM 147) These numbers actually pale beside what comes later, but you can see that large sums of money have been spent by the Kochs personally on politics.

For a look at a bigger number, consider that the health insurance industry, through its trade association transferred over $102 million to the Chamber of Commerce to fight against health care reform in 2009 to 2010. (AA 296) If it seemed to you that the Affordable Care Act (ACA), or Obamacare, was a hard fight, this gives you some idea why, despite the Democratic Party holding a majority in both houses of Congress in those years, as well as the presidency, it was a close call. Believe it or not, this number will be shown to be small change shortly.

Speaking of not-so-small change, consider this from Hacker and Pierson:

In 2009, reported lobbying expenditures – which do not include organization building, public relations campaigns or election- related activities ramped up to $3.5 billion and ticked just above record level in 2010. Leading the charge were general business groups such as the Chamber, which spent $300 million on its own between the start of 2009 and the end of 2010. But after general business spending, three sectors led the way, spending approximately $1 *billion* each on lobbying across the two years. They were health care, finance and energy.

In each of these epic battles, too, the Great Enablers did what they do best: stand up for the big guys. Republicans presented an almost unbroken wall of opposition, which, given the narrow Democratic edge and the inevitable wavering of cross-pressured Democrats, created a daunting hurdle for the Obama administration and its allies. Not a single Republican voted for the final passage of the health care bill in either house of Congress. Not a single Republican voted for the financial reform bill [Dodd Frank] in the House. (AA 296)

With not millions or hundreds of millions but billions of dollars being poured into lobbying our Congressional office holders in the space of a given year, can it be any surprise that the spenders of such sums get what they want and to hell with the rest of us? Are our elected officials for sale? If not that, then they are subject to almost unbelievable pressure. This sort of thing needs to be illegal. That is the only way the interests of those who cannot spend such sums can be protected. Standing up for the big guys has wreaked havoc on our society as the rich get richer and the poor increase.

This gets us to 2010. On January 21, 2010 the Supreme Court decision in the case of *Citizens United v. Federal Elections Commission* was handed down. Now, Citizens United was (and is) a 501(c)(4) non-profit political action committee funded by the Kochs, despite its misleadingly labeled name. In January, 2008, Citizens released a documentary critical of Hillary Clinton, then a Senator running for the presidency. It intended to run the documentary within 30 days of the election and advertise it on cable and broadcast television. It then sued the Federal Elections Commission for declaratory and injunctive relief because under the law as it stood then, Citizens would not be permitted to do that. Two years later (not much use to the 2008 campaign season, but then that's how it goes in the courts, especially that one) the Court's decision came out. By a 5 to 4 vote on the central issue, the Court held unconstitutional the part of the election law prohibiting corporations, unions and non-profit corporations from spending on election issues, not only just 60 or 30 days before an election but at all. This freed those entities to spend as much as they wanted on electioneering so long as the money was not given to specific candidates or campaigns. The ruling was that these entities were entitled to freedom of speech just as any individual is. The Court's opinion is pushing 100 pages of dense legal arguing amounting, to most laymen, to the fact that corporations, PACs and other entities that are not-for-profit may spend as much as they please on elections so long as they don't give it directly to the campaigns. The Court also upheld that part of the law requiring an entity which does this to disclose the source of its funding, which the majority cited as a check against abuse because the source of funds would always be known. On the central issue the justices who ruled in favor were Chief Justice Roberts, Justice Alito, Justice Scalia, Justice Thomas and the so-called swing member of the Court, Justice Kennedy, who wrote the "majority" opinion. (There were several different opinions.) Memorably, during the 2011 State of the Union address, President Obama spoke to the ills of dark money that this opinion would create and the cameras caught Justice Scalia shaking his head "no".

Naturally, the majority of the Court was dreaming if they thought they had protected the public interest by its affirmance of the disclosure requirement. (Of course, given the dauntingly high intelligence of these justices, I don't believe for a moment that they really thought that.) There are two types of entities other than charitable that may, under the IRS requirements, receive funding but not disclose the source to the public. These are the 501(C)(4) "social welfare" entities and the 501(c)(6) "business league" entities (such as the Chamber of Commerce). They are required to be named as sources of funding to election activities but they are not required to make public the source from which they received these funds. Thus, they stand as a barrier to knowledge of the original donors of the funds by the public. Thus are born the so-called "super PAC's". They are the source of the funds now called "dark money" and thus the title of Mayer's book. These are the entities you will see listed at the bottom of TV election attacks which generally have benign-sounding but publicly meaningless names. They have untold millions to spend and you and I will never know with certainty who gave them that money and therefore cannot judge the bias that is inherent in the ads. Thus, you get the anomaly of a PAC that sponsored ads on behalf of a Democrat whom the funder wanted to win the primary in Florida for a State House seat even though it was a Republican PAC. You probably have noticed that most of the really vicious ads are sponsored by such groups, leaving the candidates "clean" of such vitriol. Now, can this approach be used by both sides? Yes. It can be and it is used by both sides. However, two things about that. One is that the right wing has vastly more wealth to spend than the liberal or progressive wing. The other is that we shouldn't be subjected to these shenanigans no matter who is doing it. And you can tell from the fact that Hillary Clinton wanted *Citizens United* reversed by a new Court or overturned by a constitutional amendment and the Republicans don't that it is the Democrats whose ox is being gored. Should we care about this? Only if you have been paying attention to the takeover of the Republican Party by radical right wing moneyed interests.

Let me next speak of an organization that I can only call the representative of the enemy. It is the Koch's own baby. Its name is "Americans for Prosperity" (AFP). It was created when "Citizens for a Sound Economy" broke up and fractured into two subsequent organizations, one being AFP and the other being another dark money funder called "Freedom Works" under the direction of the former House Majority leader Dick Armey. AFP is one of those lovely 501(c)(4) organizations and it is one that millions get funneled through. AFP had a $2 million budget in 2004. By 2010, its budget was $40 million. In the 2012 campaign cycle, it spent $179 million! By 2014 its budget was close to $300 million. By the 2014 election, AFP had five hundred field operatives in thirty-five states – triple the manpower it had just two years earlier. You can believe that this colossus has not shrunk since then In the 2011-2012 campaign cycle the Koch network of donors raised $407 million to funnel through entities such as AFP. (All from AA 234)

Two entities serve as "banks" for the Koch network to funnel money to such other entities as AFP. They are "Freedom Partners" (FP) and the "Center to Protect Patients' Rights" (CPPR). These names are precious. Don't they sound like all-American inclusive groups? They are, too. They include some of the richest men and women in the world. The CPPR has since changed its name to "American Encore". The first name came up during the fight to pass Obamacare. FP was set up in 2011 (after *Citizens United*) and had a budget of $256 million in its first year. (AA 234) It is a 501(c)(6) organization. Thus it fits the mold under *Citizens United* to mask the source of hundreds of millions of dollars of dark money. The CPPR was a 501(c)(4) organization, or "social welfare" organization. These sources collect money from the Koch network and distribute it to the organizations such as AFP which will do the work "on the ground" so to speak. Hacker and Pierson say:

Yet Freedom Partners was no ordinary business association. According to a spokesman, the organization funds groups "based on whether or not they advance the common business interests of our members in promoting economic opportunity and free-market principles". Between Freedom Partners and CPPR, hundreds of millions flowed to campaigns, including a huge clandestine contribution from CPPR to groups in opposition to a 2012 ballot initiative in California that raised taxes temporarily to balance the state budget. The groups doled out large sums to other organizations in the right-wing orbit: $3 million to the Chamber of Commerce, $2.5 million to the National Federation of Independent Businesses, $500,000 to the Heritage Foundation's political arm, Heritage Action for America, and $6.6 million to the National Rifle Association (NRA) (AA 234-235)

As you see, the number of entities involved is numerous and I haven't even scratched the surface. Mayer has charts of some of the Koch related groups on the inside of the covers of her book. You readers should look at them. Just realize that those are only Koch-related groups and don't even touch on the Scaife entities, the Bradley entities, etc. It was never intended for anyone outside the Koch circle to know them all or to know their relationship to the Kochs. That Mayer knows is a tremendous tribute to her skill and perseverance.

Two other organizations are of interest. They are "American Crossroads" and "American Crossroads GPS". These are right wing organizations associated with the political professional Karl Rove. According to the Wikipedia article on these two entities, American Crossroads GPS and AFP together outspent all other categories, including political parties, PACs, super PACs, unions and trade associations, for televisions ads in the 2012 election cycle, quoting from a Pro Publica article by Kim Barker on August 12, 2012. Think of the power here!

Hacker and Pierson provide another stunning statistic about campaign spending:

Between 1980 and 2012, the share of campaign contributions coming from the richest 0.01 percent of donors rose from 15 percent to 40 percent. And, of course, these official figures track only public contributions, not the huge amounts of dark money. (AA 228)

Get that, the richest one hundredth of one percent of all donors gave 40 percent of all donations! Look, it's not illegal and they can afford it. What can't be afforded by our society is for such a tiny part of our population to wield such power over 300 million people!

In the 2012 election cycle, there was a traceable $7 *billion* spent on the presidential campaigns. One donor alone, Sheldon Adelson, who vowed to spend "as much as it takes" spent nearly $150 million, $92 million of which was disclosed. Of that amount, $15 million went to the Koch's group. (DM 331) Not only that, but the Koch network vowed to raise and spend $888 million on the 2016 cycle, although they didn't seem too enthused over Donald Trump. (DM 317)

As you can see, once the controls were off, the spending on the right in elections has jumped sensationally. Their power to lobby Congress is phenomenal. When billions can be spent and are spent to bend the politics of this country in favor of the richest, the politics will bend. We, as voters, can be and are hornswoggled by these lovely-sounding organizations and by the allegedly authoritative output of think tanks and the purchased media of the right into believing black is white and white is black. We are being led to believe that tax cuts (which always benefit the rich more than the rest of us), deregulation (set the wolves loose) and smaller government (no one big enough to control the wolves!) are in our best interests. How could they be? Will supply-side, trickle-down economics help the general public?

Hell no! It never has and it never will. When we allow the money to first go to the top, it will never willingly "trickle" down to the rest of us. They don't even want to pay the measly share of taxes they are paying now. As Donald Trump recently stupidly said in a televised debate, if he can make millions and still not have to pay taxes, that just makes him smart. He's right, too. He is a smart predator. And we are his victims.

Only a strong central government can help the general public. And despite the right's adopting his name in their own behalf, James Madison, one of the principal authors of the Constitution, was not an advocate of small government. He, after all, wanted a strong central government to replace the hopeless confederation that preceded the federal Constitution. There is a lot of information on the beliefs of Madison in *American Amnesia* and I strongly recommend reading it. Or, you could, if you are really ambitious, read *The Federalist Papers* and the detailed history of the creation of our present form of government. You will certainly see that the right is taking Madison's name in vain. But we will not get the government we need if the right continues to bulldoze it and our politics. We need to find political candidates who are interested in the general public and against having the money of the right wing buy them off. At the very least, we need to stop voting for candidates who openly say they want to cut taxes, deregulate and minimize government. As is set forth in the next section, our government is actually too small, not too large.

Chapter 12

The Effect on Politics

Like everything else in this book, there is significant overlap from one section to another. Some of the effects of the efforts of the right wing on our politics have been alluded to already. However, in this section I will deal specifically with that subject. It is a truly fascinating if disturbing story.

By 1980, the effect of think tanks made itself felt. Ronald Reagan sent the Heritage Foundation playbook to all the members of Congress. He obviously believed in it and he is the one who started our government on the search for a supply-side economic policy. Even then it was referred to as "trickle-down" and that was said with some pride by its conservative adherents. (During the 1980 presidential campaign, George H. W. Bush, who was then running against Reagan, called supply side economic policy "voodoo economics" and indeed it has proven to be that.) The right would have us believe that as corporations and businesses gain in income and profits, that will result in more jobs and more wealth for everyone which would then be spent on the products of business and all boats will be lifted. This overlooks the fact that as corporations in particular gained profits, they spent them buying back their own stock, paying their executives hundreds of millions and increasing payments to their stockholders (who are overwhelmingly the rich). None of that money has gone to the employees who produced the products and services and it has gone less and less into research and development for future improvement in the products of the corporations. There is also the theory of the right that as they become richer and richer, they will return some of that money to the needy by way of charity. Some of them will do that, but it will be too little to make any difference. Further, as they gut the IRS and the tax law so that they don't need charitable deductions any more, there will be less incentive for them to be charitable. In any event, the details of the effect of the right's efforts on our politics so far goes on.

Speaking of the effects of the various right wing groups and entities I have discussed on politics, Hacker and Pierson say:

These hugely resourceful and organized groups are the first of the Great Enablers. They have made common cause with the second: a Republican Party that has embraced and encouraged the Randian turn of the nation's new economic elite. In the process, the GOP has abandoned not just its prior moderate commitments but also its willingness to work constructively with other political actors to update and strengthen the mixed economy. Indeed, the GOP has learned how to win politically by fostering dysfunction, to achieve its policy goals not by brokering agreement but by breaking government. With positive conceptions of government's essential role marginalized and demonized in political discourse – denounced by Republicans and defended feebly by Democrats – Republicans discovered the benefits of self-fulfilling prophecy: They could simultaneously cater to narrow corporate interests and denounce "crony capitalism," feed political dysfunction and win by railing against it, undermine the capacity of government to perform its vital functions and decry a bungling and corrupt public sector. (AA 166)

This may seem like a harsh and one-sided analysis, but wait until you see what follows.

During the Clinton presidency, the Chamber of Commerce was at first willing to work with the administration to advance Clinton's economic goals. Two of the Chambers executives, Richard Lesher, president, and William Archey, vice president, were called to a meeting with Republican Congressional leaders and the following is described by Hacker and Pierson about that meeting:

Ascendant conservatives within the GOP pushed back, with Congressman John Boehner [future speaker of the House eventually run out of that position for being too willing to compromise to accomplish progress] leading the charge. Boehner reportedly declared at a meeting with Archey and Lesher that it was "the Chamber's duty to categorically oppose everything that Clinton was in favor of." House minority leader Robert Michel – long an advocate of compromise but now under fire from his right – sent Lesher a fierce letter signed by the rest of the House GOP leadership (including the triumvirate of Gingrich and Texas congressmen Dick Armey and Tom DeLay [Gingrich and DeLay would eventually leave Congress under a cloud] that would soon lead a Republican-controlled House). The letter warned that the Chamber's position on Clinton's economic program was unacceptable and the "ramifications could be quite severe". Describing "a rapidly spreading frustration with the Chamber's failure to take an aggressive posture on the Clinton economic program," the Republican leaders suggested a need for a course correction "before we pass the point of no return." (AA 216)

As an aside, Newt Gingrich all by himself went a long way to crippling the ability of the GOP to work with the Democrats and poisoning the relations between the two parties as will be evident as we go along. In any event, here we have an example in the early 1990's of the push to the far right by the Republican Party and its unwillingness to compromise in order to make government work. If Clinton wanted it, the Republicans (and the Chamber of Commerce!) must be categorically against it. With an attitude like that, no wonder there was so much friction between the parties during Clinton's administration.

About the "Gingrich effect", Hacker and Pierson say:

The "middle way" that Eisenhower staked out gained strong bipartisan support. Forty years later, Clinton received zero votes from the opposition on his highest-priority goals. Under the direction of House GOP leader Newt Gingrich, Republicans waged a scorched-earth campaign against the president's agenda. Within two years, they had brought down the president's health plan, blocked his public investments, and then converted public discontent with Washington into a Congressional majority. (AA 164-165)

One of the strong business voices in the 90's was the Business Round Table (BRT), made up of a group of corporate CEO's. Republican leaders became dissatisfied with the BRT for donating to some Democrats and hiring Democrats on its staff. Hacker and Pierson report:

The conflict came to a head in a 1997 meeting between the GOP leadership (including DeLay and House Speaker Gingrich and twenty CEO's .... The Republicans expressed displeasure that BRT companies continued to donate to the Democratic Party and the BRT continued to employ Democrats in important staff positions. The *Wall Street Journal* reported that the GOP offered an ultimatum: "stop donating so much to the Democrats and become more involved in partisan politics, or be denied access to Republicans in Congress." (AA 207-208)

So, here you have two instances of Gingrich involved in telling outside parties what they had to do and that was be "partisan" and give no quarter to any Democrat or any Democrat ideas. They are saying, "You guys can't even *employ* a hated Democrat if you want access to any Republican". Notice that they presumed to speak for every Republican Congressman whether they all agreed with that position or not. The basic message is that there will be only Republican ideas allowed in Congress, no matter who was in charge of the government or how good their ideas might independently be.

Hacker and Pierson:

Once the Republican Party could be counted on to work with Democrats to restrain the growth of federal health spending by using Medicare's bargaining leverage to hold down provider charges. ... Beginning under Gingrich, Republicans renounced these once bipartisan efforts to control costs within the health care industry. Instead, GOP leaders focused their proposals on cuts in benefits, even ones that would in practice have little impact on overall costs. ...They [Republicans] refused to support *any* tax increases in budget packages. In fact they went further. On numerous occasions they insisted that "deficit reduction" include (deficit raising) tax cuts. Clinton's 1993 budget plan – similar to the agreement reached with George H. W. Bush in 1990 – received no Republican votes. ... From 1994 on, a simple principle seemed to dictate GOP tax stances: the more a particular tax fell on the wealthiest Americans, the more important it was to cut it. (AA 243)

There you have it. The GOP did not then (and has not since) allowed Medicare to try to control its outlays by looking to the cost of care. Instead, their solution was, and is, to cut benefits. What they want is to cut taxes on the wealthy. And this started with Gingrich (although, in fairness, he was not alone obviously.)

Speaking of Republicans who joined the House after 1978 (when Gingrich arrived) and then later won election to the Senate, whom they say political scientist Sean Theriault calls "Gingrich senators", Hatcher and Pierson say:

Gingrich senators aren't just more conservative than other Republicans (though they are, even when representing the same state.) They are more obstructionist. They are more confrontational. They are allergic to cooperation with Democrats, not only on matters large, such as budget deals, but on matters small, such as participating in Secret Santa gift exchanges. They are, in short, committed partisan warriors who reject the postwar bipartisan approach to economic policy. And they are the modern GOP. (AA 248)

Gingrich set forth guidelines for hate speech to be used toward all Democrats and their policies:

Gingrich used apocalyptic rhetoric. Democrats were "the enemy of normal Americans." His PAC sent out tapes to Republican candidates explaining how to "speak like Newt." As one relatively moderate Gingrich ally recalled, the tapes were "all about how to demonize the opposition, how to use invective and scary language. It wasn't that he trained them to have a better understanding of foreign policy or economic policy. They were techniques in how to wage a nasty partisan war against your opponent." One Gingrich tape, *Language: A Key Instrument of Control,* offered a long list of "contrast words" to be used against Democrats: *betray, corrupt, sick, decay, incompetent, disgrace, traitors, pathetic, obsolete.* (AA 260)

There you have the mind-set that invaded the Republican Party as it adopted the rich as its constituency. Use words like "traitor", "betrayers", disgrace", "pathetic" and "corrupt", even though Gingrich obviously did not and could not know whether there was any basis in fact for ever using even one of those terms against a particular candidate. What Gingrich fostered was the concept that Democrats were not "the loyal opposition", but were actively enemies of America as he saw it. Unfortunately, the man infected the whole GOP and it has not only never recovered, but it has gotten worse as time went on. This approach obviously not only does not care what the truth is, those who use it wouldn't recognize the truth if it bit them in the ass.

If none of this is getting your attention, try this from Hacker and Pierson:

Gingrich's break with George H. W. Bush [a Republican president] over a bipartisan deficit reduction bill that raised taxes as well as cut spending was fateful for the GOP and fatal for Bush's reelection. "The number one thing we had to prove in the fall of '90," Gingrich later explained, "was that if you explicitly decided to govern from the center, we could make it so unbelievably expensive, you couldn't sustain it." To Tom DeLay, a leading ally, "The only way we could take over Congress and be a party of prominence was to have a very clear distinction between the Democrats and the Republicans. The Bush administration wanted to work with Congress rather than beat Congress. And so it was contrary to what we were doing. We were trying to build a party and take over Congress. The Bush administration was trying to run the country and be reelected. "(AA 261)

Well, we can't have people trying to govern from the center or trying to run the country! That might get in the way of someone's political ambitions! Such utter horrid crap. It doesn't matter about the country, folks. It only matters to have power so that the rich can be protected.

Another poisonous politician in the Republican Party is Senator Mitch McConnell, present and previous majority leader in the Senate. Unlike the loud, boisterous, pushy Gingrich, McConnell is a political mastermind and lord of the intricacies of the running of the Senate. He knows that voters know nothing about the workings of Congress or the policy positions of even their own representatives. He also knows that voters often punish or reward political leaders for things over which they had no control. Most Americans thought Obama was in control from the White House. They had (and have) no idea how hard it is to get anything accomplished in Congress with a committed opposition who will use every trick to defeat any and every effort of a president in order to prevent him from getting anything he wants done and to prevent him from getting credit for anything good. McConnell was dedicated, even when he was only the minority leader in the Senate, to delay and disrupt every Obama effort. He raised the filibuster to new levels. As Hacker and Pierson say:

The persistent gridlock brought on by endless filibusters meant little or no adaptation. [Adaptation to changing contours of dynamic markets] It also meant, McConnell recognized, little or no accountability.

For filibusters leave no fingerprints. When voters hear that legislation has been "defeated." Journalists rarely report that this defeat meant a minority had blocked a majority. Not only does this strategy produce an atmosphere of gridlock and dysfunction; it also chewed up the Senate calendar, restricting the range of issues on which Democrats could progress. McConnell knew proposals lost support the longer they were out there, subject to attack. He knew constant delay would drive down the approval ratings of Democrats. In the case of health care, for example, McConnell encouraged a handful of Republicans to "negotiate" for months. According to a close friend of his in the Senate, Bob Bennett of Utah, this was all part of McConnell's plan to smear the bill: "He said' Our strategy is to delay this sucker as long as we possibly can, and the longer we delay it, the worse the president looks. … We're gonna delay it, and delay it as long as we can.' … We dragged that sucker out until December." (AA 264)

Like Gingrich, McConnell had found a serious flaw in the code of American democracy: Our distinctive political system gives an antigovernment party with a willingness to cripple governance an enormous edge. With the strategic guidance of these two congressional leaders, Republicans launched a self-reinforcing antistatist cycle. First they made the government less functional. Then they highlighted that dysfunction to build political support. The capacity to generate and then benefit from voter alienation reinforced all the other potent factors that encouraged the GOP's rightward shift. (AA 263-264)

I take it for granted that you readers know that it takes a 60 vote majority to break a filibuster. (Except for consenting to the nomination of a Supreme Court justice since the Republicans used the "nuclear option" for Judge Gorsuch.) Thus, even a party in the majority can't force a Senate vote unless they have a 60 vote majority. In any event, here you have it. The Gingrich/McConnell strategy is to cripple the Congress and then use the inability of that body to function to play up to voters that they need new (Republican) leaders in Congress to break up the stalemates which they themselves created. This works because who among us ordinary Americans knows what actually happened? This leads to what Hacker and Pierson call "the rule of 60". They mean that you can't get anything done unless you have a 60 seat majority. Fifty-nine seats won't do it. Then, of course, you need to be sure that all 60 of your party are for the bill. Things like this also lead to the practice of government by parties, not by the elected representatives. Never mind voting your true position, step in line with the party. That is a bad, bad thing for our government.

You may be wondering what this political maneuvering of Gingrich and McConnell has to do with the right wing. Let me quote from Mayer:

Among the new power brokers [after the 2014 elections], few, if any, could match the political clout of the Kochs. The reach of their "integrated network" was unique. One reflection of their singular status was their relationship with the new majority leader [after the 2014 elections gave the Republicans a majority] of the Senate. Mitch McConnell had been an honored speaker at their June donor summit. There, he had thanked "Charles and David" and added, "I don't know where we would be without you." Soon after he was sworn in, McConnell hired a new policy chief – a former lobbyist for Koch Industries. McConnell then went on to launch a stunning all-out war on the Environmental Protection Agency, urging governors across the country to refuse to comply with its new restrictions on greenhouse gas emissions. (DM 371)

How much clearer could it be? McConnell is the Koch's man. Bought and paid for. And, to be sure he gets it right, he has their lobbyist in his staff to keep him on the "right" path. And his assault on the EPA is in perfect concert with the Koch's energy industry position on greenhouse gases. This guy McConnell is an American enemy.

Another guy is also in the crosshairs here. This is Eric Cantor, who is the House majority leader and before that was the minority whip. He has labeled himself and his followers "the young guns". He has no interest in compromising in order to get things done. He only wants what he wants and everyone else can go to hell. As he was about to become the minority whip, Mayer says he:

…told a handful of trusted allies in a private planning meeting in his Washington condominium. "We're not here to cut deals and get crumbs and stay in the minority for another forty years." Instead, he argued, the Republicans needed to fight. They needed to unite in opposition to virtually anything Obama proposed in order to deny him a single bipartisan victory. The group, which included his deputy, Kevin McCarthy, called itself the Young Guns. The strategy of obstruction that they adopted won the Republicans the nickname the Party of No. (DM 172)

The Party of No. No bipartisan victory.

Mayer says:

At their first official leadership retreat in January 2009, the model that the House Republicans chose to emulate was the Taliban. The Texas congressman, Pete Sessions, the new leader of the Republican House campaign committee, held up Afghanistan's infamous Islamic extremists as providing an example of how they could wage "asymmetric warfare. *The country might be in an economic crisis, but governing, he told his colleagues, was not the reason they had been elected.* As he flashed an economic crisis through a slide presentation at the Annapolis Inn, he asked his colleagues, "If the Purpose of the Majority is to govern ... What is Our Purpose?" His answer was simple: "The Purpose of the Minority is to become the Majority." That one goal, he said, was "the entire Conference's mission." (Italics mine) (DM 172)

There you have it. The Republicans didn't (and don't) want to govern. They may have been elected to govern, but they didn't care what the voters thought or wanted. *They* wanted power and they were willing to oppose anything the other side tried to do, even though the American electorate had made the other side the majority. Who cares what the people may want?

Not convinced yet? Try another quote from Mayer:

The Republican leadership, according to an anecdote related by Grunwald, told GOP members of the House that, as one of them, Jerry Lewis, a member of the House Appropriations Committee, put it, "We can't play." David Obey, the Democratic chairman of the House Appropriations Committee, was incensed at the lack of cooperation. "What they said right from the get-go, he said< was that "it doesn't matter what the hell you do, we ain't going to help you. We're going to stand on the sidelines and bitch." (DM 173)

Here you have it again. Although it is the duty of the elected members of Congress to govern and to forward the business of the people, which always has and always will require cooperation and compromise by both major parties, the new Republican agenda is to refuse to do that both when in the minority and in the majority. Democrats are enemies and anything they may want to do needs to be fought and demonized. It is not the Democratic politicos so much that suffer from this. After all, they are also big shots who are well paid and catered to personally. It is the people who elected them and even the people who elected the Republicans who are the losers.

Another story that Eric Cantor and the Young Guns star in is that about the fight over the bill to raise the debt ceiling in 2011 and the budget bill. The Tea Party faction (which included Cantor) backed the fight. With respect to raising the debt ceiling, this made the Young Guns look like they were fighting the free-spending Democrats, but what they were really doing was making it impossible for the government to pay for expenditures which the Congress *had already approved.* This approach resulted eventually in the shut-down of government services and having Standard & Poor's downgrade America's credit rating for the first time in the country's history. It also paralyzed the functioning of the government for days. According to our friend, Eric Cantor, the debt ceiling fight was "a leverage moment." (DM 296-297)

That same year there was a big fight over the budget for the following year. Obama was ready to make concessions that many Democrats decried. A "grand bargain" was in the works between Obama and John Boehner. One of the issues was closing the loophole known as the "carried interest" provision of the tax code that I have mentioned before as seriously benefiting hedge fund managers and other Wall Street types. Cantor was strongly opposed to cutting that loophole and he was the recipient of large support from securities and investment firms. The fact that closing that one loophole would raise $20 billion over a decade from those making hundreds of millions per year, was the motivation for Wall Street and Cantor to oppose the budget bargain. At the last moment, Boehner reneged on the grand bargain and claimed that it was Obama's fault. In truth, the answer was different. As Mayer says;

Cantor later told the real story to Ryan Lizza of *The New Yorker.* Blowing up the grand bargain, had been his idea. He said it was a "fair assessment" to say that in the critical final moments he had talked Boehner out of accepting the deal for purely political reasons. Cantor had argued, why give Obama a win? Why aid his reelection campaign by helping him look competent? It would be more advantageous to sabotage the talks, regardless of the mess it left the country in, and wait and see if the next year's presidential election brought them a Republican president who would give them a better deal. (DM 299)

The result of this machination by Cantor and his allies was that the Congress and the president could not fashion a budget and instead relied on a horrible deal called "the sequester" which involved draconian slashes in government spending on a categorical basis. According to the Congressional Budget Office, the sequester would cost the economy 750,000 jobs per year and hurt millions of people who were reliant on public services. (DM 299) Boehner himself made a statement that helps explain what was going on. He said, "The American people will not accept, and the House cannot pass a bill that raises taxes on job creators." (AA 316) Where did Boehner get that idea? He got it from his right-wing backers. In fact, almost all Americans think that the rich need to pay more taxes, whether you call them "job creators" or not.

After the debt ceiling fight, Obama's policy director, Neera Tanden said that he

> … finally understood what he was up against. "I think he came in truly trying to be post-partisan," she said. "I think it took the debt ceiling fight to make him see that they hated him more than they wanted to succeed. It was an irrational deal, driven by their funders." Two and a half years into his presidency, she said, "he finally realized that they would rather kill him than save themselves." (DM 300)

Was she right? Consider that in a March 2011 op-ed piece in *The Wall Street Journal,* Charles Koch stated that he regarded any raise of the debt ceiling as simply a way to "delay tough decisions". Mayer says:

Pushing the Young Guns forward toward the financial cliff was Americans for Prosperity the Koch's political arm. Some forty other Tea Party and anti-tax groups also clamored for all-out-war. Among the most vociferous was the Club for Growth, a small, single-minded Wall Street-founded group powerful for one reason: it had the cash to mount primary challenges against Republicans who didn't hew to its uncompromising line. (DM 197)

Thus, there is no question but what the Republican Party by 2011 belonged wholly to the right-wing money as it still does. And, yes, there are Democrats who do as well, but there are far fewer of them and it is because they represent areas that have strong industrial or other financial interests who can put pressure on those Democrats. Very few, if any, Democratic politicians share the apocalyptic vision of the right wing.

Another "poster boy" for craziness is Mark Meadows, a congressman from Western North Carolina elected in 2012. Mayer tells the tale:

After only eight months in office, Meadows made national headlines by sending an open letter to the Republican leaders of the House demanding they use the "power of the purse" to kill the Affordable Care Act, By then the law had been upheld by the Supreme Court and affirmed when voters reelected Obama in 2012. But Meadows argued that Republicans should sabotage it by refusing to appropriate any funds for its implementation. And, if they didn't get their way, they would shut down the government. By fall, Meadows had succeeded in getting more that seventy-nine Republican congressmen to sign on to this plan, forcing Speaker of the House, John Boehner, who had opposed the radical measure to accede to their demands.

Meadows later blamed the media for exaggerating his role, but he was hailed by his local Tea Party group as "our poster boy" and by CNN as the "architect" of the 2013 shutdown. The fanfare grew less positive when the radicals in Congress refused to back down, bringing virtually the entire federal government to a halt for thirteen days in October, leaving the country struggling to function without the most vital federal services. In Meadows's district, day-care centers that were reliant on federal aid reportedly turned distraught families away, and nearby national parks were closed, bringing the tourist trade to a sputtering standstill. National polls showed public opinion was overwhelmingly against the shutdown. Even the *Washington Post* columnist Charles Krauthammer, a conservative [and then some!] called the renegades "the Suicide Squad".

The suicide squad indeed. Suicide for good sense, but not suicide to their political aspirations. We keep electing enemies like these who just do not care what they break in trying to get their own way – a way not good for average Americans, but good for them and their rich bitch backers.

For rich bitch backers? Is that fair? (Although by now, I hope you know the answer to that.) Consider this, Hacker and Pierson report; "Since federal lobbying disclosures began in 1998, pharmaceutical manufacturers, medical device makers, health insurers, hospitals and medical professionals have reported spending more than $6 billion." (AA278) Think of that! $ 6 billion! Did it do any good? The fight over the Part D drug cost provisions for Medicare (sponsored by George W. Bush!) helped answer that question. Hacker and Pierson quote former Reagan adviser Bruce Bartlett on that issue:

Republicans were keen to make sure that the legislation enacted was theirs, because the Democrats were certain to include cost containment for drugs in their legislation. It was widely believed that if the federal government used its buying power to pressure drug companies to cut drug prices, the cost of providing drugs to Medicare recipients would be substantially reduced.

But forcing down drug prices would diminish drug companies' profits and Republicans were adamantly opposed to that. Consequently, despite their oft-repeated opposition to new entitlement programs, they got behind the new drug benefit, now known as Medicare Part D and made sure there was no cost containment provision. (AA 278-279)

There you have it. Who cares what the consumers pay or the government gets billed? So long as those who spent $6 billion pressuring them, not to mention the vast right wing dark money behind their campaigns, our elected representatives chose to benefit the rich to the cost of the citizens and the government. Where was their concern about the deficit then? This is why Americans pay more for prescription drugs than any other country in the world. And make no mistake, if you have ever used Part D, you know that the benefits to the people are small and the benefit to the drug companies is large indeed.

One way the right has crippled the government is to refuse to properly fund its functions. The agency probably most hated by the right (even more than the EPA and that's saying something) is the IRS. Hatcher and Pierson introduce us to Senator Ron Johnson from Wisconsin, a Tea Pary favorite elected in 2010 and backed by Koch Industries. He has lead a crusade against the IRS, crippling its function by refusing to adequately fund it and leading the fight to slash its budget. In 2014, Johnson and his House counterpart slashed the request of the IRS Oversight Board's request for $13.6 billion to less than $11 billion. Hatcher and Pierson say about that:

If $11 billion seems like a lot to spend on tax administration, keep in mind that the IRS collects around $3 *trillion* in taxes. More important, every $1 spent on IRS enforcement yields $6 in recovered taxes, as well as at least three times more in indirect gains due to the deterrent effect on tax evasion. (Targeted enforcement efforts that focus on high-income taxpayers produce more than $47 in recovered taxes for every $1 spent.) Still, the IRS estimates that one in six tax dollars goes unpaid – a loss of nearly $450 billion (in 2015 dollars) each year. (AA 306)

Now, no one likes to pay taxes and most of us have some fear or distrust of the tax man. Nevertheless, without a functioning IRS, the government cannot be funded, to include such essential functions as defense and the operation of the government itself. It is a canard that we are the most highly taxed nation on earth. We are nowhere close to that. Look it up for yourself if you doubt that, given the bloviations of Donald Trump and his ilk. Look who benefits most from crippling the IRS. It is the big dollar earners who spend a fortune on their tax attorneys to avoid paying taxes that they can well afford, but would rather cheat on. Look at the figures! The IRS recovers $47 for every $1 spent on enforcement on the high income earners. Why is that? Well, I give you the poster boy, Donald Trump. But, truthfully, I don't know about his taxes because he won't tell us. What could we do with that extra $450 billion if it were only collected? Well, that is the lion's share of our yearly repayment and interest on the national debt, for one thing. It is also the lion's share of our defense budget. Why don't we have it? Cheaters is the answer. Why shouldn't we send the IRS after them? And what do you think Johnson's backers, the Kochs' position is on this? We actually know that because they are Libertarians and they want the IRS closed down. Folks, the IRS is not our enemy. Almost all average Americans willingly pay their taxes. Why should we let the cheaters get away with it? It should not be because of idiots like Ron Johnson or right wing kings like the Kochs. As I have previously said, audits of rich people have declined drastically but audits of the poor receiving earned income tax credits are still being vigorously audited. The IRS can no longer provide accurate and timely help to taxpayers because they are so short of personnel. Who is this hurting?

You folks probably remember the furor in 2013 when the IRS inspector general reported that lower-level staff had applied special scrutiny to conservative political groups seeking tax exempt status. Joe Scarborough, the House Republican who took up as an MSNBC host called it "tyranny" (see AA 308) Jon Stewart took after Obama on his show after that report. Hathcher and Pierson say:

The takedown [Stewart's] was humorous, but it wasn't accurate. Subsequent investigations showed that the frontline IRS officials who had questioned the nonprofit designation were acting substantially on their own. Moreover, their net of scrutiny had ensnared liberal as well as conservative groups; in fact, the only group flagged by the IRS that ultimately had its tax-exempt status denied or revoked was a *left-leaning* one .After the inspector general report, the officials responsible were reprimanded and the federal supervisor of their division compelled to resign. President Obama forced the IRS's head to step down as well, even though he had not been in charge at the time, a Bush appointee had been.

What's more, the underlying issue *was* complicated. The Supreme Court's *Citizen's United* ruling had opened the door to new organizations that claimed tax-free status yet acted much like traditional political groups that are taxed. A year later, a Republican-appointed federal judge dismissed all the lawsuits brought against the IRS. What was portrayed as a witch hunt carried out by a partisan agency turned out to be mostly an ill-conceived screening process developed by a short-staffed IRS grappling with ambiguous law. (Thanks to the GOP attacks, however, the IRS would essentially give up policing the increasingly murky lines between charitable non-profits and those dedicated to political advocacy.) (AA 308-309)

In case you folks were thinking the IRS was a monster because of this particular incident, you can see that it was vastly overplayed (mostly by Fox News). All of these so-called nonprofit entities ought to be scrutinized closely no matter which way they lean. They are a scam by and large and they allow dark money to be poured into our political system tax-free to the tune of what is now billions of dollars. If you think there was some kind of cover-up, you can be sure that the subsequent lawsuits filed by the conservatives would have produced the facts and proof, but instead, those suits were dismissed which is a legal way of saying there is nothing at all to your suit, so go away. No trial on this garbage. Nevertheless, watch for the Republican Party's 2016 platform wherein they describe the IRS as a rogue agency. (The Republican platform is discussed in some detail later in this book.)

Next, we consider the 2014 Ebola scare and the way the right treated it. In January of that year a Liberian named Thomas Duncan was admitted to Texas Health Center with the disease and died quickly. You may recall that an epidemic of the disease was going on in Africa at the time. Ebola, while a hideous disease, is not airborne. Coughs and sneezes won't spread it. This got lost in the rhetoric. Ultimately there was one death in this country and only a few diagnosed cases. How did the right react? The moderate critics were suggesting a lack of trust in the agencies responsible for public health. Hatcher and Pierson (I just love these guys) tell it:

And these were the *moderate* voices. Within hours of Thomas Duncan's diagnosis, talk radio and Fox News filled up with right-wing commentators spouting ever-more outrageous conspiracy theories. Glenn Beck suggested that Dallas, Texas, was the first US city to experience the disease because it leaned Republican. According to Rush Limbaugh, Obama and the left have this attitude, "Well, if they have it in Africa, by God, we deserve to get it because they're in Africa because of us and because of slavery." Not to be outdone, Michael Savage – whose show, *The Savage Nation* has over five million listeners – said Obama's actions regarding Ebola rose "to the level of treason; it actually exceeds any level of treason I've ever seen. … Obama wants equality, he wants fairness," Savage continued. "It's only fair that America have a nice epidemic or two or three or four, in order to really feel what it's like to be in the third world." …

Conservative celebrities are in the outrage industry, of course. But, it was a strikingly short distance from their apoplectic warnings to the criticisms lobbed by prominent GOP politicians. With the 2014 midterm looming, leading Republicans – including presidential hopeful Rand Paul (a doctor) and former Massachusetts Senator Scott Brown, who was locked in a tight race for governor in New Hampshire – warned that a disease centered in West Africa and never seen before in Latin America would soon cross the Mexican border. Paul and other top GOP politicians also claimed that President Obama's decision to provide military support for efforts to fight the disease in Africa would lead to mass infection of American troops. Raising the specter of a "whole shipload of soldiers" infected with Ebola, Paul suggested the CDC had "understate[d] the transmissibility "of Ebola and "political correctness" was standing in the way of "sound, rational, scientific decisions. (AA326-327)

This kind of media attack and political attack gives rise to such things as a wing-nut religious web site accusing Obama of deliberately spreading Ebola to attack Christians. The paranoid in this country only need this sort of filth to stoke their fears. It is clear that the right wing media and its idiot spokesmen such as Beck, Limbaugh and Savage have taken Gingrich speak to a whole new and scurrilous level. But what is worse is Paul, a physician, suggesting that the "transmissibility" of Ebola was understated by the CDC. He knew better or damn well should have done so. All of this crap helped spread widespread fears of an epidemic of Ebola in the US which was never likely and even had it been, it would in no way have been the fault of the government. Whose fault would it have been? Interesting question.

Listen to Hacker and Pierson:

The biggest and most telling tragedy of the Ebola scare is that it might well have been avoidable. Over the prior decade, funding for the National Institutes of Health declined by $5 billion after inflation – a drop af almost a fifth in the NIH's budget. Even more striking, the CDC's budget for disaster preparedness, always small, was slashed in half over the same period. These cuts amid the economic downturn contributed to more than forty-five thousand job losses within state and local health departments just between 2008 and 2012. And the cuts continued after the Ebola scare. The so-called sequestration legislation that ended the debt-ceiling standoff put in place tough automatic cuts in discretionary spending (again, the kind of spending that finances many of the most vital investments in America's future, such as infrastructure, medical research and education), further squeezing the NIH and the CDC. (AA 327)

Thus, the Republican drive to cut the government cripples vital functions, but when it does so their politicians blame the resulting falloff in services on the Democrats and the President. It works every time even though the fault is that of the party that says "no" to compromise and won't hear of taxes on the rich. Hacker and Pierson end their coverage of this Ebola issue with this tidbit:

In retrospect, the most shortsighted cuts were for funding of a vaccine to prevent Ebola (which, at the start of 2016 looked finally to be on the horizon.) Since 2010, the NIH's funding to develop a vaccine dropped by half. (AA 328)

So, cut the funding to do important tasks, then blame lack of progress on the agencies that have been shorted and whose capabilities have been slashed. Then wrap it all up by calling the president a traitor. It makes me sick.

There are many other agencies that have been treated the same way. The FDA, for instance, has been cut so much that its food inspections have fallen by 61 percent between 1972 and 2007. Thus, every year nearly 48 million people are sickened by food-borne illnesses. Only one percent of food crossing our borders is inspected and more and more food comes to us this way. Again, Hacker and Pierson tell it:

> By 2010, the problem had grown so bad that Congress passed a law updating the FDA's enforcement strategy. Unfortunately, the funding to implement the new law was slashed. Fierce lobbying by the food industry meant that user fees proposed by the FDA were a political nonstarter. Meanwhile Congress appropriated less than half the total that the Congressional Budget office said the FDA needed. "We have good plans for going forward," said a top FDA official in 2015. "The problem is we don't have the money." Nearly half of the job openings in its crucial overseas offices remain unfilled. (AA 321)

So, did you have food poisoning? It must be the FDA's fault, right? Nope. It is the fault of those right wingers who think they have done a good thing by cutting the government's budget.

There are many other such stories. The EPA has suffered extravagantly at the hands of Republicans who are now talking about "the war on coal". The Federal Elections Commission has been slashed. Etcetera.

Hacker and Pierson point out that from the administration of Dwight Eisenhower, when there was one federal worker for every 78 Americans, to the present when the number is around one federal worker for every 150 Americans, the relative size of the US government workforce has dropped precipitately. As they say:

Assume that the number of federal workers had risen in line with the US population since the late 1970's. By 2009 in this alternative reality, the Agriculture Department would have employed 83 percent more workers than it did. The US Department of Health and Human Services – the agency responsible for two of the fastest growing programs, Medicare and Medicaid – would have employed 60 percent more. Treasury (which certainly has its hands full, too) would have employed 39 percent more. All told, to get the employment-population ratio back to its pre-1980 levels, the federal government would need to increase its workforce by around 80 percent over the next twenty years.

Yet the loudest voices in Washington are calling for the opposite. After the 2010 midterm, GOP leaders vowed to cut the federal workforce by at least a tenth within five years. Not content with that goal, two Republicans in the House introduced the Federal Workforce Through Attrition Act, which would limit new federal hires to one worker for every three who left government. "Real, productive job creation takes place on Main Street America, not in the bloated federal government," declared one of the bill's authors, Wyoming Republican Cynthia Lummis. (AA 321-322)

As you can see, not only is the federal government not bloated, it is being systematically stripped of its ability to do the job of protecting average Americans so that the one percent and big corporations can reap the benefits. The federal government is the only ally average Americans have that can really protect us from the wolves and see to the general welfare as our Constitution demands that it do.

Hacker and Pierson also discuss the fact that most government jobs are paid less than similar jobs in the commercial world. This leads to massive brain drain in the government and provides business with the people who know how to stifle the government. They conclude:

The dirty little secret is that essential government responsibilities don't disappear when federal workers do. They just get farmed out to private contractors or pushed down to lower levels of government. Study after study has concluded that excessive reliance on outside contractors magnifies complexity, reduces performance, and impairs accountability. For the federal government's most complicated tasks – guiding scientific inquiry, managing medical payments, overseeing complex financial transactions – talented public workers are vital. "Today's federal civil service is not bloated," concludes John DiLullio, the public administration scholar who worked on George W. Bush's faith-based initiatives. "It is overloaded." To be effective, he argues, the federal government needs to hire one million new workers – a 50 percent increase in its workforce – in the next twenty years. Dilulio might still be working on faith-based initiatives. It will take divine intervention to achieve that goal. (AA 322)

Yes sire. Private contractors, of course! I especially like the private contractors running schools and, in Florida, many of our prisons. The hideous result for the prisons is that they are ticking time bombs. Not only that, but they are full of people who never should have been sent there in the first place or, in the alternative, not for so long. Furthermore, they are full of a far lopsided number of blacks and Hispanics proportionately who don't get the breaks that whites do. As for private schools, which our Republican pols love (after all, their constituency includes the private school industry), Hacker and Pierson say this:

But there's one part of the higher-education sector that has received more and more largesse: for-profit colleges. Almost a seventh of college students are now enrolled in for-profit schools; in 1993 it was just 1.6 percent. And for all their emulation of the private commercial sector, these profit-making enterprises are basically creatures of the federal government. The fifteen largest firms receive, on average, 86 percent of their revenue from the feds. All this would be less troubling if they were revolutionizing education in the ways their rhetoric suggests. But the outcomes are dismal; Fewer than a quarter of students graduate in six years; the median debt of the students who actually graduate is $33,000; tuition is twice what public institutions charge; and job market outcomes are bleak, which makes those big debts more of an economic yoke than a smart investment. But the industry has become a major lobbying power in the higher-education arena and Republicans have garnered most of the industry's campaign donations. Once upon a time, Republicans criticized the for-profits. Reagan's education secretary, William Bennett, rightly called them "diploma mills designed to trick the poor into taking on federally-backed debt" Since the mid-1990's, however, GOP leaders – and plenty of Democrats on key congressional committees who have raked in the for-profits' donations – have eagerly backed the rent seekers. [Hacker and Pierson's term for those seeking to make excessive income, especially at the expense of government] (AA 302-303)

Will the right wing insistence that "Main Street" does it better or that the "free market" does it better even try to encompass these rotten deals in their thinking? No, they won't. It ain't profitable for them. If it screws the little guys to the advantage of the big guys, it must be good for America. Right? What's good for General Bullmoose is good for America, to steal from an old comic book, which is a takeoff on "what's good for General Motors is good for America." That can actually be true if General Bullmoose is willing to share with his workers and not try to own the government.

As Hacker and Pierson point out, there is a book by Thomas E. Mann and Norman Ornstein called *It's Even Worse Than it Looks* which helps understand what is going on. Thomas Mann is a fellow at the non-partisan Brookings Institute and Ornstein is actually a fellow at American Enterprise Institute, which is a conservative think tank. These authors refer to the tactics of the Republican party with the term "the new nullification". Hacker and Pierson say:

The phrase comes from the ugly history of state resistance to federal laws. Yet, Mann and Ornstein apply the term to a range of contemporary tactics that opponents use to cripple democratically enacted laws. These include coordinated assaults on those laws' constitutionality [by lawsuits], denying funds necessary for their implementation, and "blocking nominations, even while acknowledging the competence and integrity of the nominees, to prevent the legitimate implementation of laws on the books." (AA332)

Who cares whether we couldn't prevent the law from being enacted? We'll just refuse to do what our oath requires us to do and we will cripple the law of the land.

An example that Hacker and Pierson give is the Consumer Financial Protection Bureau which was part of the Dodd-Frank financial reform legislation. The Bureau was intended to provide some protection to consumers when dealing with complex financial services. Hacker and Pierson say:

When the CFPB was included in President Obama's financial reform legislation, The Chamber of Commerce and Wall Street tried desperately to kill it. The head of the Chamber's Center for Capital Markets Competitiveness vowed to "spend whatever it takes" to defeat the proposal. [Remember, this was all happening in the ashes of the catastrophe that Wall Street inflicted on our economy in the form of the great recession of 2007.] Despite all the spending, however, the opponents lost – which would usually mean the agency would go into operation. Yet Republicans refused to confirm a head to the CPFB unless President Obama agreed to changes that would weaken it greatly. When Obama refused, Republicans threatened a filibuster to block the intellectual architect of the bureau, Harvard law professor Elizabeth Warren, from becoming the agency's first director. … Obama then nominated Richard Cordray, a former Ohio attorney general. Republicans acknowledged that he was qualified, but they did not budge from their nullification stance: no changes in the agency, no head of the agency.

It is worth pausing here to consider just how audacious this demand was. The CPFB was law. The Republicans didn't have the votes to repeal it. Yet the GOP still felt it could win the war by refusing to carry out its constitutional role of advise and consent. (AA 332-333)

Does this resonate with the empty Supreme Court seat we have as of this writing in October 2016? [Subsequently filled by Trump nominee Justice Gorsuch.] Who cares if it is our duty to do it? We ain't gonna do it and you can't make us. So there! By the way, Cordray did eventually become director.

In this context, there was an interesting column in the *Tampa Bay Times* on June 7, 2016 which they reprinted from the *New York Times.* Entitled "Investor Protections in the Crosshairs", it dealt with law suits filed by industry groups to prevent the implementation of a rule by the Department of Labor, one upon which the Dodd Frank Act specifically called for study and rules. The rule set forth a best-interest standard. The column says about that standard:

A best-interest standard, also known as a fiduciary duty, would end the common industry practice of steering clients into high-priced strategies and products, even when comparable lower-cost options are available. Such steering generates an estimated $17 billion in excess fees and inflated commissions, a bundle the industry is desperate to preserve.

The groups' legal arguments are vacuous. For example, the rules require advisors to disclose compensation incentives or conflicts of interest that might induce them to recommend one strategy or product over another. That is basic disclosure for a fiduciary. But one suit says such disclosures would violate advisers' right to free speech by forcing them to discuss things they would rather not discuss.

Whoa! Did you know that your broker (if you have one or would like to have one) could recommend stuff to you that he or she knows is more expensive or less favorable just because the broker would profit by it without even telling you about that? Their suit position is that "we want to protect our right to freely speak lies and misleading sales pitches to screw our customers so we can personally profit." How sweet of them. In case you thought brokers had a fiduciary duty with your money, sorry about that, sucker. [And I am one of you.] Just think of it: a $17 billion rip-off every year. But, you know, we should deregulate Wall Street so they can make us all richer! Which is true if you define "us all" as "Wall Street swells". It takes a set of brass balls to actually put this stuff in writing in a lawsuit. On the other hand, how much influence do you suppose this column had on the lawsuits?

Well, back to nullification. When Obama entered office, the National Labor Relations Board had only two of five directors. That board, as you readers probably know, is intended to adjudicate labor relations disputes. The Republicans hate unions, which are the participants versus industry in these disputes. Obama followed precedent and nominated one Democrat and one Republican. The GOP refused to act on any of Obama's appointments to the board. Hacker and Pierson say:

Again, the NLRB was established by law to play a specific role. Again, business lobbies and Republicans disagreed with that role. And again, unable or unwilling to change the law [which has been around for eighty-five years] through the normal democratic process, they threatened to make the agency dysfunctional. After a complaint against Boeing in 2011 by the NLRB's general counsel (who acts independently of the five-member board), Senator Lindsey Graham of South Carolina vowed to block all nominations to the board. "The NLRB as inoperable could be considered progress", he declared. … In July, 2013, Mitch McConnell made clear the basis of GOP objections by making a remarkable demand: He would support Obama only if he agreed to a board with a Republican majority. Nullification or capitulation – those were the choices. (AA 333-334)

Can it be any clearer than this? We don't care that the voters have elected a Democratic majority, we will filibuster and we will refuse to advise and consent on appointments and we will refuse to fund what is enacted and we will block any rules and laws in the courts if we possibly can, because we will not govern nor will we permit you to govern, Democrats, no matter what it does to the government or the country. By the way, we are going to blame the lack of progress on you even though it is our fault and part of our plan to become the majority and take all power for the right.

Another issue and one that is particularly troubling is the recent spate of voter-restrictive laws coming out of the states. This includes voter ID laws, limiting early voting, placing polls in difficult places and any other contrivance that the fertile minds of the Republican state legislatures can devise. This sort of thing is very recent and relates to the takeover of many state legislatures by Republicans. Hacker and Pierson explain that the claim that these laws are intended to prevent fraudulent voting is "absurd on its face." Think about it. When was the last time you read about voter fraud in which someone fraudulently voted too many times or impersonated someone else or did something to affect the voting machines? It has never happened in my area to my memory in 55 years of voting in the Tampa Bay area. As Hacker and Pierson say:

There is nothing partisan about observing that voter restrictions are partisan. Republicans have spearheaded these initiatives, and they and their organized supporters have trumpeted a mythical narrative to justify them. A recent statistical analysis by two University of Massachusetts Boston researchers concludes that the proposal and passing of voter restrictions are highly partisan, strategic and racialized affairs. New restrictions are more likely where there is a large minority population, where minority turnout has increased, and where Republicans control legislatures. These findings, the authors conclude, "are consistent with a scenario in which the targeted demobilization of minority voters and African Americans is a central driver of legislative developments (AA 345-346)

There you have opinions from Hacker and Pierson and two U. Mass. researchers. Is it really true? Let us see what Jane Mayer has turned up. She speaks of the same issue and refers to an instance in which an African American woman named Teresa Sharp in Ohio received a summons from elections authorities requiring her to prove her legitimacy as an Ohio voter at a public hearing. The summons was as a result of the Ohio Vote Integrity Project policing rolls. In Ms. Sharp's case they had mistaken a vacant lot for her address. Mayer says:

The national outbreak of fear over voter fraud appeared a spontaneous grassroots movement, but beneath the surface there was a money trail that led back to the usual deep-pocketed right-wing donors. To target Sharp, for instance, the Ohio Voter Integrity Project had relied on software supplied by a national nonprofit, True the Vote, which itself was supported in different ways by the Bradley Foundation, the Heritage Foundation and Americans for Prosperity [the Kochs!].

True the Vote described itself as a nonprofit organization, created "*by* citizens *for* citizens," that aimed to protect the rights of legitimate voters, regardless of their political party." But its founder, Catherine Engelbrecht, a Houston Tea Party activist, was guided by Hans von Spakovsky, a Republican lawyer and fellow at the Heritage Foundation who had made a career of challenging liberal voting rights reforms. Heritage had an ugly history on the issue. The think tank's founder, Paul Weyrich, had openly admitted, "I don't want everybody to vote." In 1980, he told supporters, "As a matter of fact, our leverage in elections goes up as the voting populace goes down." (DM 329)

Does it get any clearer than that? The sponsors of these voter restriction laws are right wing Republicans. Why? Not because of voter fraud. That is a lie. It is because the Republican Party does better when minorities, who are strongly Democratic, don't vote. So, rig the laws against them. It doesn't take much to make a small fractional difference in voter turnout. Look how close the 2000 presidential election was.

Hacker and Pierson quote from Mann and Ornstein's book in a quote that I suggest is a perfect statement of the point I have been trying to make:

However awkward it may be for the traditional press and nonpartisan analysts to acknowledge, one of the two major parties, the Republican Party, has become an insurgent outlier – ideologically extreme; contemptuous of the inherited social and economic policy regime; scornful of compromise; unpersuaded by conventional understanding of facts, evidence , and science; and dismissive of the legitimacy of its political opposition. When one party moves this far from the center of American politics, it is extremely difficult to enact policies responsive to the country's most pressing challenges. (AA 335)

This and the rest of their book got Mann and Ornstein ousted from their perches as respected media spokesmen, but it spoke powerfully of the truth.

Where does the Republican Party stand now? Hacker and Pierson say:

Old-time Libertarians might look at the marriage of the the Koch network and the GOP political establishment and worry that the brothers had sold out. In truth, it was more that the GOP had bought in. Charles and David Koch hadn't left the fringe to come to the Republican Party. The Republican Party had come to them. (DM 237)

Remember, I started this book by pointing out the ways that the Libertarian Party is the enemy of almost all Americans. Later, I will work through the Republican Party platform for 2016 and show you how tightly it adheres to that 1980 Libertarian manifesto. Folks, it is sickening.

Then there is this from Mayer: "By 2015, the acrimony had broken out into the open as Katie Walsh, the chief of staff at the RNC [Republican National Committee], all but accused the Kochs of usurping the Republican Party." (DM 369) They have indeed. The party of the Great Emancipator, Abraham Lincoln, has become the tool of racial profilers, apologists for thieves and also the tool of the rich against the rest of us – the new and "improved" Republican Party.

Once more I quote from Hacker and Pierson (who better?):

To Mann and Ornstein, the problem was the continuing insistence that both Republicans and Democrats were equally to blame for government dysfunction. Mann marveled at the degree to which the well-funded campaign by Pete Peterson [of Wall Street] and others to elevate the deficit as the nation's number one concern had led many journalists to conclude that American government was overextended – and Democrats, in denial about this alleged reality, at least as complicit as the Republicans in the failure to address the problem. "The Peterson world, I think, has given journalists the material to keep doing what they're doing," he said.

Seeing both parties as equally at fault seems hardheaded and superficially suggests objectivity, but it's an abdication of responsibility. "If voters are going to be able to hold accountable political figures, they've got to know what's going on," explained Ornstein. "And if the story that you're telling repeatedly is that they're all to blame – they're all equally to blame – then you're really doing a disservice to voters and not doing what journalism is supposed to do. ... If one side is tearing down government, it's a deep problem when those writing about American politics are convinced that the mess is thoroughly bipartisan. (AA 336)

The mess is not bipartisan. That is not to say that Democrats have been nearly as effective dealing with it as we could have wished. It is, however, the far, far right co-opting the Republican Party through the Gingrich, McConnell and Tea Party politics, the purchase of the government by billionaires who want to tear it down to free them from constraints, and the billions poured into lobbying by business, industry, Big Pharma, Wall Street and the fossil fuel interests. None of these interests are Americans' interests. In fact, they want to be free to exercise their freedom of speech to lie to us about our own investments. By now I hope you see that I am not making this up.

Chapter 13

What about the Climate?

This section could easily have been put into the last one, but I feel very strongly that this is a critical issue and have decided to treat it separately. The question is what the right is doing now to affect this issue. Having just recently watched the vice-presidential debate between Kaine and Pence (with some discomfort about Kaine's performance, I must admit), I saw the newest on that front. Mr. Pence referred to "the war on coal." This is a neat way to avoid using the word "climate" at all and to cast the criticism of fossil fuels as a war against coal and, no doubt, it will be cast in terms of trying to deprive coal miners and coal towns of their livelihoods. Frankly, the fossil fuel industry could burn all the fuels they wanted if they would spend the millions that they have poured into fighting the climate change debate into ways to capture and use the CO2 they emit. But, they would rather spend the money on devastatingly dangerous fighting. So, what are they doing?

It is interesting to note that, before the 2008 election, both presidential candidates had spoken in favor of fighting climate change. That obviously changed on the Republican side. Speaking of research done by Kert Davies, the director of research for Greenpeace, Mayer says;

What he discovered was that from 2005 to 2008, a single source, the Kochs, poured almost $25 million into dozens of different organizations fighting climate reform. The sum was staggering. His research showed that Charles and David had outspent what was then the world's largest public oil company, ExxonMobil, by a factor of three. In a 2010 report, Greenpeace crowned Koch Industries, a company few had ever heard of at the time, the "kingpin of climate science denial."

The first peer-reviewed academic study on the topic added further detail. Robert Brulle, a Drexel University professor of sociology and environmental science, discovered that between 2003 and 2010 over half a billion dollars was spent on what he described as a massive "campaign to manipulate and mislead the public about the threat posed by climate change." The study examined the tax records of more than a hundred nonprofit organizations engaged in challenging the prevailing science on global warming. What it found was, in essence, a corporate lobbying campaign disguised as a tax-exempt philanthropic endeavor. Some 140 conservative foundations funded the campaign, Brulle found. During the seven-year period he studied, these foundations distributed $558 million in the form of 5,299 grants to ninety-one different nonprofit organizations. The money went to think tanks, advocacy groups, trade associations, other foundations, and academic and legal programs. Cumulatively, this private network waged a permanent campaign to undermine Americans' faith in climate science and to defeat any effort to regulate carbon emissions.

The cast of conservative organizations identified by Brulle was familiar to anyone who had followed the funding of the modern conservative movement. Among those he pinpointed as the largest bankrollers of climate change denial were foundations affiliated with the Koch and Scaife families, both of whose fortunes derived partly from oil. (DM 204-205)

Sorry for the long quote, but her words are right on point. More than half a billion dollars spent to fight the science of climate change. Why? Profits now, to hell with later.

Speaking of the opinions of the Kochs themselves on climate change, Mayer says:

But in one interview, David Koch suggested that if real, it would prove a boon. "The Earth will be able to support enormously more people because a far greater land area will be available to produce food", he argued. Charles's thinking was reflected in the company's in-house newsletter which featured an article titled "Blowing Smoke". "Why are such unproven or false claims promoted?" it asked. Rather than fighting global warming, the newsletter suggested, mankind would be better off adapting to it. "Since we can't control Mother Nature, let's figure out how to get along with her changes," it advised. A similar line was subtly argued in the David H. Koch Hall of Human Origins at the Smithsonian's National Museum of Natural History in Washington which opened in March 2010. The message of this exhibition, funded by his fortune, was that the human race had evolved for the better in response to previous environmental challenges and would adapt in the face of climate change, too. An interactive game suggested that if the climate on earth became intolerable, people might build "underground cities" and develop "short, compact bodies" or "curved spines" so that moving about in tight spaces will be no problem. (DM 215-216)

Well, gosh let's look at these wonderful arguments for a moment. First, "far greater land area will be available to produce food". Baloney. As land closer to the poles warms up, what happens to food growing areas closer to the equator? Temperatures there are already getting to be intolerable in the summer. Further, if we are going to grow food further to the poles, what about the people living there now? And this completely overlooks the enhanced storms, fires, rising seas, deaths from heatstroke and social upheavals as all of this occurs. Then, Charles suggests that Mother Nature is to blame for the climate change. That is one of the great lies of the climate change deniers. The reason is the near doubling of CO2 in the atmosphere which is a purely human result from burning fossil fuels in the past couple centuries. Because it is a result of Mother Nature, Charles says, we can't do anything about it. Another great lie. We can do something. We can stop pouring CO2 into the atmosphere (along with methane from natural gas production). Then we have David's little production at the Smithsonian. I can't believe that the Smithsonian allowed it, but that is another matter. It is true that we evolved under the stress of adverse conditions. This is in the line of "what doesn't kill us makes us stronger". The problem is that on more than one occasion, the human race nearly died out as a result of past climate changes. Yes, the race survived and got better able to cope. But, this only happened at the cost of the loss of most of our people. Do we want to pay that price again so these wolves can keep pumping CO2 into the atmosphere for fun and profit? And we can build underground cities? Gee, won't that be fun? How much will that cost and how many billions of us will die first? And how many folks will we be able to fit into these things anyway? Forget the stars, dig in! Finally, we will develop short bodies or curved spines? I got news for David. We don't have time for that sort of evolution even if we wanted to do it and I sure don't. You see the price these guys are willing to have the human race pay so that they can have a "free market" that lets them poison our planet for profit.

Mayer goes on to recount incidents in which congressmen were bombarded by correspondence from normally liberal groups such as the NAACP and the American Association of University Women railing against their climate change positions. It was found that the letters were forgeries sent on behalf of a coal industry trade group. Another approach was to send hecklers into the appearances of congressmen. Put up to it by an official of the Virginia office of our old friend AFP. (See DM 217)

Then you get the outright garbage mouths:

Fanning the flames were the right-wing radio hosts. "It's not about saving the planet," Rush Limbaugh told his audience. "It's not about anything, folks, other than raising taxes and redistributing wealth." Glenn Beck [ugh] warned listeners it would lead to water rationing. "This is about controlling every part of your life, even taking a shower!" Torquing up the fear, Republicans in Congress quoted from a study by the Heritage Foundation [our old friend] that predicted it [the proposed cap and trade bill] would add thousands of dollars to Americans' energy bills and lead to devastating unemployment. The nonpartisan Congressional Budget Office put out an authoritative study contradicting this, demonstrating that the average cost to Americans would be the same as buying a postage stamp a day. But John Boehner, the Republican minority leader in the House, dismissed the real numbers, suggesting that anyone who believed them could "go ask the unicorns." (DM 217-218)

Has anyone seen a peer-reviewed study from an accredited scientific source funded by Glen Beck or Rush Limbaugh – or anyone else for that matter – that supports their position? Hell no. And don't quote some Heritage Foundation study to me. They have no proper peer-reviewed science behind them and I wouldn't believe them if they presented one until it was vetted by other outside scientists. They manage to disappoint peer reviewed studies by the hundreds from all over the planet with their crap. Has John Boehner got any peer reviewed studies to cite? The only effort ever made was a single National Academy of Sciences study that ignored its scientists in favor of an economist and which has been superseded by many later National Academy of Sciences studies supporting human caused climate change. They don't have the facts, so they throw money, propaganda and lies at it masquerading as thoughtful positions. Why do I keep saying peer-reviewed? Because that is how science is done. Once the authors of a scientific article have submitted it for publishing in any reputable publication, it is sent out to experts in the same field who review it to see if it stands up to rigorous standards. Then and only then, if the article stands up, is it published. That is the gold standard in *any* scientific field, not just climate science. Heck that is even the standard for publishing in many legal journals, as I can attest personally.

In 2010, the Republican Party gained a majority in the House. Speaking to the House Energy and Commerce Committee, the committee responsible for dealing with the energy and climate change issues, Mayer says:

In the previous Congress, the panel had been chaired by Henry Waxman, the liberal Democrat from California who had quarterbacked the House's successful passage of the cap-and-trade bill, only to see it die in the Senate. Now the new Republican leadership stacked the committee with oil industry advocates, many of whom owed huge campaign debts to the Kochs. Koch Industries PAC was the single largest oil and gas industry donor to members of the panel, outspending even ExxonMobil. It had donated to twenty-two of the committee's thirty-one Republican members and five of its Democratic members, too. In addition, five out of the six Republican freshmen on the committee had received "outside" support from Americans for Prosperity.

Meanwhile, many of the new committee members had signed an unusual pledge swearing fealty to the Kochs' agenda. They promised to vote against any kind of carbon tax unless it was offset by comparable spending cuts – an unlikely scenario. The "No Climate Tax" pledge was invented by Americans for Prosperity [No! Can it be?] in 2008 when the Supreme Court cleared the way for the EPA to regulate greenhouse gases, as it did all other pollutants. (DM 273-274)

It is, of course, routine for a party gaining a majority in either house of Congress to pack the committees with its own and I, frankly, could not nit-pick that. But look at the overwhelming influence, not of the Republican

Party here, but of the Kochs. Look at the pre-judging going on concerning issues that the new members haven't even heard testimony about. The Kochs own the place, not the American people. And AFP is seeing to it.

Speaking of AFP, listen to this from Mayer:

At the end of 2011, only twenty of the sixty-five Republican members of Congress who responded to a survey were willing to say that they believed climate change was causing the planet to warm. Tim Phillips [president of AFP] gladly took credit for the dramatic spike in expressed skepticism. "if you look at where the situation was three years ago [when most thought it was causing warming] and where it is today, there's been a dramatic turnaround," he told the *National Journal.* "most of these candidates have figured out that the science has become political," he said. "We've made great headway. What it means for these candidates of the Republican side is if you … buy into green energy or you play footsie in this issue, you do so at your political peril. The vast majority of people who are involved in the (Republican) nominating process – the conventions and the primaries – are suspect of the science. And that's our influence. Groups like Americans for Prosperity have done it." (DM 278)

So, folks, you may have thought your vote mattered, but it doesn't matter as much as AFP's does, even if AFP doesn't itself vote. What's happening is that billions are being spent to lie to us and take our government away from us so that it can be stripped of the power to look to the general welfare or control the wolves.

And what of the climate these days? Well, I have already spoken of the records being set for heat year after year on an annual basis lately. I have already alluded to Ile de Jean Charles which is being relocated by the federal government due to rising waters. I may have mentioned that Miami Beach is having to raise road beds due to rising seas. However, there was a recent article in the *Tampa Bay Times* on September 21, 2016 that caught my attention. It was entitled "Brutal Summer Takes Toll". It lists floods, droughts and storms costing billions and taking hundreds of lives all over the globe. Temperatures in Kuwait and Iraq reached 129 degrees Fahrenheit in July. Localities in the US broke 15,000 daily records for hot nighttime minimum temperatures from May to September.

Another *Tampa Bay Times* article on October 9, 2016 is relevant. The article was written in the wake of Hurricane Matthew [which is still churning in the Atlantic and headed back toward Florida as I write this]. It states, correctly, that no one storm can be related to global warming, but studies have shown that it can be related to the severity of those storms. Matthew came to Florida as a category 4 hurricane which is unusual for October. The strength of these storms depends in no small part on the temperature of the water. The Atlantic waters where Matthew bred are one degree Celsius warmer this year along with all other global temperatures. And although our Republican governor, Rick Scott, was big on appearing on television alerting Floridians to the danger of the storm and requesting federal [federal!] help, he also refuses to accept that global warming is happening and even banned the Florida Department of Environmental Protection from using terms such as "climate change" and "global warming". Hey, Gov., you are the leader of the state considered most at risk for rising sea levels!

So, what about the climate, you ask? It is heating up faster and faster. The CO2 levels are rising faster and faster. The science has been well-settled for decades by scientists all over the world, including all the most authoritative American scientists and groups such as the National Academy of Sciences, not to mention the Intergovernmental Panel on Climate Change (IPCC0. The seas are rising and that is recognized by many different agencies, including the city government of Miami Beach and the federal government in its treatment of Ile de Jean Charles. Climate change and global warming are facts. We have poisoned our air so as to bring this on ourselves. We need to stop doing it. Will we? Will the rich and powerful let us? That is up to us. If not us, who? Only the massed votes of the American people can salvage a better result for our posterity.

Chapter 14

How About that Republican Platform?

You folks will recall that this book started with a look at the 2014 Libertarian platform. I described those folks as the enemy and I went into detail based on their platform. Since 1980 , the Republican Party has been shoved farther and farther to the right to the extent that it has been described as having been usurped by the far right. Is that true? I suggest that a reading of the 2016 Republican Party platform will answer that question definitively. I have read it repeatedly. I have analyzed it, annotated it and mused over it. I have also had to do battle with my sense of nausea as I did this. It is, to me, a sickening document. I will share with you why I say that. However, it is 58 pages long and I have annotated nearly every page of it. It would be cruel and unusual punishment for me to try to cover every one of those annotations with you patient readers, so I will not do that. The document is full of slurs on the Democratic Party and especially on Barack Obama, one of politics in America's finer voices and more grown-up people. It is full of accusations of failures by Obama that are, in fact, the result of the war on him by the Republican Party. These are, by and large, the sorts of things I am going to ignore in discussing this platform because I can see that I would just be accused of being biased as a left-wing Democrat, which

I actually am, although I have tried to prove in this book that my point of view is correct. There are many detailed points in this platform with which I disagree but will elide over because they are not important to the central issues. Nevertheless, I am going to go into some detail with this platform. Enough. Let's get on with it.

The document is labeled "Restoring the American Dream." It starts out with a heading of "Rebuilding the Economy and Creating Jobs." What this document, Donald Trump and the Republican candidates all over the map overlook deliberately is that the economy was driven into near collapse as a result of George W. Bush's Iraq war and the deregulation of Wall Street by the Republicans. Obama took office just in time to inherit the worst economic disaster since the great depression. And remember, there had not been such a disaster since the 1929 because Wall Street had been reined in by the government. Once it let go of the reins, depending on the good sense of the "free market", greed and crazy short-term profit taking in the housing finance market drove the whole enterprise off the cliff. Since Obama took over, the economy has climbed out of the hole. The stock market is booming. Millions of jobs have been created. The unemployment rate has plummeted. And in 2015 middle class income improved for the first time in years. The Republican Party believes it can convince Americans that we are in an economic disaster because of Obama and the Democrats just by saying so over and over again. And remember, the Dodd-Frank re-regulation legislation has been hamstrung by the Republicans to the point that we are beginning to see the same craziness in the housing market that set this all off in the first place.

Under "Our Tax Principles" in the platform, there is some drivel and a couple of very important points. The drivel includes a criticism of judges who "order higher taxes". That is simply silly. Judges don't and can't do that. I suspect they are talking about judicial approval of taxes that have come up some other way. They say that charities, religious organizations and fraternal benevolent societies should not be subject to taxation and donations to them should be tax deductible. That is silly because that is already the law. The hidden point is that they want to open all such organizations to being able to participate directly in political activity. That has long been forbidden and should be. That does not prevent such organizations from contributing to other organizations that can actively politic. That is what is happening now with all the dark money. We don't need to loosen these strings, we need to tighten them massively.

The important points here relate to the desire of the party to restructure the federal tax system. They don't say it, but it looks as though they are talking about a favorite idea of a flat tax. Under such a tax, the folks near the bottom lose a percentage of their income which they desperately need while those better off can lose that percentage and sail on without a care. They speak of the "hypertaxation" of the American people. The party has been trying to sell this bogus idea that Americans are the most taxed people in the world and it is a lie. It is not a fib. It is a lie. Look it up if you don't agree. The fact checking organizations have debunked it over and over again. It is true that our corporate tax rates are among the highest, but corporations have so many ways to reduce their taxes with deductions that the effective tax rate is much lower. So as not to shock you folks, I will let you know now that in the final chapter of this book I will be recommending ways out of the morass and that will include more taxes on those who can afford them to include the upper middle class (of which I deem myself a member).

Finally, the platform advocates the repeal of the sixteenth amendment – the amendment that legalized the income tax. Instead, they refer to a "value-added tax" or a national sales tax, which is six of one and half dozen of the other. These ideas are deadly. The federal government cannot sustain itself on a value-added tax or a national sales tax. That may very well be the way that the Republicans believe they can drastically downsize the government. That raises the question how they would pay for the defense department, which they propose to beef up. If it be by way of a national sales tax, beware. Sales taxes are regressive. Everyone pays them regardless of their income level. Admittedly poor people pay less of them because they can't afford to buy as much, but they still pay them out of what little they have. Further, because almost all states have sales taxes, the burden of regressive taxes will be doubly hard on the poor.

The platform says, under the heading "A Competitive America", that there needs to be a lowering of corporate taxes because they are a drag on the recovery of the economy. That is a great talking point, but it has never been proven and I say it ain't true After all, look at the stock market currently. In fact, what I say we need to do is keep taxing American companies that move their incorporation to other countries for tax avoidance. They can do this and they do it. If they couldn't get away with it, we would stop losing American jobs and tax revenues. Lowering corporate taxes is no panacea. Big corporations get away with all sorts of dodges to avoid taxes. What might make sense would be to lower taxes on small corporations and start-up corporations for a period of time. But remember this: lowering taxes is a Republican mantra and has been at least since the Reagan years and their approach to it has never helped anyone but the rich. This plank of the Republican platform is much like the Libertarian approach.

Under 'A Winning Trade Policy", the platform advocates "a worldwide multilateral agreement among nations committed to the principles of open markets, what has been called a 'Reagan Economic Zone", in which free trade will truly be fair trade for all concerned." The platform suggests that prior agreement (such as NAFTA, I suppose) have not been properly negotiated to protect American interests. They would do it right and protect American interests and sovereignty. Interestingly, they voted for the NAFTA treaty and they have controlled Congress for most of the last two decades. Such multilateral agreements are very difficult to negotiate and every nation is vying to "protect its own interests". Nevertheless, this platform plank is much like the Libertarian position and it is just as difficult to do as it has ever been. At heart what they want is the upper hand over other countries and an open door to compete in those countries without restraints they see in this country. That will benefit the big businesses and the rich, not the rest of us.

Next comes a section that I cannot adequately express my disgust for. It is labeled "Freeing Financial Markets." I quote:

Unfortunately, in response to the financial institutions crisis of 2008-2009, the Democratic-controlled Congress enacted the Wall Street Reform and Consumer Protection Act, otherwise known as Dodd-Frank. They did not let the crisis go to waste but used it as an excuse to establish unprecedented government control over the nation's financial markets. The consequences have been bad for everyone except federal regulators.

Rather than address the cause of the crisis – the government's own housing policies – the new law extended government control over the economy by creating new unaccountable bureaucracies. Predictably, central planning of our financial sector has not created jobs, it has killed them. It has not limited risks, it has created more. It has not encouraged economic growth, it has shacked it.

What utter garbage! How can they say such things with a straight face? Folks, the great recession was caused by financial institutions lending money for houses to people whom they knew or should have known, had they done any due diligence at all, did not qualify and then bundling the resulting mortgages into investment vehicles that large institutions such as Lehman Brothers poured money into until so many of the loans underlying those mortgages defaulted and the packages were exposed for what they were. A better regulated Wall Street would not have done that and it used to be better regulated until the Republicans deregulated it to the point of stupidity. Dodd-Frank did not reinstate all the prior regulatory protections and, as I have set forth, the Republicans have done everything they could to emasculate the bill and hamper it ever since. Thus, today, it is still possible for the same financial stupidity to occur and it does.

The platform goes on to say that Dodd-Frank has caused a loss of community banks and has helped contribute to the "slow economy we all endure today." Well, gee whiz. It is too bad that we now have the highest stock market performance in history. It is too bad that we have added millions of jobs. By the way, the platform says that community banks have fallen from 13,000 in 1985 to only 1900 today and that, I guess, is the fault of the Democrats. Does it matter to them that from 1985 to 1993 and from 2001 to 2009 Republican administrations were in power? How about the fact that during most of those years Republicans controlled Congress? How about the fact that deregulation of banking allowed interstate banking and the big banks have eaten up thousands of smaller banks?

The platform then attacks the Consumer Finance Protection Bureau, an entity created by Dodd-Frank specifically to protect consumers from predation by financial institutions and which the Republicans have been fighting ever since the legislation was enacted. They call this central planning of our economy. That, folks, is the language of socialism. Of course, nothing in the Dodd-Frank or any of the previous safeguards on the financial sector have anything to do with central planning of the economy. The government does *not* have control of the means of production nor does it tell business what to do with its money. Government only prohibits those practices by the financial sector which destabilize the economy or cheat investors. We the public need that protection. Just read one of their financial prospectuses and try to understand what the institutions are doing to you. Only government has a chance of keeping Wall Street less dishonest, not to say honest because they won't ever be that. This sort of big-business-friendly crap is what the Libertarians want to see.

Next, we get the section entitled “Responsible Homeownership and Rental Opportunities.” There is so much crap in it that I will ignore some of it. But, get this:

Our goal is to advance responsible homeownership while guarding against the abuses that led to the housing collapse. We must scale back the federal role in the housing market, promote responsibility on the part of borrowers and lenders, and avoid future taxpayer bailouts.

So much utter dreck is contained in those sentences. Their goal is to promote “responsible homeownership”. Hey, it was their buddies on Wall Street who caused this mess. They want them unbound to do it again. And look at the emphasis on the homeowners. Yes, it was homeowners who bought all those houses they couldn’t afford, but who told them they could afford it and bombarded them for years urging them to buy or refinance homes? It was the financial institutions. If we scale back federal regulation, it will happen again. In fact, if you have been paying attention to the advertising by lenders lately, it already is happening again. And with respect to taxpayer bailouts, those first happened on George W. Bush’s watch. Remember? Yes, Obama and the Democratically controlled Congress enacted legislation to help consumers, but the bailouts were necessitated by the excesses of the Bush administration in war and in finance. This position, however, is right in tune with the Libertarian approach that it is a *caveat emptor*, buyer beware world that they want.

They go on to attack the federally sponsored entities Fannie Mae and Freddie Mac as being responsible for the problems in the recession and also complains that they have been in conservatorship for nine years. Yes, nine years since the Republican caused disaster of 2008. There is no doubt that these two entities got crushed by the collapse and that they are of somewhat dubious operation. However, they were operating that way before 2008 under a Republican administration. The Republicans did it, but they are averse to owning up to their own failures and the plan is always to blame them on the Democrats. There is no question that Fannie Mae and Freddie Mac are exactly the sort of entities that the Libertarians would abolish, even though they do make it possible for those who need help to get a home. They also complain about the fair housing standards of Fannie Mae and Freddie Mac. This is, of course, in line with their (and Libertarians') desire to do away with the efforts of government to give minorities and disadvantaged people a hand - a position the Libertarians completely endorse.

The next section is entitled "America on the Move." I want to argue with all of it, but I need to move on. Thus, two quick points. They take credit for having "secured the longest reauthorization of the Highway Trust Fund in a decade." Then they bitch about the fact that some of its funds are used to help with urban mass transit. Maybe they did extend the Fund, but they haven't properly funded it for a long time. As to mass transit, that provision has been there through the Bush administration and during the last six years when they had partial or complete control of Congress. The second point is that they want to repeal the Davis-Bacon law. That was enacted in 1931 under a Republican president. It specifies that the government will pay "prevailing wages" on federal contracts of a value over $2,000. Well, heck, let's don't let anything that might benefit a laborer go uncut! If they hate it so much, why has it been law for so long under so many Republican administrations?

Skipping ahead, we come to the section entitled "Start-up Century: Small Business Entrepreneurship." The platform notes that more businesses are closing in this country than are opening. That is true. However, it has been going on for decades. It owes much to the monopolistic tendencies in our country that are not sufficiently restrained. How many small businesses, especially in rural areas, have been put out of operation by the siting of a new Wal-Mart store? How many even larger businesses such as Sports Authority have been squeezed out by larger businesses? How much have prior

Republican administrations done about the problem? They go on to decry over-regulation and Dodd-Frank for strangling business. You know, I have never seen a large scale study of the facts to support this mantra. Certainly Dodd-Frank hasn't had diddly to do with it. The answer they provide for this problem is that the country's "incubators of unconventional thinking" such as the National Labs (in the department of Energy, I suppose), the National Institutes of Health and NASA as well as the Defense Department have the potential to form partnerships with small businesses to create an American Star-Up Century. How cynical! They have been steadily cutting back funding for the Department of Energy, the National Institutes of Health and NASA. And then they say that these entities should be the motor for the "American Start-Up Century"! Have they been paying attention to their own people who want to do away with the Department of Energy or slash funding to NASA? Besides, isn't using the government to spur economic growth exactly what they swear they want to see stopped? Do they think we are stupid? Oh, and by the way, the Department of Defense? Who does business with it? Big business mostly. Beside which, they have cut its budget substantially with the sequester and now they are complaining about the cuts. Folks, even if they had not cut the budgets of these entities, they couldn't possibly employ enough small business contractors to spruce up a whole century – or even a year.

Under the rubric "Workplace Freedom for a 21st Century Workforce", the party makes clear its distaste for unions. They say their ambition to create jobs "impels us to challenge the anachronistic labor laws that limit worker' freedom and lock them into the workplace rules of their great-grandfathers." They want to do away with unions. They will claim that unions are not needed because in this enlightened time, employees don't need to be encouraged by government to organize in order to protect their rights. Well, it is sure true that labor unions are fading to a large extent. Let them go away wholly and see if the lack of their potential to affect the employers has any effect on how employees will be treated. Remember the West Virginia miners whose safety ought to sacrificed for higher wages according to West Virginia Republicans? This anti-union sentiment is a staple of the Libertarian Party, although it is a fairly standard position for Republicans for decades. This, however, is the first time I have seen them come out in favor of eliminating the labor laws

Along the lines of limiting the benefits or rights of workers, in the same section the party advocates the elimination of the federal minimum wage. After all, if employers could pay less, well, more people would be employed! The platform excuses this position by saying that it should be a state matter. If the states had handled it responsibly, there wouldn't be a federal minimum wage. And, the federal minimum wage of $7.25 is already below survival level as it is. As Reich says, slave labor is a full employment arrangement. This sanctimonious hiding behind the states' rights is nothing but a way to get rid of the minimum wage altogether which is a Libertarian position taken on by the Republicans.

Next, we get "A Federal Workforce Serving the People". In this short section, the Party complains about the non-cash benefits of the federal worker and promise to cut them as well as firing the federal employees who are bad workers, tax cheats and scammers. Now, you will note there is no mention of reducing their salaries. That would be because federal employees are paid less than their non-governmental equivalents. Where this "bad workers, tax cheats and scammers" thing came from they don't say. However, by that measure, we should get rid of quite a few *elected* officials whom we know fit that description. What we are really seeing here is the "smaller government" mantra that the Libertarians invented but the Republicans now love.

Then comes "Reducing the Federal Debt". I think every American believes this should be done. The Republicans want to do it by creating "a strong economy" and say that "spending restraint is a necessary component that must be vigorously pursued." Just how "a strong economy" is supposed to do this I suppose is by increasing our tax revenues. If they keep cutting taxes, how will the strong economy help? If any individual finds that she or he is in financial trouble, the usual approach to the problem is two-fold. One approach is, indeed, to spend less. The other is to find some way to increase income. Republicans strongly resist the second approach. They will not countenance raising taxes to increase income. In fact, Donald Trump claims he will cut the middle class tax rate 20% and the business tax rate from 35% to 15%. (This looks like the same cut for both, but the middle class cut is 20% of the rate and the business cut is 57% of the rate.) Such an approach would beggar the government. There wouldn't be enough left to pay the interest on the debt and fund the Defense Department. He would fund this, he says by eliminating the carried interest loophole. Much as I agree the loophole needs to go, the CBO estimates that will save $17 billion over a decade. Not much per year - $1.7 billion. Cutting taxes to the bone is not a long-time Republican position. It comes about as of the Reagan era and the drift to the right.

The platform's next section is entitled "A Rebirth of Constitutional Government." I guess that the previous Republican administrations and Congressional majorities have stood by while the Democrats acted unconstitutionally. Such nonsense. They say in this section that they want to "restrain executive lawlessness." I think that means they don't like the executive branch promulgating rules and regulations, even though that is exactly what it is supposed to do and it is done pursuant to laws enabling it. They also say that "forty-eight Democrats in Congress, for instance, voted to amend the Bill of Rights to give government officials control over political speech." I suppose they are talking about their right to dark money pursuant to *Citizens United.* They also claim that "Democrats in Congress have likewise proposed bills that would limit religious liberty, undermine property rights and eviscerate the Second Amendment." I think they believe that it is a constitutional right to deny someone access to goods and services based on religious bigotry. Somehow, that seems backward to me. It especially bothers me when they take the position that a clerk of court may refuse to issue a marriage license to a gay couple as an exercise of the religious liberty of the clerk. But, I digress. Actually, the Libertarians don't have this religious bigotry position. They are very open and accepting of all religious beliefs.

Under "The Judiciary we see some very disturbing material. It doesn't come from the rich right position. It comes from the religious right. The Libertarians, actually, don't have this hang-up. Take this sentence: "Only a Republican president will appoint judges who respect the rule of law expressed within the Constitution and the Declaration of Independence, including the inalienable right to life and the laws of nature *and nature's God* as did the late Justice Antonin Scalia. (Italics added) A couple of points. While I revere the Declaration of Independence, it is *not* part of the law of the land. Second, and this is only a forerunner of what is to come, we in this country are not under the laws of *nature's God.* Our ancestors came to this country to obtain freedom from governance by someone else's idea of what God's laws might be. They go on to say that they need the chance to have their party appoint up to five new Supreme Court justices. They want those justices to overturn the Roe, Obergefell and Obamacare cases. As you probably know, Roe upheld the right of women to seek abortions, Obergefell held that gay couples have the right to marry and, of course, the Obamacare cases upheld the constitutionality of the Affordable Care Act (Obamacare). Where is this desire to reverse *Roe* and *Obergefell* coming from? Again, the religious right. They want to impeach judges who rule against what they believe. In other words, they want to have veto power over the third branch of government. They say many other irritating things here, but tempus fugit.

Under "Defending Marriage against an Activist Judiciary" they say, among other things: "In *Obergefell,* five unelected lawyers robbed 320 million Americans of their legitimate constitutional authority to define marriage as the union on one man and one woman." There is so much wrong with this statement. First, those "unelected lawyers" were Supreme Court Justices duly appointed and affirmed by the US Senate. They were exercising their constitutional duty to rule on the case in question. Both the word "unelected" and the word 'lawyers" were deliberately pejorative. Mind you, two of those "unelected lawyers" were in the majority in the *Citizens United* case. It is craziness to suggest that the Congress has any business having power over the judiciary based on the substance of their decisions. Further, the Supreme Court, or any other court, can only exercise its jurisdiction on cases that are brought to them. No matter how much the justices may personally disagree with something going on in another branch of government or anywhere else in the country, they cannot do anything about it unless someone brings a case before them. So, what does "activist" even mean? Then, the 320 million Americans referred to didn't *have* a constitutional right to define marriage as a union between one man and one woman. That's what the court said and our system of government gives the power to make such decisions to the Court. Finally, just as an aside, polls at the time showed that a majority of Americans favored the gays having the right to marry. What this crap from the Republican Party shows is a scary adherence to a religious bent to their politics.

Under "The First Amendment: Religious Liberty", we get this, among much else:

Ongoing attempts to compel individuals, businesses and institutions of faith to transgress their beliefs are part of a misguided effort to undermine religion and drive it from the public square. As a result, many charitable religious institutions that have demonstrated great success in helping the needy have been barred from receiving government grants and contracts.

Government officials threaten religious colleges and universities with massive fines and seek to control their personnel decisions."

Now, most of this is not just bluster, it is lies. The control by government is all aimed at preventing the forcing of religious views on citizens by governments or by the contractors of government or those operating under government grant from doing that. The other arena has to do with the next subject

The platform calls for the repeal of the "Johnson Amendment". That amendment was proposed by Lyndon Johnson while a member of the House. It amended the tax code to prevent 501(c)(3) charitable institutions from engaging in campaign politics. The provision has been partially obviated by *Citizens United* which allows donations to someone who will get involved in political campaigns. The only "control" by the government has to do with tax exemptions. Anyone who doesn't want to abide by the restriction may certainly do as they please, but they will forfeit the tax exemption. That only seems right because all citizens are affected by these exemptions in that their taxes are affected and they may very well not share the views of the charitable institution. What the Republicans mean by religious freedom is the freedom to shove ones religion in the face of others with government help, especially if that religion happens to be some form of Christianity. The repeal of the Johnson Amendment would set loose the dogs of dark money in full force.

Yet another quote from this section:

Our First Amendment rights are not given to us by the government but are rights we inherently possess. The government cannot use subsequent amendments to limit First Amendment rights.

“Rights we inherently possess” sounds perilously like “God-given rights” doesn’t it? When it comes to political rights, which is what the Constitution grants, the Constitution is the source of those rights, not the government. The power to change the constitution is given to the people and they must vote on such amendments. Should they choose to vote to amend the Constitution, it is amended and the rights affected are affected, period. There is no such thing as an inherent right granted by the Constitution that cannot be affected by an amendment to the Constitution. If we start dealing with “God-given” rights, we will be in the fight of our lives among many religious views of God and His laws. Once again, we see the Republican Party playing with theocracy. The citizens of this country should not be confronted by a political party that wants to rule by the law of God. That is what is so desperately wrong in the Middle East today.

It gets worse:

We support the public display of the Ten Commandments as a reflection of our history and our country’s Judeo-Christian heritage and further affirm the rights of religious students to engage in voluntary prayer at public school events and to have equal access to school facilities.

No one in our government has ever kept any church or other religious organization from publicly posting their sentiments. The problem relates to the judge who posted the Ten Commandments at the cost of the state government in a courthouse. Many citizens and taxpayers of that jurisdiction were not Christians or Jews and they had no say in whether they wanted that religious sentiment mounted in their publicly funded place. This is the opposite of the freedom of religion. It speaks again to the affinity of the Republican Party to the evangelical right.

Next, we have the section entitled “The First Amendment: Constitutionally protected Free Speech”. This two-paragraph section has more gotchas in it than I would have believed until I saw it. First, they oppose requiring private organizations to publicly disclose their donors to the government. This despite the fact that the Supreme Court's reasoning for the *Citizens United* decision rested in part on the fact that the corporations and organizations they set loose to donate to campaigns would have to disclose their donors. Frankly, this thought is just one more evidence of the Republican love for dark money. They also want to raise the limits for political donations or repeal them altogether. Again, open the floodgates wider. They want to end the "Fairness doctrine" which is supposed to keep our media unbiased. They want the media to be just as biased as it wants to be. Given Fox News and the right wing radio phenomena, they pretty much have that now. What would it be like if all restraint were removed? They are against the forced funding of political candidates through union dues. They do truly hate unions. However, I think I agree that even in unions, the members should not have to support candidates they don't personally favor. Look here, I am actually agreeing with them on something.

Then we get: "The Second Amendment: Our Right to Keep and Bear Arms." The NRA is the source of this concern and if any single entity has more influence on the Republican Party, it could only be the Kochs. The Supreme Court has given the arms argument by the NRA many victories. However, the Court has said that some regulations of arms is permissible. The Republican platform says that they oppose "ill-conceived" laws that would restrict magazine capacity or ban the sale of the most popular and common modern rifle. Folks, there is no reason any civilian needs a magazine that can hold twenty or thirty rounds. That is the sort of capacity that allows massacres like the one at Pulse in Orlando. If one is hunting, and doesn't make a hit with one or two rounds, the prey is long gone. If one is target shooting, the need to reload after eight or ten rounds means nothing. The issue seems to be that if legislation bears on guns and restricts them in any way, it is a major assault on the Second Amendment. It is not and the Supreme Court has said that some regulation is permitted. Insofar as the "most popular and common modern rifle" is concerned, that is a euphemism for what is commonly known as "assault rifles" including such weapons (note the term) as AR15's and AK47's. These weapons were designed for the militaries of the US and the USSR to kill in combat and the AK47 has probably killed more people than any other single rifle in history, followed shortly thereafter by the military version of the AR15 – the M16. The only difference between the military versions of these weapons and the civilian versions is that the civilian versions are not (supposed to be) fully automatic, albeit, it is easy to convert the civilian versions so that they can be fired on full automatic. Why do we need to allow these weapons? The Second Amendment does not mandate it. Furthermore, look at the weapons favored by the mass murderers lately and you will see a preference for the assault weapon profile. Why? Because you can kill more people faster that way. We had these bans after Reagan was shot but they expired. We could have them again if the Congress had the guts to stand up to the NRA. It is clear the Republicans have no such guts nor do they want them. They would rather frighten gun owners with the fantasy that Democrats want to take away their weapons.

Next, they decry "frivolous lawsuits" against gun manufacturers and the "current Administration's illegal harassment of firearm dealers." They oppose federal registration of "law-abiding gun owners", registration of ammunition, and restoration of the ill-fated Clinton gun ban. You know, it is impossible to know at the time of purchase whether a gun purchaser is "law-abiding" or not. If there is no registration, there is no way at all to track down weapons that have been purchased.

Skipping ahead, we come to the section entitled: "The Fifth Amendment: Protecting Human Life. This is basically a straightforward anti-abortion screed. They include a ban on federal funds to Planned Parenthood or any other organization that provides or refers for abortions. Thus, although the

Supreme Court has ruled that women have a constitutional right to choice on this matter, they want to make it as hard as possible until they can somehow get *Roe v. Wade* overturned. I agree that they have every right to try to get *Roe* overturned, but their approach to defunding is an illegal effort to restrict a Constitutional right determined by the Court. Never forget that is what they are doing and they are cheered on by the evangelical right. This is once again an area where the conservative political right as a whole deviates from Libertarians who don't seem to have a dog in this fight. The platform calls for the appointment of judges who will "respect traditional family values". They will get their wish if enough of them are elected.

They are against "euthanasia and assisted suicide". With respect to non-consensual euthanasia, who could disagree? With respect to consensual euthanasia and assisted suicide, we already have both going on and assisted suicide is specifically legal in some states. Do states have rights or not? As far as consensual euthanasia is concerned, what is it that happens when a competent adult decides that if they are deemed terminal, they wish to have all life support measures discontinued and nothing but palliative care rendered? Isn't that a form of euthanasia? It goes on all the time everywhere in this country. This looks a lot like forcing the federal government's nose into very private personal decisions. I thought they were against that?

They are against partial birth abortions and against failing to provide care to infants born alive. You know what? I agree with them on this one as well. Others apparently do not. But it seems difficult to me to undertake to kill an infant who is alive and independently functioning. It sounds a lot like murder to me.

Under "The Fifth Amendment: Protecting Private Property" they say they are against "the taking of water rights and the taking of property by environmental regulations that destroy or diminish the property's value." This is one of many ways they seek to eviscerate the power of the government to regulate the environment. When the EPA makes rules about the damaging use of private property that affects the environment either locally or generally, that does limit or somewhat encumber the use of that property. If, for instance, the EPA requires emissions controls on automobiles, that causes the automakers to make a more expensive product. If the EPA rules that one may not dump certain substances into the waterways, that limits the use of the producing property. If the EPA bans the use of certain substances, that affects the businesses that produce or use those substances. (Think DDT) If the EPA bans the use of certain procedures to produce extractive materials, such as banning strip mining, that affects the value of the property for the purpose of extracting those materials. That, folks is the price we pay as a society in order to have a safer country and world. The Republicans don't want the environment protected by the federal government. They claim the free market will adjust and protect the greater interests. The fact that it never does that except under the lash doesn't seem to affect the Republican position. In this way, they are exactly aligned with the Libertarian Party.

Then we skip to: "The Tenth Amendment: Federalism as the Foundation of Personal Liberty". This is basically a condemnation of the federal government in relation to all their favorite peeves. This includes "bullying of state governments in matters relating to voter identification laws." I have already discussed the various ways the Republicans want to restrict voting. The use of federal regulation in such agencies as the Federal Elections Commission is the gist of this complaint. Well, gee, isn't that what the FEC is supposed to do? There is an item about "forced educational curricula" which puzzles me. Are they talking about, do you suppose, the restriction against forced religious education in institutions where federal support is provided? When they later say they want to permit public schools to offer an elective course in Bible study do they feel a little bit hypocritical? Naw. The federal government does not force education curricula and it should not.

They also decry federal government grants for "matters that should be the exclusive responsibility of the states." Recognize that there may be just the tiniest disagreement about what is the "exclusive responsibility of the states." In particular, they are against the requirement of matching funds by the states for some programs. The most significant by far of these is Medicaid. Look, states are not required to accept federal Medicaid funds, but if they do, they are required to match funds to some extent. How many Medicaid recipients (of whom there are tens of millions) are ready to give up the program or, more significantly, are able to give it up? Frankly, I agree that Medicaid is a klunky mess, but it needs central government direction or it will disappear at the state level. If we had a single-payer system, much of this could be streamlined. But simply turning funds over to the states without further requirements, as the Republicans would like to do in block grants will not help. As a resident of Florida, I can tell you that the state governments cannot be trusted to do the right thing.

I love the section on: "Honest elections and the Electoral College." They say that they oppose the "National Popular Vote Interstate Compact" and any other scheme to distort the procedures of the Electoral College." They go on to say: "An unconstitutional effort to impose National Popular Vote would be a grave threat to our federal system and a guarantee of corruption, as every ballot box in every state would offer a chance to steal the presidency." I will be damned if I know where this distrust of our voting system came from, but there is absolutely no evidence of any systematic corruption in the system. Furthermore, the bitch is not about corruption. The bitch is that the Electoral College allows situations over in which a presidential candidate wins the popular vote, sometimes by a large margin, but loses the election. (Sound familiar, Hillary? Ooh, look whose goat actually got gored.) This system was set up to help the less populous states have a more equal say in the presidential election. However, it also causes the election of presidents who receive fewer votes than their competitors and dilutes the votes of those in more populous states. The Republicans do better in those less populous states, so they don't want the system changed in any way, even if a majority of voters are disregarded by the system. Whatever your position is on this issue, just recognize the nature of the position of the Republican Party. It ain't about the voice of the people, it's about Republican power.

Under "Honest Elections and the Right to Vote", they go on and on about their claims concerning the right to vote, by which they mean the right to vote by their constituency and the right to limit the ease of voting for everyone else. Read it and you will see. I need to move on.

We come to a major section of the platform entitled "America's Natural Resources: Agriculture, Energy and the Environment." As you might expect, there is a strongly pro- right wing slant here which would be admired by the libertarians. Under "Abundant Harvests, they speak of "bogus science" in reference to the FDA. As in other areas, one suspects that the science that is bogus will be that of the right. Remember, the Republicans have so gutted the FDA's budget that it can't even perform a tithe of the inspections it should such that we have the huge numbers of food poisoning cases in this country. They oppose mandatory labeling of genetically modified food. Why? What harm can it do? Could it be that Monsanto objects? Complaining about the EPA and the Army Corps of Engineers, they say: "We must never allow federal agencies to seize control of state waters, watersheds, or groundwater. State waters, watersheds, and groundwater must be the purview of the sovereign states." (Sovereign so long as they agree with Republican views.) Now, the Corps of Engineers deals with navigable waters only. The EPA deals with issues that are of interstate importance or that have an impact on public health on a large scale. What this platform means by "state waters" is not stated, but would need to be. In fact, this is really just another complaint about the regulation of issues of national importance by a party other than theirs.

They complain about how long it took to enact the last Farm Bill and state that the delay was due to the Democrats' efforts to expand the provisions popularly known as food stamps. As we have already seen, the Democrats were fighting slashes in that program. However, slashing programs that benefit the poor is a Republican (and Libertarian) priority. They don't want to say that outright, however. Instead, they speak of the Democrats playing politics with farm security. Who gets the farm subsidies? Do any large corporations get them? You bet they do. If it goes to big business, it is for "farm security" and if it goes to the people, it is "welfare" and it is evil. Or, so they would have us believe. Yay Monsanto.

The next section of the Republican platform is one of my favorites, as might be expected from the title: "A New Era in Energy". They say, "Together, the people of America's energy sector provide us with power that is *clean,* affordable, secure and abundant." (Italics mine) I even agree with all of that but for the word "clean". It is manifestly *not* clean if by that we mean not harmful to the environment and the global climate. It is hard to see how they can say that with a straight face. That is especially true of the current (mid-October 2016, the heat of the Trump, Clinton campaign) advertisements talking about "clean" coal. This is the heart of the problem between the energy sector and those who decry global warming. This is what causes the right to slander the science of climate change and its practitioners. It doesn't need to be this way, but it is.

They go on to say, "…we support the opening of public lands and the outer continental shelf to exploration and responsible production, *even if these resources will not be immediately developed.*" (Italics mine) Why should we agree to that? Why should we chance another Deepwater Horizon or allow extraction on public lands even if we don't need it now? The only gainer here will be the energy companies. Until and unless they can show responsible use of these resources and responsible extraction of them, we should not. Further, they should not extract such resources from public lands or the outer continental shelf without a substantial payment to the government, because they expect to profit substantially from the energy sources they extract. However, allowing any further use of fossil fuels without a plan in place and under development to prevent the release of greenhouse gases, such thoughts should never even be entertained.

Next, we see a theme that owes more to libertarianism than any other political thought. They say: "Congress should give authority to state regulators to manage energy resources on federally controlled public lands within their respective borders." Federally held public lands belong to the entire country and its whole population. Such lands have been a part of the assets and posterity of all America. They made the development of the West possible. They remain a major asset of the country as a whole. I would no more trust Florida's state government with control of such assets than I would trust a private business with such control. Frankly, I believe that our present governor thinks he is still running a private business. (Note that his prior business, of which he was CEO at the time, was found to be overbilling Medicare and federal health programs by billions.)

They say that the Democratic Party's energy policy is "keep it in the ground." If you are paying attention to the Democratic Party's plans as set forth in Hillary and Tim's book, *Stronger Together,* they did *not* make any such claim or plan. Frankly, I think they were too timid in their approach to the energy sector, but they certainly don't say "keep it in the ground." What I think should be done is in the end of this book, but the Democratic Party does not have the position attributed to it. That statement is a scare tactic.

Next, we get this:

The Democratic Party does not understand that coal is an abundant, *clean,* affordable, reliable, domestic energy resource. Those who mine it and their families should be protected from the Democratic Party's radical anti-coal agenda. (Italics mine)

It is true that the Democratic Party does not understand that coal is "clean" because it is not. That it is essential for now is inarguable, but that it is clean with respect to CO2 emissions is a canard of the highest degree. There are answers to this problem, but they lie in technology that needs to be developed, not in lying about the problem and ignoring it. With respect to protecting the miners and their families, I would refer the reader back to the love affair of the legislature of West Virginia with a book advocating that miners should want higher salaries rather than safety. I would also remind the reader about the Republican position on unions such as the United Mine Workers. The Republicans care about the Kochs and ExxonMobil, their rhetoric to the contrary notwithstanding. Miners are not their concern.

They bitch that only three nuclear power plants have been permitted in the past three decades. Does it occur to them that in the past three decades, (1986-2016) we have had 14 years of Republican presidential administrations? Frankly, our present nuclear power plants are nearing the end of their lives. When that happens, you get a real mess, as we in Florida have reason to know. We also have the problem of dealing with spent fuel rods that will be viciously radioactive for millennia. I am not against nuclear power per se, but if we would get on the ball, we would not need it.

They complain that the government granted loan guarantees of $500 million to the solar energy company Solyndra that eventually went bankrupt. They say taxpayers will "not soon forget" that. Frankly, I doubt many remember it even now or ever knew it.. Furthermore, the government has subsidized energy production back to the inception of the oil business in the early twentieth century. Far more government money has been poured into the fossil fuel industry over the years than has been put into renewable energy sources. Even today there is a $5 billion subsidy of the fossil fuel industry by way of annual tax breaks. The industry says this is not a subsidy, but is needed for them to profitably develop new resources. Well, hell, the renewable energy industry needs the same. Further, if we pursue the data on the program that made the guarantee, we find that the Department of Energy loan program in question, is now turning a profit. That program was initiated by the George W. Bush administration in 2005. The Obama administration added the renewable energy component of the program in 2011. If it was OK for all other sources of energy, why not renewables? Further, it is inevitable that not every government program of that sort will end in success. If the program is making a profit, what is the bitch? If it was good enough for fossil fuel energy programs, why not renewables?

They oppose a carbon tax. Gee, no, really? In fact, in years past, they were for it, being worried something worse might come down the pike. But, I admit there are other approaches. They go on to urge that the private sector focus on the development of carbon capture and sequestration technology. You know what, I absolutely agree with this!! Imagine! But, it ain't going to happen unless there is a goad or a carrot. I support both as I will say later.

Next, we get their section entitled "Environmental Progress". This section is full of the Big Lie. It is so blatant, I really want to take it line by line, but I won't. Let me start with this: "We assert that private ownership has been the best guarantee of conscientious stewardship, while some of the worst instances of degradation have occurred under government control." I suppose it's not really a lie to say you believe this if you do, but the belief is stupid. The Deepwater Horizon incident is only the latest major evidence of this point. Then there was the Exxon Valdez in Alaska. Then there was the Love Canal. Then there were all the instances you find in *Dark Money.* Then there is the vicious, lying campaign against the science of global warming. We cannot trust private ownership to steward the general good. It isn't geared to it. Private business is geared to profit. Unless it is compelled to be a good steward, private business generally won't do it.

Even with the sanctions that exist, we still get these disasters. To eliminate the controls in place, we will get worse disasters. And unless we curb the increase of CO2 in our atmosphere, which is put there almost exclusively by private free market forces, our children and our posterity will pay the price. The idea, which is the main and favorite point of libertarians, that the free market will protect the general welfare, is brain dead. That is why the federal government was given the constitutional authority to see to the general welfare. No, folks, we cannot trust General Bullmoose – or the Kochs – to protect our world. They prove it to us over and over again.

The platform states that the environment is too important to be left to the "radical environmentalists". Given what has happened in Congress on global warming, I suggest that it is fair to say the environment is too important to the world and the American people to be left to those who spout the Big Lie that global warming is a "hoax." They go on to say that the "environmental establishment" has become a self-serving elite stuck in the mindset of the 1970's, subordinating the public's consensus to the goals of the Democratic Party. Folks, ask yourselves, what is in it for this "elite"? And, how did the recent "consensus" about global warming come about? There is no discernable profit to the climate scientists who say what their studies show. There is a major profit to the climate change deniers. They, in fact have funded the public relations campaign of lies that produced this evanescent "consensus." We are perilously close to being totally unable to deny the rising temperature of our world. And, *no one can deny the rapidly rising CO2 levels in our atmosphere.*

Next, we get the assertion that the environmentalists rely on "shoddy science, scare tactics, and centralized command-and-control regulation." Well, folks, read *Merchants of Doubt* ,*This Changes Everything* and *The Hockey Stick* as well as many of the other works I refer to in this book. The shoddy science comes from such places as the Heritage Foundation and non-peer-reviewed "scientific" journals. The real environmental scientists publish in peer-reviewed journals and share their science with others all over the world. This claim by the Republicans and the far right is another Big Lie. Do environmentalists depend on government regulation? Of course they do. Who else has the power to require that the activities in the market poisoning our world stop doing it if it is profitable?

They say:

We propose to shift responsibility for environmental regulation from the federal bureaucracy to the states and to transform the EPA into an independent bipartisan commission similar to the Nuclear Regulatory Commission, with structural safeguards against politicized Science.

Well, tell us, please Republicans, how would a state agency deal with regulating water or air pollution that comes from another state? How would it deal with CO2 emissions coming from across the whole country? That is why we have a federal government. With respect to this "politicized science", folks, we are being lied to big time here. It is the climate change deniers who use politicized science.

So, what would the Republicans do? They say:

We will enforce the original intent of the Clean Water Act, not its distortion by EPA regulations. We will likewise forbid the EPA to regulate carbon dioxide, something never envisioned when Congress passed the Clean Air Act. We will restore to Congress the authority to set the National Ambient Air Quality Standards and modernize the permitting process under the National Environmental Policy Act so it can no longer invite frivolous lawsuits, thwart sorely needed projects, kill jobs, and strangle growth.

Well, that's a mouthful. You know, the Supreme Court has ruled that the Clean Air Act *did* empower the EPA to control CO2 emissions. Further, Congress has never lost the authority to set standards. It has delegated that to the EPA because, like everything else that must be actually administered, environmental administration cannot be done by Congress. It cannot seem to do its own job, much less administer the country, which is, after all, the reason we have an executive branch to be the "administration".

They speak of improvements in the environment, which I agree have happened. These include the emissions controls on autos, the ozone hole problem, the acid rain problem, and a few other issues. But, you will note that industry fought every one of these improvements as hard as they could and poured senseless millions into fighting them. For the Republicans to now intimate that these happened as a result of voluntary or even industry-sponsored activities would be another major lie. All of it is overwhelming proof that without government regulation, the environment is a goner.

Then we get this:

Congress shall immediately pass universal legislation providing for a timely and orderly mechanism requiring the federal government to convey certain federally controlled public lands to states. We call upon all national and state leaders and representatives to exert their utmost power and influence to urge the transfer of those lands identified in the review process, to all willing states for the benefit of the states and the nation as a whole. The residents of state and local communities know best how to protect the land where they work and live.

Well, taking the last first, folks don't work and live on the lands we are talking about. Those lands are a part of the national heritage. We no longer live in a confederation and have not done so for centuries. For my part, I wouldn't trust the government of Florida with those lands. Our present state government in Florida would immediately sell them or rent them so that it could benefit buddies, "cut taxes" and turn our state parks into "profit centers". I am not talking about state property where the areas are uncontrolled and hunting is allowed, I am talking about parks. These areas already contribute by way of visitors and tourists who add to our state economy. Every time the state had a little budget problem, those lands would be fair game. I will say it again. Those federal lands are part of the assets of our whole nation. If more parks are needed, that can easily be done with the cooperation of states and the federal government. But to turn them over to the states would be a grave disservice to the nation as a whole. This is part of an attempt to minimize the federal government. It stinks of a libertarian motive.

Next comes this, which just enrages me because it is a fine example of the Big Lie in support of destroying the earth's environment so that the elite may prosper:

Information concerning a changing climate, especially projections into the long-range future, must be based on dispassionate analysis of hard data. We will enforce that standard throughout the executive branch, among civil servants and presidential appointees alike. The United Nations Intergovernmental Panel on Climate change is a political mechanism, not an unbiased scientific institution. Its unreliability is reflected in its intolerance toward scientists and others who dissent from its orthodoxy. We reject the agendas of both the Kyoto Protocol and the Paris agreement, which represent only the personal commitments of their signatories; no such agreement can be binding upon the United States until it is submitted to and ratified by the Senate.

To start with, I actually agree with the statement that prefaces this paragraph to the effect that projections of any sort at all by scientists must be based on hard data. The problem is that for the last thirty years, the data collected by climate scientists has accumulated and enlarged massively. As it has done so, it has debunked the favorite theories of the deniers concerning the medieval warm period and the many bogus "scientific" papers by deniers that are not peer reviewed and do not depend on any hard research data produced by those "scientists" – some of whom are anything but scientists – such as lawyers and lobbyists for the fossil fuel industries. If you read up on it, some of the scientists who complain that they were ignored were not, in fact, ignored. Their opinions and papers were reviewed. If you read *The Hockey Stick,* you will get a tutorial on the vast and continuing collection of data, construction and use of computer projections and, unfortunately, the ongoing evidence that the world is warming up and the CO2 content of our atmosphere is increasing rapidly. The IPCC is not a "political mechanism", it is a collection of hard scientists practicing in the area of climate research from all over the world. The, to borrow a word from Spiro Agnew, "nabobs" of denialism are political lackeys and hirelings. This plank of the platform alone should tell any intelligent person that the Republicans don't care whether the actions of the fossil fuel industry are damaging our planet's ecology so as to cause permanent and increasing catastrophe. Our nation's shamefully disregard of things like the Kyoto Protocol tells the world that we will do whatever we want even though the world as a whole will pay the price. I think that is enough, given that I have said so much already about the climate issue. The rest of the crap they spew about the environment in this section is just that - spew.

Under the major heading "Government Reform", the Big Lie continues. Under "Balancing the Budget", they contend that the Obama administration is responsible for increasing the national debt from $10 trillion to $19 trillion and it is true that it did increase to that extent. Overlooked is the fiscal catastrophe that the Bush administration left behind for Obama to clean up. They say the administration systematically crippled economic growth and job creation. This overlooks the fact that the Dow was at incredible highs during the last days of the Obama administration and that many millions of jobs had been created during Obama's years. But worst of all, they blame the government shutdowns on the administration. I have been at some pains in this book to show that the government shutdowns were the deliberate policy of the Republican Party as "leverage" to hold the operation of government at ransom to further their own agenda even when they couldn't enact that agenda legitimately. To see them blame the shutdowns on the administration is nauseatingly lying. Furthermore, the deficit has no chance of coming down unless the Republicans are willing to see some increases in tax income along with their constant cutbacks in funding.

They call for a constitutional amendment requiring a balanced budget. That sounds great, but the fact is that emergencies and wars come along regularly requiring spending that was not budgeted. It is unworkable and will put the government in a straitjacket that can only cripple its functioning. They also want an amendment requiring a super-majority vote in Congress for any tax increase. Given the cowardice of Congress to raise needed tax income as it is, imagine how impossible that provision would make governing. It would be beloved by libertarians, albeit they would consider it only a good first step.

They proceed to "Preserving Medicare and Medicaid". In this section they say they want to do this, but the devil, as usual, is in the details. They want to leave Medicare as it is for those 55 or older and then "Give others the option of traditional Medicare or transition to a premium-support model designed to strengthen patient choice, promote cost-saving competition among providers, and better guard against the fraud and abuse that now diverts billions of dollars every year away from patient care." Buried in this quoted language is privatization of Medicare by option (to begin with, anyway). What that does is enriches private insurers at the expense of the patient. Who among us has not had to fight tooth and nail with their health insurer over benefits as it is now?

They also want to set a "more realistic age for eligibility for Medicare in light of today's longer life span. Believe it or not, I agree with that need.

The system needs to be viable. On the other hand, I should say that I favor a single payer system for our whole population to do away with the great injustices of the present system.

They wish to avoid "cuts to Medicare providers." Look, we have already examined the problem with drug costs that occur because the government is not allowed to use its spending clout to get the best prices for drugs, which leads to Americans paying more for drugs than anyone else on earth. Let me give you a personal example as to hospital costs. Several years ago while I was still practicing law, I had a client who suffered an accident and went to an ER where he received CT scans of the neck, mid-back and low back. He was in the hospital three hours. The bill was $18,000. You have no doubt read about the ridiculous charges by hospitals all over the country. The same thing is going on with physician groups as they grow bigger and the shortage of doctors continues due to the incredible cost of a medical education. Why shouldn't the government use its spending power to seek and if necessary require more reasonable charges? The Republican answer is that it interferes with the incredible profits of these industries that are their supporters.

When it comes to Medicaid, they want to turn all control over to the states. They also piously point out that they "respect" the authority of the states to exclude abortion providers from their Medicaid programs. This is, of course, aimed particularly at Planned Parenthood, which offers those services among many others. Of note, this is a break with libertarianism in that the libertarians don't care about abortion, although they would object to the government paying for it along with everything else. This position by Republicans is a nod to the religious right which is not any part of libertarianism.

There is a very short paragraph entitled "Saving Social Security" in which they "accept responsibility" to preserve "and modernize" Social Security.

But, when it comes to spelling out how they would do that, they only say, "As Republicans, we oppose tax increases and believe in the power of markets to create wealth and to help secure the future of our Social Security system". The power of markets indeed. Here you see the privatized social security system writ large. Leave it to the workers and private markets to handle this. The fact that many people cannot do this is the very reason that Social Security exists in the first place. Who would benefit? The financial industries, that's who. We trust them don't we? Why isn't there more about this in the platform? Because they would have to admit that they don't have an answer that is acceptable to most citizens. The obvious first answer is to increase the limit of income on which Social Security taxes are levied to perhaps as much as $1 million annually. Those in this income level can afford it and they should pay for it. After all, they will be eligible for Social Security themselves. This position by the Republicans is one that libertarians would agree with ,although the libertarians would like to see the program abolished.

Under "Immigration and the Rule of Law" there is a blast at Obama and the position that they "stand with the victims of his [Obama's] policies, especially the families of murdered innocents." This is a Trumpian position, of course. Funny enough, you never get any figures on the number or proportion of aliens who murder. That is because the figures won't support the danger of these aliens as compared to our own citizens. They oppose any amnesty programs. This, of course, would leave us with the problem of many families with children born in the US who have never lived anywhere else being deported to a strange land, among other various human problems that would create. Here again they are at odds with the libertarians who have no problem with immigrants, but only because they would not want government involved in the problem. What this position does is put the platform in agreement with Trump's position, which I think is reasonable from the Party's perspective, even if not from mine.

The platform goes on at great length decrying the horrors of illegal immigrants and the need for a complete wall across our southern border. The one non-Trump plank is that they don't claim they will make Mexico pay for this wall. The fact that walls don't stop illegals from burrowing under, sailing around or flying over them doesn't seem to register. The only similar behavior I can think of would be the Korean DMZ and the Berlin Wall. That puts us in good company with North Korea and the USSR. It might also be of importance to consider that all of the horrors caused by the illegal drug trade including the drug cartels is a direct result of the great demand for those drugs in the US. If our own populace did not demand those drugs and pay outrageously for them, then the problem would not exist in the first place. This problem is a fine example of what truly "free" market will accomplish, no matter what damage it causes.

Perhaps more puzzling yet is that the platform calls for the Department of Homeland Security to use its "authority to keep illegal aliens off our streets and to expedite expulsion of criminal aliens." Note this is not directed to the Department of Immigration and Naturalization. So, what is being proposed is for the Department of Homeland Security to become a huge and pervasive national police force, which, as an executive body, would be under the direct control of the president. How we would pay for that is hard to imagine. How a governmental-adverse party could stand for it is beyond amazing. Here are true "jackboots." They also want any deported alien who returns sentenced as a felon. That will certainly do great things to our federal prisons (which are already overcrowded and too expensive).

Next they say: "…we urge the reform of our guest worker programs to eliminate fraud, improve efficiency and ensure they serve the national interest." Once again we are talking about executive functions – to which they are allegedly averse, except when it suits them. The goals stated sound great. Who should decide what substantively these "reforms" would consist of and what would make these reforms more efficient exactly? Shall we depend on President Trump for that "efficiency"? Folks, what this platform plank consists of is generalized junk that could lead to pogroms and national police like what happened in many totalitarian states. And this from the "small government" party! Enough of this subject.

Under "Internal Revenue Service" there is the hatred the Republican Party has exhibited for that agency. They call it toxic and say that it has become an "ideological attack dog". This refers to the attempt by the agency to audit new 503 (c)(5) and other entities pouring dark money into the system which did in fact have a tilt against conservative entities and which was rooted out. Remember that the only entity that lost its tax exemption was a liberal one. They then say:

We also support making the federal tax code so simple and easy to understand that the IRS becomes obsolete and can be abolished."

Yay libertarianism. The IRS not only administers the collection of taxes, but it enforces the tax laws. Who will do that when it is gone? The libertarians don't want the tax laws enforced at all. Folks, the government cannot survive without the IRS function, no matter what you call the entity that performs that function. And this country cannot exist without its federal government. Furthermore, the "simplified" tax code the Republicans want is a flat tax. Such a tax would be a pox upon all poor and middle class citizens and a boon to the rich. It is a regressive tax and anathema to the nation. And even such a tax would have to be collected and tax evaders would still have to be detected, caught and punished. The idea is still a pie-in-the-sky favorite of the right wing.

We skip to "Improving the Federal Workforce". It should be no surprise that they want to limit the extent of unions in the federal workforce. They don't want mere employees to have any method of redressing grievances with their federal employer. They then say:

We call for renewed efforts to reduce rather than expand government responsibilities, and we urge particular attention to the bloated public relations budgets of the departments and agencies. The federal government spends too much of the people's money telling them what they should do.

Mind you, these are the same people who just got done telling us how the Department of Homeland Security should become a national police force and the immigration rules should be made more "efficient" at getting rid of people who are deemed illegal aliens. As for the "public relations budgets" of governmental agencies, that would include, of course, the myriad publications by the government that tell us how Social Security works, that warn us about new disease problems like Zika, that tell us how to comply with tax collection and hundreds of other such efforts. Come on, now. The public relations budgets are no big deal in our federal budget.

Under "Regulation: the Quiet Tyranny" we get what one would expect. They decry the extent of regulatory power of the executive branch. You may be sure they will sing a different tune in the administration of every Republican president. They are just mad that Obama could use the regulatory authority to accomplish some environmental aims and they take no time at all to blast the EPA. All of this is vintage far right noise. They say one thing that astonishes me and (gasp) with which I agree. They advocate reinstating the Glass-Steagall Act of 1933 which prohibits banks from engaging in high-risk investment. This, of course, would give more power to the agencies involved in monitoring Wall Street! Do they now admit that Wall Street was involved in causing the great recession? Anyway, I agree with this odd plank.

Their section entitled "Crony Capitalism and Corporate Welfare" is an amazing example of the hypocrisy of this platform. They say: "When government uses taxpayer funding and resources to give special advantages to private companies, it distorts the free market and erodes public trust in our political system." Of course they specifically refer to Solyndra. What they don't discuss is the annual farm support bills that go a long way to prop up large agriculture businesses. They ignore the history of subsidizing the railroads in the past or the oil and gas subsidies that continue to this day. They overlook the billions being spent by the far right on lobbying for favorable treatment and getting it. They elide over the legislation prohibiting the Medicare system from seeking competitive prices for drugs, And so forth. The Republicans are the major party most involved in crony capitalism and corporate welfare and they don't appreciate it if anyone other than their pets gets a break from government. Don't be confused by the bluster.

The next major section of the platform is entitled "Great American Families, Education, Healthcare, and Criminal Justice". In that section under "American Values" is a bunch of blather about our great American values and how they have been corroded. They say, "For several generations, an expansive federal regime [regime!] has marginalized and supplanted the institutions holding our society together." Those several generations have included decades of Republican administrations and Republican control of Congress as well as Democratic ones. This statement is really just a condemnation of central government by any party.

Under "marriage, Family and Society" we get the expected paean for marriage only by one man and one woman and a determination to make the law require that. They say every child deserves a married mom and dad. They decry single parent families. They decry children being born out of wedlock. For some reason they think that having the law define marriage as the union of one man and one woman will solve these societal problems. Perhaps they have overlooked the fact that the law did define marriage the way they wanted for centuries and that didn't prevent the problems they identify. They seem to think that the solution to these issues is government intervention. Are they listening to themselves?

Under "A Culture of Hope", they decry our federal welfare programs and say that they want work requirements in such programs as Medicaid to avoid the "false compassion" of past welfare programs. The fact that many of the people on Medicaid are there because they are disabled doesn't seem to matter. The fact that many people at the bottom can't get jobs that would support them and their families doesn't matter. These people are the Republicans' despised "takers".

They say:

We call for removal of structural impediments which progressives throw in the path of poor people. Over-regulation of start-up enterprises, excessive licensing requirements, needless restrictions on formation of schools and day-care centers serving neighborhood families, and restrictions on providing public services in fields like transport and sanitation that close the door to all but a favored few. We will continue our fight for school choice until all parents can find good, safe schools for their children.

They use the cant of over-regulation but they don't tell us what they are talking about. Are they talking about public safety regulation? Are they talking about usury laws? Are they talking about the requirement that private schools teach the basics of science, mathematics, language and history? What transport and sanitation regulations are they talking about? Should we not have safety, educational standards, usury laws and other public protections? And, by the way, much of this is aimed at the requirements for private schooling, which they want to foster to allow the private school industry to proliferate. What we get from that is lousy private schools for those who are poor which are unregulated and do nothing to improve education as we have seen in the proliferation of private for-profit schools to date.

Then we get to the heart of the evangelical republicanism: "To protect religious liberty we will ensure that faith-based institutions, especially those that are vital parts of underserved neighborhoods, do not face discrimination by government." What they are talking about they do not say. They seem to say that government may not regulate activities of "faith-based" organizations whether they affect the public welfare or not. While this seems particularly well aimed at private schools, it may well be aimed at religious hospital efforts, drug rehabilitation efforts, adoption efforts and similar activities. Should these be allowed to go unregulated? Do we trust these groups to do the right thing without any oversight? If we do, then why have oversight of these activities at all? Hell no.

Then we have: "Education: A Chance for Every Child." They say:

Parents are a child's first and foremost educators, and have primary responsibility for the education of their children. Parents have a right to direct their children's education, care and upbringing. We support a constitutional amendment to protect that right from interference by states, the federal government, or international bodies such as the United Nations."

There is so much buried in this language. First off, if no government can "interfere" in the education of children, then compulsory education is history. Will all parents undertake this obligation in a "responsible" way? Of course not. If the parents can direct the education of their children can any public school system avoid anarchy as it tries to educate the society's children while each child's parents can interfere in the administration of that education? Should the government allow each child to be taught any religion's theories including young earth, Christian Scientism, the darker aspects of Islam and any other "education" the parents want regardless of whether it is part of the curriculum? That is, at heart, both a libertarian approach (which does not want the government to pay for schooling) and a religious right approach (which does not want its children taught science if it conflicts with their religious doctrine). This is no way for this nation to forge into the twenty-first century and beyond,

Next we come to the part of the Republican platform that I cannot believe is there except when I am looking right at it. It goes like this:

A good understanding of the Bible being indispensable for the development of an educated citizenry, we encourage state legislatures to offer the Bible in a literature curriculum as an elective in America's high schools.

The Bible has no business in a political platform. This country was founded on the basis of the freedom of religion. When one major party declares a bias for the Christian religion and wants that bias enacted into law, it flies in the face of the freedom of every citizen to make his or her own choices about religion. I have no problem with offering an elective in high schools that teaches the substance and history of religion, but if it is to be done, then most of the major religions, at the very least, must be part of that study. When the state chooses only to teach the Bible at public expense, that state is endorsing one religion to the exclusion of all others. It is spending public money on a study that many citizens do not agree with and do not want their money spent on. This may well be the scariest thing in this incredibly tone-deaf platform. Yes, it is useful in a majority Christian nation to know something about Christianity, but not more so than to know about Judaism, Islam, Buddhism, Taoism, Hinduism, etc. To suggest to naïve high school students that the only religion that matters is Christianity is repugnant to the fundamental precepts on which this country was founded.

In the same section, there is, of course, an English First endorsement for schools, which doesn't surprise me nor does it really bother me, although it does seem rather xenophobic. But in that same paragraph, we get this:

We renew our call for replacing family planning programs for teens with sexual risk avoidance education that sets abstinence until marriage as the responsible and respected standard of behavior. That approach - the only one always effective against premarital pregnancy and sexually-transmitted disease – empowers teens to achieve optimal health outcomes.

Have they noticed that the abstinence approach does not work? Teens will not adhere to it on a universal basis and the ones who do not, need to know how to best prevent pregnancy and disease if one is going to engage in sexual activity. They want to prevent the teaching of those measures and force the only approach to be abstinence which a certain proportion of our youth absolutely will not do and that is the reason that family planning programs were created in the first place. This is another plank from the religious right asking for what cannot work.

The following section is about Title IX, the sexual nondiscrimination legislation applying to colleges and universities. Therein they abjure the interpretation of sexual discrimination as including discrimination based on sexual orientation "or other categories". I guess they think it would be OK to discriminate against gays, lesbians and transgender people. Their plank is repulsive and only tells us that the bias and xenophobia that seems to be a Republican standard is in fact such a standard. They don't mind prejudice against some minorities, apparently.

Under college costs we see the bias toward private schools that is producing the plethora of diploma mills we are already suffering with. They say, "...states should be empowered to allow a wide array of accrediting and credentialing bodies to operate." Funny thing, states can already do that. The problem is that the federal government will only recognize a few proven outfits. That relates only to federal issues such as funding and grants from the federal government. Folks, if every private fly-by-night accrediting agency is allowed, there will be no standards in education at all.

The diploma mills will reign supreme. Any accreditation agency that really does a good job should, of course, be given room at the table. However, there is no reason that the federal government can't set its own standards when doling out federal money. What they want is the right to turn all higher education into a private school mecca wherein the poor behavior we have already seen in such schools as set forth earlier in this book will be the norm. We won't get education out of that, we will get scams.

The next section is entitled, "Restoring Patient Control and Preserving Quality in Healthcare." This is the section dealing with the Affordable Care Act (Obamacare). Almost everything they say about it is untrue. It does not, for instance, impose a "Euro-style bureaucracy" to manage its "unworkable, budget-busting, conflicting provisions." Under the Affordable Care Act (ACA), twenty million people have health insurance who didn't before. We got rid of the pre-existing conditions disqualifications. The Congressional Budget Office has said repeatedly that the ACA will not "bust the budget". It is certainly true that prices in the program are going up recently. Check out what is happening to the prices of non-ACA health insurance. Does anyone remember that health insurance costs have been going through the roof for decades? There is no doubt that the ACA is a kludge. It can certainly be improved. However, what we really need is affordable protection for all of our citizens. Even the ACA cannot provide that, so millions of Americans do not have health insurance because they can't afford it and they also obviously cannot afford the price of medical care itself. They are the ones who clog our emergency rooms where they are treated regardless of their ability to pay and the rest of us bear the burden of that care anyway. Even that approach by the uninsured is a poor one because many people will not go to a hospital and others just ignore their health until that kills them.

The platform says they want to "… recover the traditional patient-physician relationship based on mutual trust…." That would be like what happens now in our HMO's? That is the private health care system we have today. Is there a person reading this sentence who has not been screwed in one way or another by the HMO mentality? Our (private) insurance companies think they know better than our physicians what medical care we need. In my case, my insurer (Humana) has refused to pay for blood tests ordered by my physician as part of an annual checkup and refused to pay for blood tests ordered to help diagnose a neurological problem when those tests were ordered to try to avoid (successfully) more expensive tests. I think that is typical. *That* is what the free market gives us for the traditional patient-physician relationship.

There is a lot of blather in here that is infuriating, but I need to get moving on. I will just cite to one other prize specimen: "We believe that individuals with preexisting conditions *who maintain continuous coverage* (my italics) should be protected from discrimination." How nice of them. Do they know that most breaks in coverage are the result of financial inability to keep continuous coverage? Someone who loses his or her job and cannot immediately pay for coverage extension from their employer will have a break. Those who fall on hard times and can't pay for health insurance but who then regain that ability will have a "break" in coverage. These are exactly the problems that the preexisting condition exclusion applies to and the pious statement by the Republican platform about this issue is the insurance company position that will throw people out of coverage just like it happened before the ACA. In other words, the Republicans believe in the sanctity of the preexisting conditions exclusion.

The section "Protecting Individual Conscience in Healthcare" sets forth expected biases. They support not forcing health care professionals "...to choose between following their faith and practicing their profession." Now, it seems to me that any health care professional is perfectly within his or her rights now to refuse to provide medical care he or she believes is immoral or sinful. However, when they make that choice, they need to let the patient know what they are doing and give the patient references to other providers who can provide the care. And there are and should be some limits. For instance, a health care provider is not free to tell someone seeking birth control options that there is no such thing or tell them that it doesn't work. Lying to the patient is not and must not be an acceptable approach to dealing with the provider's own faith beliefs. Naturally, they oppose any federal spending on health care providers for abortions. Thus, the poor will not have access to the right to choose because they won't be able to afford it if this is the rule. That is, of course, what they want to happen. This way only those who can't afford a new child will have no option but to have one.

Under "Better Care and Lower Costs: Tort Reform", they want state and federal legislation to cap non-economic damages in medical malpractice lawsuits on the theory that these suits are drastically affecting the cost of health care. Experience in California and Texas which have had such legislation does not bear that out. Furthermore, in Florida (where I defended doctors and hospitals in malpractice suits for decades), the frequency of such suits has declined substantially for reasons not clear to anyone.

Under 'Advancing Research and Development in Healthcare" they laud recent advances in medicine such as MRI's and CAT scans as well as other developments. They say:

This is the consequence of marrying significant investment, both public and private, with the world's best talent, a formula that has for a century given the American people the world's best healthcare."

Well, first off, they are the ones who have been consistently cutting the budgets of the NIH and the CDC which have been active in creating the advances the party is bragging about. Second, the MRI and the CAT scan are among the developments in question, the development of which owed a large degree of enablement from the federal government. Finally, the US *does not have and has not for many years had* the world's best health care.

(See prior coverage of this issue in this book.) We certainly do have some cutting edge research going on, but it is not "trickling down" into our health care system adequately or affordably and things like an Ebola vaccine which could already be in our arsenal are not because of the cuts to the CDC's budget by Republicans. Their pious concerns are so much hot air.

Next we get; 'Putting Patients First: Reforming the FDA." They are bitching about how long it takes for the FDA to approve a new drug. Guess who wants the system "streamlined"? Could it be big Pharma? Actually, it is possible that the system could be improved. However, there have been drugs that were approved and then turned out to be a bad idea. A balance has to be struck. As for the rest, they are just bitching about the "burden of government regulation". Folks, those regulations help protect our safety. And the reference by the platform to returning the FDA to "hard science" is another call to the quacks who support the industries opposition to the FDA and the EPA among others. The agencies have the hard science, not the Republican Party and its donors. On the other hand, I actually agree with their call for "right to try" legislation allowing terminal patients the right to try experimental treatments.

Skipping to "Securing Safe Neighborhoods: Criminal Justice and Prison Reform." There is some vicious language here with a threat to prosecute Department of Justice personnel who "have violated their oath of office." This is a very dangerous approach. They will not only refuse to cooperate with Democrats in governing the country, they will undertake to prosecute those they disagree with. Very Trumpian of them. The peaceful transition of power in this country is in peril with this crap.

They say: "The power of career civil servants and political appointees to criminalize behavior is one of the worst violations of constitutional order perpetrated by the administrative state." This is just stupid. Yes, there are regulations that create unlawful behavior definitions and set penalties, most of them fines. That is how the law is actually carried out by the administration (any party's administration). And how do they think they would set up their Homeland Security police force without such regulation? What it amounts to is they disapprove of administrative regulations when a Democratic administration sets them and not when they do it. Don't be confused.

Speaking of stupid, try this: "We call for mens rea elements in the definition of any new crimes to protect Americans who, in violating a law, act unknowingly or without criminal intent." So, from now on new crimes can be defended by "I didn't know it was illegal" or "I didn't know that would be the result of what I did". Baloney! Speaking as one who prosecuted people in the Army JAG Corps, I can tell you that this is just crap some politico dreamed up because it sounded good. Fortunately, platforms are not laws.

They favor mandatory minimum sentencing and want any deviations from those sentences to take place in only a very small category of cases. Folks, our prisons are breeding grounds of recidivism. Further, as I have said before, we have a larger proportion of our populace behind bars than any other first world country. Anyone who has studied this closely will tell you that the mandatory minimum sentencing approach is a blunt force object preventing judges from using their good judgment with respect to individual defendants. The mandatory minimum sentencing approach has also put a disproportionate number of blacks is prison, contributing to the racial unrest in this country.

They say: "Public officials must regain control of their correctional institutions, some of which have become ethnic and racial battlegrounds." Really, Sherlock? Do they know why this is happening? In almost every jurisdiction in America, the budgets of prisons have been cut and cut. In Florida, we have a number of privately administered prisons which are just leaky hell-holes. Between sending more folks to prison with mandatory minimum sentencing and cutting prison budgets, a crisis is coming. Besides which, if we were honest about it, when we send someone to a penitentiary, we should tell them that they are sentenced to so many years of being abused and battered by their fellow inmates and to repeated rape in many cases. And that doesn't even count the lousy health care, the crappy food and the abuse by the correctional officers. Look, Republicans, you can't send more and more people to prisons while cutting the prison budgets and expect a good result. The problem is your fault.

The next major section of the platform is called: "America Resurgent." It starts with a section entitled, "A Dangerous World". Of course, it begins by claiming that the world is more dangerous for America because of the Obama administration. I violently disagree, but that is a matter of perspective and I don't intend to try to defend Obama. It would take too long. They say:

We are the party of peace through strength. We believe that American exceptionalism - the notion that our ideas and principles as a nation give us a unique place of moral leadership in the world – requires the United States to retake its natural position as a leader of the free world. (Not working very well is it, Mr. Trump?)

We Americans suffer from a very inflated sense of our own probity and power. We still are the premier military power in the world. We will continue to be that for a long time. However, our place as the premier military, industrial and economic power of the world was bound to be reduced as the world recovered from World War II. Further, the morality of what we do needs to be considered carefully. What we did to Vietnam and especially to Laos and Cambodia during the Vietnam War is almost totally unforgivable. What we have done in Central and South America over the years is hard to read about. I suggest that those who are interested read Noam Chomsky's book *Who Rules the World?* We have no particular moral right to rule the world. Further, we can't afford to do it. The platform's call to "rebuilding the U. S. military into the strongest on earth, with vast superiority over any other nation or group of nations in the world" deliberately ignores the fact that we are already the preeminent military force on earth and we already spend more on our armed forces than any other nation or group of nations on earth. What they are suggesting, including their recommendation that we beef up development of our nuclear ballistic missiles and our "Midcourse Defense system" would cost an incredible amount of money. That sum would drastically inflate our national debt unless, of course, we stop spending money on all the programs that directly benefit our own citizens. And, by the way, does anyone remember the "Strategic Defense Initiative", Reagan's anti-missile system? We didn't have the technology then to intercept a ballistic missile in flight and we don't have it today. And their blaming defense cutbacks on Obama will not fly. They forced the sequester and they can't live with it, so will blame Obama.

Under "Confronting the Dangers", they say, among other things, that we need a "Reagan-era" military that can "...fight and win two-and-a-half wars ranging from counterterrorism to deterring major power aggressors." Look, we haven't won a war since WWII. We aren't going to "win" guerrilla wars or terrorism wars. We are going to be fortunate if we can suppress this type of "war". They also call for a ramp-up in border protection which goes along with their Homeland Security Police" as well as harking to Trump's position.

Under "Supporting Our Troops: Standing by Our Heroes", they reiterate their intent to pour money into the military. They don't talk about how they intend to pay for all this, but you can bet they want to take it from the domestic budget and from the poor and disadvantaged. But what blows my mind is this:

We support the rights of conscience of military chaplains of all faiths to practice their faith free of political interference. We reject attempts by the Obama Administration to censure and silence them, particularly Christians and Christian chaplains. We support an increase in the size of the Chaplain Corps. A Republican commander-in-chief will protect the religious freedom of all military members, especially chaplains, and will not tolerate attempts to ban Bibles or religious symbols from military facilities.

What? "Particularly Christians and Christian chaplains"? What the hell is this about? Did someone on a military base put up a big crucifix on a building or something that led to this? And why "particularly Christians'? Once again the "freedom of religion" contemplated by the Republican Party seems to mostly mean the freedom of Christians to be first and foremost in religion while others come after and only if it doesn't inconvenience any Christian consideration. I absolutely do not believe the Obama administration banned Bibles from military facilities or religious symbols, although I could believe that it might have banned religious symbols outside buildings, especially in the Middle East battle areas where those symbols, particularly Christian ones, could cause those areas to become targets. Come on, guys, a little reality here wouldn't hurt would it?

The Republicans want to reinstate the exemption of women soldiers from direct ground combat units and infantry battalions. They claim that the inclusion of women in combat units by the Obama administration was an imposition by the White House on military cohesion. You know, they still see women as inferior beings who need to be protected by them regardless of the women's wishes. There are no units in our military in which women are forced into a combat role. It only happens by the choice of the woman and only if she can qualify for it just as men must do. Yes, it does introduce sexual issues into those units, but the women who are there chose to be there and as time goes by, they will not be unusual in such units which will help the problem.

Under "Honoring and Supporting Our Veterans: A Sacred Obligation", they have a lot of fluff. Ask them who has been in charge of funding the Veteran's Administration.

In the section "U. S. Leadership in the Asian Pacific" (yes, I skipped ahead), they suggest that China is aggressively pushing into the South China Sea and building a navy far out of proportion to defensive purposes. Hey, guys? The Republic of China is a nation of well over a billion people with one of the most dynamic economies in the world. The South *China* Sea didn't get named that by accident. Are we the only nation allowed to have a military larger than needed for defensive purposes? And who decides that the Chinese military is that big? China will push, at least in Asia. What would we think if they were setting up bases in Cuba and Central America? That's what we have done to them, especially in Taiwan, which by everything I can learn, does not want us there anymore. We don't own the world. Get used to it.

Next we get, "Family of the Americas". I think the intentions of the Republican Party are well limned here. Basically, they feel we have the right to dictate to the nations of Central and South America what form of government they will have. Consider this:

A Republican president will never embrace a Marxist dictator, in Venezuela or anywhere else. The current chief executive has *allowed* that country to become a narco-terrorist state, an Iranian outpost threatening Central America, and a safe haven for the agents of Hezbollah." (Italics mine)

Allowed? Obama "allowed" this? Even if we accept that this description of Venezuela is correct, which is open to question, what right did the US have to interfere in the Venezuelan government? For that matter, what right do we have to interfere in the government of Cuba? Interfering in the governments of our hemispheric neighbors is a sin we have committed time after time. The government of Juan Peron, for instance is stark evidence of the unwisdom of our doing that. People, the US government has no business telling other countries how to govern themselves. Our many missteps in that regard have killed millions of people. We need to stop.

Next, we get "Sovereign American Leadership in International Organizations." As you might expect, there is a severe condemnation of the United Nations (which we were a prime mover in creating). I especially like this language:

We do not support the U. N. Convention on Women's Rights, the Convention on the Rights of the Child, the Convention on the rights of persons with Disabilities and the U.N. Arms Trade Treaty, as well as various declarations of the U.N. Conference on Environment and Development. Because of our concern for American sovereignty, domestic management of our fisheries, and our country's long-term energy needs, we have deep reservations about the regulatory, legal and tax regimes inherent in the Law of the Sea Treaty.

It is interesting, is it not, that they especially dislike conventions protecting women, children, and persons with disabilities. They have "deep reservations" about the Law of the Sea Treaty which has been around for a while. One of their concerns is our long-term energy needs. Look, if they would just go with renewable energy that would not be a problem. We have plenty of fossil fuels in the ground and on the continental shelves to last us until we make a complete transition to renewables. But, as we know, the fossil fuel industry owns the Republicans lock, stock and barrel. (And barrel?? Oops.)

They also do not accept the jurisdiction of the International Criminal Court. I understand that because they don't want it trying our military members for war crimes (even if we did it). I kind of understand that as one who went to fight in Vietnam. Hey, I even volunteered – I was Special Forces. I'm glad I can't be tried for it.

They have a section entitled "Defending International Religious Freedom." They propose to protect religious freedom in, among other areas, the Middle East. Hey, ISIS, big brother America disapproves of your depriving people of religious rights by killing them. Come on, people, religion is at the center of the fighting over there , although power is the real motivator – power for one or another religion or sect. We can't possibly enforce religious freedom in international affairs and we should not try. We will only make of ourselves a greater pariah than we already are.

Thus, the Republican Party platform for 2016. Many of its precepts are aimed at the betterment of the "free market", meaning their big money sponsors. That part would make the Libertarian Party proud. Part of it will warm the cockles of the religious right. Part of it is just scary such as the Homeland Security police force on immigrants and the drum beating to upgrade our nuclear weapons. Much of its criticism of the administration of Obama and the Democrats is a Big Lie, blaming on their opponents what they themselves have done such as shut down the government and force the sequester. All of it is clearly indifferent or hostile to the domestic needs of our own people. Much of it is clearly calling for things which cannot be done and would not work if it were done. I admit that it is, after all, a political document. Nevertheless, any thinking person armed with the facts can only see this platform and despair for the American people that a major party could be that dense and combative with its opposition. For me, this platform inspires fear and loathing.

Chapter 15

The Catastrophe of November 8, 2016

As I stated in the foreword, I don't intend to try to analyze why the presidential election turned out the way it did nor do I intend to try to detail my detestation of our new president. It has astonished me that so many apparently intelligent and kindly people, some of whom I even know, were able to justify voting for the spoiled child in the white house. I try to tell myself that there is something there that I don't see or understand. Unfortunately, I haven't been able to sell that to myself. However, for the purposes of this book, I will not be focusing on the personal shortcomings of Mr. Trump, although they are many and I am tempted to write a separate book on the topic. The issue I will deal with here briefly is how the present administration will affect the dominance of the far-right wing and what that means to the many issues that I have covered thus far.

As I am sure we all remember, Mr. Trump campaigned as a friend of the middle class and promised that his administration would provide relief to the overlooked Americans. There would be cheaper and better health insurance, there would be safety in our cities from criminal elements of the immigrants and undocumented aliens in our midst. The economic inequality of our society would be addressed. And, he would "never, never let you down". (Of course, he also said he would never, never lie to us, but that is a different issue.) For so many of us to believe these promises is amazing to me. He is, after all, a billionaire and his view of society from the vantage point of the lifelong rich person is now proving, as it always should have been expected to do, to be far removed from the one the rest of us have. I fear that the real reason he was so popular with so many people was his bloviating about "making America great again" and what that seemed and seems to mean. Many of us who are older, including my generation and the baby boomers remember a time when America bestrode the world as the unquestioned premiere world power with a burgeoning (white) middle class in which we were all doing better and better. There is no question that vast numbers of us white, middle and upper middle class whites voted for Mr. Trump because of his promise to treat the world as though we owned it and to expel the "criminal" alien elements among us. The not-so-hidden xenophobia of Mr. Trump's blather was, I fear, another selling point to those of us white middle class and upper middle class folks who voted for him.

Unfortunately for the fond memories of those of us who believed in Trump's "great America" of the past is that it was always a mirage. We bestrode the world in the late 1940's and the1950's because the rest of the advanced nations lay in ruins from war while we simply became stronger in our safety across the oceans. What we don't now remember clearly is the Korean War, the development of the hydrogen bomb by the USSR and being taught to get under our desks at school in case of a nuclear attack (as though that would matter). We don't remember the House Un-American Activities Committee and Representative Joe McCarthy. We don't remember the terrible turmoil of the 60's with the war we clearly lost in Vietnam and the riots in our cities. We don't remember stagflation in the seventies and the Ayatollah Khomeini. We don't remember the Japanese wiping out our lead in the auto industry in the 70's. We don't remember that the years in question were far kinder to us than to the blacks, the poor and other minorities. The "greatness" we remember is a chimera that has a much rosier cast in retrospect than it ever possessed in real life. Thus, I fear that all too many of us who voted for Trump were voting out of xenophobia and jingoism than I would like to believe.

So far (I am writing this in late March, 2017) it appears that those of us who are "Trumpies" and those of us who are not cannot conduct sober and polite dialogue on the subject of Mr. Trump and hos policies. Over time, I hope we will be able to do so. In the meantime, however, I firmly believe that Mr. Trump is the most devastatingly bad thing to happen to the US since World War II or perhaps even the Civil War. So, let me set forth on this very short exposition concerning Trump's effect on the American society. To be clear about it, however, I will not address the influence of Russia on our election, the inability of our president to recognize the truth or to care about it, the temper tantrums and self-centeredness of the man, not the hatred he spews toward anyone or anything that contradicts his view of the world or his own ego. I will not address Mr. Trump's infantile behavior nor the jingoism and xenophobia he fosters. That is all for another time and place.

It is fair, I think, even at this early stage to conclude that Mr. Trump belongs heart and soul to the far right. If there were no other indicator of that than the appointment of Steve Bannon, former executive with Breitbart News and big proponent of the so called "alt-right" as chief White House strategist on a par with his chief of staff, that would be enough in itself. If you examine the online materials about the alt-right, you cannot help recognizing that, despite their arrogant belief that they are smarter than the rest of us (and many of them are), they still belong to the far right; they are just a different and scarier flavor of that end of the spectrum. The president's appointment of Bannon to the Security Council and dismissing of the chairman of the Joint Chiefs of Staff and the Director of National Intelligence from that body should give us all shivers. Bannon wants the regulatory side of government dismantled. This is a paean to the song of the Kochs. Bannon may be, and I am far from the first person to say this, the most dangerous man in the world today. That we elected as president a man who wants to take his advice on governing from this right wing crazy is terrifying to me.

Let me just touch on a few points and then get on with this book as I originally planned it in ignorance of the new "president". First let's talk about his cabinet. He has appointed many billionaires and millionaires to his cabinet. He has appointed some people to head agencies and departments who clearly want to destroy those entities. He has appointed people to positions who have dubious ties to foreign powers. And, he has nominated a judge to the Supreme Court who is a clear right wing conservative. In Judge Gorsuch's defense, however, much as I dislike his conservative and religious views, he is a consummate jurist and I could not in conscience vote against him if I were on the Senate myself. Nevertheless, the nomination of Judge Gorsuch is a clear indication of Trump's position on the political spectrum.

Now some details. Our new Secretary of State is Rex Tillerson, ex-CEO and Chairman of Exxon Mobil. He is reputedly worth $150 million with a retirement package coming from Exxon Mobil in an amount perhaps greater than that. He is a confidant of Vladimir Putin and has received a medal from Putin. He has been deeply involved in the oil business in Russia. Further, as a life-long employee of the fossil fuel industry, his position on global warming and the place of fossil fuels in that problem is a danger to the environment.

Then, in no particular order with respect to the importance of their department or agency, we have Betsy DeVos, appointed to head the Department of Education. Mrs. DeVos is a member of the DeVos Amway family with a net worth in excess of $5 billion. The DeVos folks are staunch members of the Koch network and are far on the right wing. Mrs. DeVos herself is a strong proponent of "school choice", which I have previously described as a way to privatize education. She was vigorously opposed by the Democrats, but, as we know, the Democratic Party has suffered almost total disempowerment as a result of the 2016 election. There is good reason to believe that Mrs. DeVos will do her best to decrease all public funding for schools and to encourage state governments to do the same.

Then we have the appointee for Department of Commerce, Wilbur Ross. Mr. Ross has a net worth near $2.5 billion. He has been a banker and an investor. He specialized in leveraged buyouts and has been referred to as a "vulture capitalist" and the "king of bankruptcy". He has a history of being sued and settling a lawsuit alleging fraud on his part and been fined for that in another case. It is not hard to imagine that he will wish the Dodd-Frank law and its regulations eliminated and a loosening of the rules on Wall Street.

For Secretary of Labor, Trump first nominated Andrew Puzder. Mr. Puzder. According to a New York Times article, quoted in the *Tampa Bay Times* on December 12, 2016, Mr. Puzder was chief executive of the company that operates the fast food chains Carl's Jr. and Hardee's. He has opposed efforts to expand eligibility for overtime pay and is an outspoken opponent of the minimum wage. He opposes Obamacare because he says that the rising premiums have left middle class and working class people with less money to spend dining out. Yet, President Trump has said he has a "record of fighting for workers. Mr. Trump has the same complete cluelessness to the concerns of workers as he has for everything else. By the way, Mr. Puzder is a multimillionaire, but his net worth is apparently not publicly known. Fortunately, he withdrew his name and Alexander Acosta was nominated. He held the position of dean of the law school at Florida International University at the time of his nomination. While there are gripes that can be had about Mr. Acosta, he is an attorney with wide experience, including a short stint on the National Labor Relations Board as well as being Assistant Attorney General for the Civil Rights Division and

U.S. Attorney for the Southern Division of Florida. He would be expected to be confirmed without the divisiveness Puzder would have caused, but Mr. Trump here showed again his disregard for the wellbeing of the departments of the government the far right doesn't like.

Then we get General Michael T. Flynn, a Marine General who was appointed National Security Advisor but resigned due to his contacts with Russian officials. He was succeeded by General H. R. McMaster, a retired Army Lieutenant General. I don't have any known complaints with General McMaster, but it is clear that the president prefers the company of generals (except maybe currently serving generals such as the Chairman of the Joint Chiefs).

The director of the Small Business Administration is Linda McMahon, who with her husband, is a billionaire arising out of their World Wrestling Entertainment company. There is good reason to believe that she will wish to see Wall Street deregulated to ease up money for loans to small businesses. There is also good reason to believe she occupies the far right.

For energy, we get Rick Perry, the longtime governor of Texas and twice failed candidate for president. Mr. Perry is a millionaire, but not on the scale of others in the administration. He has previously stated in a 2011 presidential debate that he would like to eliminate the Department of Energy. Mr. Perry is an advocate for the fossil fuel industry and can be expected to gut all of the Department's renewable energy projects.

For the Department of Housing and Urban Development, we get the retired neurosurgeon and failed presidential candidate Dr. Ben Carson. The doctor is reputedly worth upwards of $30 million. Dr. Carson has no experience in government and has been critical in the past of welfare – a subject that is central to his Department.

For Secretary of Transportation, we get Elaine Chao, the wife of Senator Mitch McConnell. Her net worth is allegedly in the millions. Further, it is impossible to believe she will not be influenced by her husband, one of our major enemies.

For the Office of Management and Budget, we get Mick Mulvaney, a Congressman from South Carolina and a well-known budget "hawk". This means that Mr. Mulvaney is a true tax-cutting advocate of slashing the federal budget on the backs of the poor.

For laughs, as Special Advisor on Regulatory Reform, we get Carl Icahn, the renowned corporate raider. Heck I thought he was dead. So, we really need a corporate raider to advise Mr. Trump about deregulating Wall Street.

There are others, but it gets depressing. So, let me get to one last appointment, the one I most detest. This is the appointment of the Oklahoma Attorney General, Scott Pruitt, to be the head of the EPA. Mr. Pruitt has been in the pocket of the fossil fuel industry for most of his career. As Attorney General of Oklahoma, he has sued the EPA repeatedly. He has been quoted as saying that he does not believe carbon dioxide contributes to global warming. He led the opposition to the EPA's Clean Power Plan which set the first national efforts on carbon pollution. Emails ordered by a court to be released show that Pruitt received drafts of letters from the fossil fuel industry which he used in his official position as Attorney General to block regulations on global warming. He recently appeared before the Conservative Political Action Conference and was asked about appearing before a group that probably wanted the EPA eliminated. He replied, "I think it's justified (to cheers). "I think people across the country look at the EPA the same way they look at the IRS". (*New York Times,* reprinted in the *Tampa Bay Times* March 9, 2017) Pruitt has stacked his agency with several former staff members of Senator Inhofe, he of the "greatest hoax" description of global warming. He has had Stephen J. Milloy on his transition team, the gentleman who runs the website JunkScience.com, a global warming denier site. (All from the same article) Short of Charles Koch himself, it would be hard to imagine a greater enemy of the EPA. Putting him in charge of it is just beyond cynical. If the "president" doesn't get us into a nuclear war, this is his most devastatingly bad action to date. Remember, Trump believes that global warming is a plot by the Chinese. In the meantime, Florida has had a winter through February 2017 that is *6 degrees Fahrenheit* above normal. We may not be giving a broken climate to our progeny; we may be giving it to the present.

Speaking of the climate, at the time of this writing, Mr. Trump has released information on the general shape of his proposed budget. In it he proposed to cut the budget of the EPA by 31%. He also proposes to cut the staff by 20%. Put together with the nomination of Mr. Pruitt, it is clear that our "president" intends to gut the EPA and leave it powerless. Just to make life interesting, Representative Matt Gaetz from (surprise!) Florida introduced house bill H.R. 861 to abolish the EPA and return the issue of environmental control to the states. That no state can handle an interstate pollution problem doesn't seem to faze these folks. What do you think? Would Trump and Pruitt back this bill? Presently the pundits don't seem to think it has a chance. I hope they are right.

The president's budget proposal also contains a cut to the State Department budget of 29%. Why talk to folks when we can threaten them? It contains a proposed cut to the budget of the Labor Department of 27%. Why let the issues of the laboring class get in the way of business? Health and Human Services is to get a cut of 18%. Who needs the National Institutes of Health and the Center for Disease Control and Prevention? I could go on, but the point is that anything that contributes to the general welfare of the people themselves is to be cut so that we can boost the budget of the Defense Department by $54 billion. (Data from the *Tampa Bay Times* March 17, 2017) Never mind that we far outspend any other single government massively in that department such that something like the next six biggest defense budgets are allegedly smaller in total than ours.

As I write this, the current news is that the Ryan – Trump American Health Care Act has just gone down in flames and the "president" has said he always contended they should just let Obamacare implode and wait for the Democrats to come to the Republicans to fix it. The man's disregard for the truth is a deliberate use of the Big Lie as a tactic to deflect the public from dwelling on unpleasant truths. Anyway, an analysis in further depth on such issues is not within the scope of this book.

Then we have Trump's avowed intent to gut the regulations of so many agencies. For instance, he signed a directive to effectively halt an Obama era Labor Department rule that requires brokers to act in the client's best interest rather than seek the highest profits for themselves when providing retirement advice. Why should the brokers the people consult be working in their clients' best interests? You folks didn't expect that silly approach did you? Certainly you thought your broker would only be looking out from him or herself didn't you? Trump was quoted as saying: "We expect to be cutting a lot out of Dodd-Frank because, frankly, I have so many people, friends of mine that had nice businesses, they can't borrow money. They just can't get any money because the banks just won't let them borrow it because of the rules and regulations in Dodd-Frank. (*Tampa Bay Times* February 4, 2017) Here you see Trump doing something (or at least wanting to do it) based on his own personal friends experiences rather than seeing the forest itself. Cronies to the fore!

But, there isn't really any problem with Wall Street and the finance industry is there? Maybe there is. Take, for instance, the report in the *Tampa Bay Times* business section on December 2, 2016 to the effect that as car loans rise, so do subprime defaults. It was the ability of Wall Street to bless subprime home lending that led to the Great Recession. What is happening with cars now, will soon happen to the real estate market again. In fact, the incredibly rising price of real estate, especially in places like Florida and California will almost inevitably lead people to cut corners and take risky chances on a grand scale.

Despite his "populist" rantings in his campaign, our president has shown no evidence whatever of being actually willing to do anything that would benefit the middle class or the working poor. We haven't yet seen his tax proposals, but he has promised to make drastic cuts in income taxes for individuals and corporations. The cuts he has talked about so far would massively favor the rich and business and would be of little real help to the middle class and of no benefit at all to those working poor struggling on the verge of bankruptcy. The preponderance of the massively rich in his cabinet tells you who he will listen to over time. The Kochs didn't know to expect this out of Trump, but they have to be chortling in their offices over this every day.

Chapter 16

Resolving this Mess

So there it is. American government at the federal and the state levels has come overwhelmingly under the control of the rich and big business. The original idea of democracy was that average citizens could prevent this from happening with their votes. Unfortunately, that has worked less and less well over the years. Today our governments are so vast and the issues addressed by them are so complex (reflecting the rapidly increasing complexity of our society) that most of us not only don't understand them, we have given up trying to do so. The farther removed government becomes from the average citizen, the easier it is for the oligarchy to control it because we never know what is happening anyway. Beyond that, we are constantly bombarded by disinformation and outright lies by the oligarchy. The Big Lie works well if it is constantly repeated and retweeted so as to inundate us in "alternative truth" (a term George Orwell would no doubt wish he had invented if he were still around). Thus, we elect politicians who promise to alleviate the inequities in our system and work for the common American instead of the special interests. They don't do that and many of them never intended to do that. For those who might have intended that, the exigencies of getting elected and the simple incompetence of many of them keeps them from achieving anything good for the multitude of us. And that does not even speak to the pressure from the party apparatuses and the outright evil such as Newt Gingrich and his vocabulary of hate. What is worse, we don't seem to recognize that the problem is that we elected people who lied to us and then didn't do what we thought they would. Whereupon we keep re-electing them! This reminds me of the quote attributed to Einstein, but perhaps apocryphally, to the effect that insanity consists of doing the same thing over and over and then expecting different results.

So, 99 percenters, whose fault is it that our country and our planet are being stolen from us? To a large degree *it is our own fault.* We hold the power to prevent it in our votes. We know this is the richest country in the world, but we don't try very hard to keep poverty, homelessness, addictions, hunger and medical-expense caused bankruptcy from plaguing our own citizenry. We allow the increasing concentration of wealth and power in the hands of a scornful few without even recognizing that we are *letting* them do it! Thus my question: *How stupid are we?* This is not really a question about innate intelligence. It is a question about willful ignorance on our part. To dredge up another well-worn quote, this one by the Irish statesman, philosopher and politician Edmund Burke: "The only thing necessary for the triumph of evil is for good men to do nothing". (I would substitute "citizens" for "men".) We can go a long way toward fixing this mess, but the question is whether we have the gumption to do so.

Look, folks, the haves will fight tooth and nail to prevent the rest of us from changing the status quo which so magnificently benefits them. They have the money and the power. They wield the Big Lie and they can pay any number of "scientists", "experts" and flacks to mislead us. But, if we look around us at what actually exists for our citizens and don't get hooked by lies, we can vote the bastards out and we can use the power of the government to see to the general welfare of the whole society just as our constitution urges. Not that long ago, average Americans survived the great depression, put 20 million men and women into uniform, fought and won the most terrifying war in human history, put up with price restrictions, food rationing, the mobilization of women into the workplace and triumphed over all adversity. We have come to call them the "great generation". They were our parents, grandparents and great grandparents. Some are still alive today. Since then? Not so great. Today we want our taxes cut. We don't want to even contemplate any hardship on our part to benefit our fellow citizens. Many of us can't be troubled to vote. Those who do vote are taken in again and again by demagogues. That happens because we can't be bothered to learn what is actually happening and why it is happening. That we are being screwed by this system is our own fault and it is not the real tragedy. The real tragedy is that our fellow humans experience deprivation and want while we bitch and whine about our "rights" and about how "great" we are as we refuse to see what we have wrought. The real tragedy is what we will bequeath to our posterity. Believe me, we will not stack up to the great generation nor the Civil War victors nor the Revolutionaries under Washington. Instead, I stink, you stink, we all stink. If we want to right what is wrong, we are going to have to stand up on our hind legs and take action. We have to endure some inconvenience. We may have to tighten our belts a little bit. What a tragedy, eh? Hey, folks, we can do it! We should do it! Let's do it! Okay, Somers, you're so smart, what are you suggesting we should do? That's a fair question. I've got the big mouth, what should we do?

The first thing we have to do is pay attention. We need to gather the facts, not from some internet troll but from credible sources and our own observations. Any politician, Republican or Democrat, who urges "supply side" economics in which the "free market" increases production, leading to more jobs and increased wealth for all is an enemy. Two very important things are wrong with that. First, when business has increased its profits, it has not shared them with the workers. Greed has kept that from happening as labor unions die. This leads to there being insufficient demand for the new production. Second, the rapid expansion of automation has rendered it unnecessary to employ nearly as many people to produce more, so there is no concomitant increase in employment. If we expect the rich to voluntarily share, we deserve what we get. And don't quote philanthropy to me. Just consider what would happen if charitable giving were not tax deductible. We have been trying supply side economics for at least 35 years and it hasn't helped a little bit. To use a term the rich love, wealth does not "trickle down", it gushes up.

A related canard is that tax reduction will help the middle class and the working poor. It hasn't, it doesn't and it won't. A family of four with an annual income of $50,000 will get so little back that it will make little difference. If that same family has an annual income of $25,000, there is no benefit at all. But, for the rich, tax cuts can mean hundreds of thousands all the way up to hundreds of millions. And then there is the outright deception. For instance the recent Republican American Health Care Act (which had failed as of this writing) was touted as saving billions in taxes. The thing is, those taxes would have been paid by the wealthy. The tax benefit to the average American was zip. Those taxes would have helped poorer Americans afford health care. We can't have that.

Then there is the favorite mantra of the right: deregulation. Deregulation decreases the ability of the government to hold the polluters, the fraudsters and the outright criminal element to rights for their transgressions. Regulations can protect our environment. Regulations can protect the safety of our food. Regulations can help protect us from the criminal greed and stupidity that led to the great recession of 2008. Regulation can help protect our privacy from the entities we are paying to provide us services. Regulation can affect the minimum amount Americans can be paid. And, only the federal government has the reach to make sure these benefits redound to all Americans. Only a government that is big enough to police its regulations can provide those benefits. Which leads to my next point.

Any politician who spouts the need for smaller government is the enemy. The government is not too big. It is too small and has been too hampered to provide to the average American the benefits that it has tried to provide. Cutting funding to schools and universities hurts America. Cutting funding to the National Institutes of Health and the CDC hurts all Americans when these agencies try to provide the research to support medical advances and fight epidemics. Cutting funding to the Department of Labor benefits only the rich and hurts the average worker. It goes on and on.

Thus, any politician who touts supply side economics or the trickle-down theory, cutting taxes, deregulation and/or smaller government is the enemy of common Americans, no matter to what party they belong. Admittedly, the vast majority of those who support these positions is Republican. Just remember, it isn't so much the Republican Party that is at fault. The fault lies at the feet of the far right who have hijacked it.

I guess by now it goes without saying that I would also label as the enemy any politician who tries to tell us that there is no global warming, or that carbon dioxide doesn't cause global warming as our current director of the EPA is alleged to have said, as the enemy.

Do not vote for these enemies. As for the ones in office now, vote them out. Make our politicians pay for being the enemy of the common American. We outnumber the bastards. Use our clout!

What else do we need to do? Well, when we common folk run up a lot of debt or can't pay our bills, we have not one but two solutions. One, of course, and the only one our enemies will consider, is to reduce outgo. Spend less. The other, which Republicans will not hear of and many sign pledges not to do, is to increase income. We common folks might get a second job. The government raises taxes. We Americans are *not* the most heavily taxed people in the world. Far from it. We all need to accept that, for those who can do it, we must pay more taxes. Poor us, hey? Nah. The increase should rest on those of us who can pay it without sacrificing our life styles. After all, the destitute don't even know what "life style" means. Bottom line: we gotta pay up! Does this involve the redistribution of wealth? You betcha. We have been redistributing upward all along, after all. It is time to redistribute some of it downward. We don't need to nor should we want to beggar the rich. But they can pay as can many of the rest of us and we should and must do it.

Another thing we need to do is to put quality assurance into the government. We need to eliminate overlapping organizations. We need to provide the departments, agencies and programs with enough personnel to investigate and root out inefficiency. We need to be sure that our benefit programs provide benefits only to those who are entitled to them under the law. This requires giving those entities to the people and computing power to do it. We need to give the IRS the people to collect all the taxes that are due and to rein in the tax evaders and scofflaws who rob the treasury and thus all law-abiding Americans. We need to get rid of the many pork barrel appropriations that come into our budget just so legislators can try to brag their way into re-election. We need to let Medicare bargain for the lowest price available for safe drugs. We actually need single payer health insurance which is not socialized medicine because the government will not own the hospitals nor employ the doctors. It will simply pay for the care just as Medicare does now. That will actually be cheaper than the "free market" approach is now and will see to it that we don't have hundreds of thousands of Americans dying every year because they couldn't afford the drugs or services they needed. We need to bite the bullet and pour money into our failing infrastructure. If taxes go up some to pay for all these changes, then so be it. We need to pay the bill while also slowly eliminating as much of the national debt as we can.

We need to stop lying to ourselves about global warming and do what is needed. This country is slowly launching on the effort to provide renewable energy and wean our vehicles off fossil fuels, but at the rate we are going now, it will be far too little too late. To accelerate the process, we need a carbon tax paid by the fossil fuel industry, by the drivers of gasoline-using automobiles and by all industries that use coal, oil and gas. We could help alleviate the cost by giving breaks to those who develop ways to sequester or, better yet, reuse CO2 and by giving tax breaks on the purchase of cars and other fossil fuel using products when they are upgraded away from that fuel or when replacements are purchased that use less fossil fuels or use none at all. Both the whip and the carrot.

There are many dozens of other things we no doubt should do. However, if we do just these things, the health of the country at large will improve drastically.

I considered dealing with the politics of xenophobia, jingoism and hate in this book but concluded that it would be just too much for me to chew after I bit it off. Perhaps another book. How does "The Tragedy of Trump" sound? Well, maybe not. By the time I could get it written, it would be a trickle in a pre-existing flood.

There you have it, folks. That is my rant. I sincerely hope that I am mistaken about how stupid we really are. Based on the history of our country, there is good reason to be optimistic, don't you think?

CLS

Bibliography

Brock, David, *Blinded By The Right,* New York, NY, Three Rivers Press, 2003.

Hacker, Jacob and Paul Pierson, *American Amnesia, How the War on Government Made Us Forget What Made America Prosper,* New York, NY, Simon & Schuster, 2016.

Klein, Naomi, *This Changes Everything, Capitalism vs. The Climate,* New York, NY, Simon & Schuster Paperbacks, 2014.

Leicht, Kevin and Scott T. Fitzgerald, *Middle Class Meltdown in America, Causes, Consequences and Remedies, 2d Edition,* New York, NY, Routledge, 2014.

Mann, Michael, *The Hockey Stick and the Climate Wars, Dispatches From the Front Lines,* New York, Columbia University Press, 2014.

Mayer, Jane, *Dark Money, The Hidden History of the Billionaires Behind the Rise of the Radical Right,* New York, Doubleday, 2016.

Oreskes, Naomi and Erik M. Conway, *Merchants of Doubt,* New York and London, Bloomsbury Press, 2011.

Reich, Robert B., *Saving Capitalism for the Many, not the Few,* New York, Vintage Books, 2016.

Skocpol, Theda, and Vanessa Williamson, *The Tea Party and the remaking of Republican Conservatism,* Oxford, UK and New York, 2013.

www.ingramcontent.com/pod-product-compliance
Lightning Source LLC
LaVergne TN
LVHW020532100826
845148LV00010B/1438

* 9 7 9 8 9 5 0 0 7 2 2 2 2 *